3D Graphics Programming: Games and Beyond

Sergei Savchenko

SAMS

A Division of Macmillan USA
201 West 103rd Street
Indianapolis, Indiana 46290

3D Graphics Programming: Games and Beyond

International Standard Book Number: 0-672-31929-2

Library of Congress Catalog Card Number: 00-100918

Printed in the United States of America

First Printing: July, 2000

02   01   00   4   3   2   1

Trademarks

All terms mentioned in this book that are known to be trademarks or service marks have been appropriately capitalized. Sams Publishing cannot attest to the accuracy of this information. Use of a term in this book should not be regarded as affecting the validity of any trademark or service mark.

This publication was produced using the Advent **3B2** Publishing System.

Warning and Disclaimer

Every effort has been made to make this book as complete and as accurate as possible, but no warranty or fitness is implied. The information provided is on an "as is" basis. The author and the publisher shall have neither liability nor responsibility to any person or entity with respect to any loss or damages arising from the information contained in this book or from the use of the CD or programs accompanying it.

ASSOCIATE PUBLISHER
Michael Stephens

EXECUTIVE EDITOR
Rosemarie Graham

ACQUISITIONS EDITOR
William E. Brown

DEVELOPMENT EDITOR
Heather Goodell

MANAGING EDITOR
Matt Purcell

PROJECT EDITOR
George E. Nedeff

COPY EDITOR
Kim Cofer

INDEXER
Eric Schroeder

PROOFREADER
Matt Wynalda

TECHNICAL EDITOR
Brett Hall

TEAM COORDINATOR
Pamalee Nelson

SOFTWARE SPECIALIST
Dan Scherf

INTERIOR DESIGNER
Gary Adair

COVER DESIGNER
Aren Howell

COPYWRITER
Eric Borgert

3B2 PRODUCTION
Cheryl Lynch

Contents at a Glance

Contents

7   Hidden Surface Removal   217

8   Lighting   253

9   Application Design   295

About the Author

Sergei Savchenko is a software engineer with The 3DO Company, which is a video games manufacturer. He has also worked on commercial flight simulators (also a variety of computer game, one might say) at Canadian Aviation Electronics. He has a master's degree in computer science from McGill University, where he also taught undergraduate computer science courses. He programs games and graphics applications both professionally and as a hobby. His interests include computer graphics, scientific visualization, automated reasoning, and game AI.

Dedication

To my parents.

Acknowledgments

I am grateful to many people for their efforts, help, comments, and recommendations, without which this book would not have been possible.

First and foremost I am deeply indebted to my parents, Nikolay Savchenko and Yanna Laevski (to whom I've dedicated this book), for their support, guidance, and sacrifice throughout the years.

Many thanks to the people at Sams Publishing, who were excellent and a great pleasure to work with. Particularly, I'd like to thank William Brown for pursuing and guiding the project and Heather Goodell for taking care of so many things and motivating so many improvements. Many thanks to Brett Hall, whose comments were always great and improved the book considerably. And of course, thanks to all the editors, formatters, and specialists who worked to produce this book, particularly Kim Cofer, Dan Scherf, and George Nedeff.

I am deeply thankful to professor Sergey Shkaraev of Kharkov Aviation Institute, who first introduced me to software development, and to everyone at Aircraft Reliability Lab, where I learned a great deal.

Many thanks to my research supervisor at McGill, Professor Monroe Newborn, for his guidance. I'd also like to thank Professors Prakash Panangaden and Lorie Hendren for giving me an opportunity to teach computer science courses at McGill, which proved to be a tremendously valuable experience. I must thank Professor Godfried Toussaint for his wonderful computational geometry course. It is thanks to that course that I can represent some bits of computational geometry in this book.

Special thanks to Sergey Lyutikov and Katia Lyutikova for reading early drafts of the book, and for their valuable help and comments.

I'd like to thank all of my former co-workers at Counselware Inc. for their support: Spencer Murray, Charles McNicoll, Addrienne DiFrancesco, Alain Hajjar, Diana Colby, and Russell Draper.

Many thanks to the guys from Canadian Aviation Electronics, particularly Tony Gerardis, Roger LaCasse, Alexander Loksh, and Alain Lavois for being good sports.

Thanks to Paul Brown from ISS Inc. for motivating the changes in the 3Dgpl library.

I'd also like to thank Charlie Wallace, Kudo Tsunoda, and Simon Everett from 3DO for showing me around the company.

Many thanks to my cousin Alexei Savchenko and to my friends, Sergey Lyutikov, Yakov Romanovsky, Kirill Filimonov, Michael Khorenko, Alexander Gurganov, Maxim Andreev, Larissa Nosalik, Rudolf Soloviev, Alexander Golovkin, Konstantin Fedotov, Ian Garton, François Labelle, Alexander Vasilevsky, Alexei Morozov, Joseph Vybihal, and Neil Grey for hanging out with me.

Last but not least, thanks go to everyone who sent their comments on the first two releases of 3Dgpl library, which were an enormous motivation to continue with this project.

Tell Us What You Think!

As the reader of this book, *you* are our most important critic and commentator. We value your opinion and want to know what we're doing right, what we could do better, what areas you'd like to see us publish in, and any other words of wisdom you're willing to pass our way.

As a Publisher for Sams Publishing, I welcome your comments. You can fax, email, or write me directly to let me know what you did or didn't like about this book—as well as what we can do to make our books stronger.

Please note that I cannot help you with technical problems related to the topic of this book, and that due to the high volume of mail I receive, I might not be able to reply to every message.

When you write, please be sure to include this book's title and author as well as your name and phone or fax number. I will carefully review your comments and share them with the author and editors who worked on the book.

Fax: 317-581-4770

Email: 3d_graphics_programming@macmillanusa.com

Mail: Michael Stephens
        Sams Publishing
        201 West 103rd Street
        Indianapolis, IN 46290 USA

Introduction

The goal of computer graphics is to generate realistic (or at least recognizable) images of virtual scenes using computer hardware. It's not surprising that these techniques are of special interest to the creators of video games. In fact, the history of computer graphics and the history of video games go hand in hand, with the former often influencing the latter and the advances in hardware paving the way for both.

Of course, there are numerous other areas where creating synthetic images of objects or scenes is of considerable interest and importance. Computer-aided design (CAD), scientific visualization, pilot training, medical imaging, and advertising all rely upon computer graphics to transfer visual information to viewers.

In many cases, 3D graphics provides a cost-effective alternative to expensive, dangerous, or impossible real-life situations. Good examples are flight simulators, which safely train pilots in potentially dangerous scenarios, and medical imaging, a non-intrusive way to look inside a patient. The introduction of computer graphics has had a profound effect on both of these areas.

Until not so long ago, the use of mainstream computer graphics was confined to a small number of very specialized fields. The appearance of inexpensive microcomputers has rapidly changed this situation. Today, the number of applications for 3D computer graphics has grown tremendously. One good example is the use of 3D graphics in the entertainment industry, computer games in particular.

3D graphics provides computer games with the same benefits that it gives to other areas. Indeed, it is often the only cost-effective way to experience things we can't see and do in real life. This encompasses many products of imagination (often *inflamed* imagination), from flying a fighter jet to cutting up unnatural creatures with a chainsaw (especially since seeking out unnatural creatures to chainsaw for entertainment purposes proved to be unfruitful and was mostly abandoned by the Middle Ages).

Implementing algorithms of 3D computer graphics has its share of complications. The main reason for this is the constant quest for higher speed and visual realism with limited resources. As computer hardware improves, it triggers interest in doing more and more complex graphics, so the game of priorities and tradeoffs never stops. Yet a lot of fundamentals remain. Very often, knowing these fundamentals is the key to well-organized and optimized programs.

What Is in This Book and What You Need to Know

This book discusses the fundamentals of computer graphics, concentrating primarily on the techniques suitable for developing computer graphics for 3D games. A lot of the material is of a generic nature and will be helpful in other graphics applications as well.

It is not, however, a book on how to design a game, but rather on how to build graphics routines for one, which is only one (although, perhaps, quite large) part of the overall task.

The discussions that follow are not tied to any single platform or toolkit. Although some platforms are briefly looked at and some popular libraries examined (OpenGL and Direct3D, for instance), this book concentrates on the algorithms and underlying problems. It could be argued that with a good understanding of the latter, mastering particular toolkits and libraries should be a much easier task.

Thus, if you are interested in developing your own graphics libraries that work from scratch or are built on top of other toolkits and libraries, you will find this book of use.

It is assumed that you are comfortable with basic concepts of software development and have a good command of the C language, which is used in all code examples. Certain fluency with mathematics will also help, although practically all mathematical concepts used in the book (beyond the most straightforward ones) are explained from the ground up.

Book Organization

The first chapter, "Hardware Interface," begins with a brief overview of the history of computer graphics and video games. It also discusses computer hardware and its effect on the structure and design of interactive graphics applications. Of particular interest is how computers display images and how application programs interact with the user. This chapter also looks at several computer platforms, both general-purpose systems and those that have been specifically built for video games.

Geometric transformations, including projection transformations, are discussed in Chapter 2, "Geometric Transformations." Transformations allow for the manipulation of sets of points in space, which is the foundation for the representation of virtual objects, descriptions of motion, as well as projections of objects to screen.

Chapter 3, "Rasterization," talks about drawing primitives such as line segments and polygons on the computer screen. Several techniques that enhance the appearance of primitives are also discussed, notably shading and texture mapping. The chapter also briefly discusses the inherently discrete nature of raster graphics and the visual degeneracies it causes.

The computer screen is limited in size, so Chapter 4, "Clipping," examines the techniques for clipping the primitives to the dimensions of the screen. Similarly, not all points from the virtual scene can be seen. The projections of many points fall outside the screen. Therefore, techniques for volume clipping are examined.

Transformations, the drawing of the primitives, and clipping are fundamental techniques in the viewing process. Chapter 5, "Viewing," looks at two different approaches to viewing: the *world-to-screen* and *screen-to-world* methods.

The objects that you usually want to display in the virtual world often consist of many primitive parts. Chapter 6, "Modeling," discusses ways of modeling various entities using such primitives as polygons or simple curved patches.

Viewing sophisticated objects is also complicated by the fact that the different primitives that make up the objects can obscure one another. Chapter 7, "Hidden Surface Removal," discusses algorithms that permit you to render objects with correct visibility.

Geometric visibility to the viewer is not enough to draw the scene realistically, however. Color and illumination are fundamental to our perception of reality. Chapter 8, "Lighting," will show you how to introduce illumination into virtual scenes. The presence of multiple objects in the virtual world gives rise to such global illumination effects as shadows and environmental reflections. Chapter 8 discusses how to compute these effects in the world-to-screen and screen-to-world viewing processes.

Finally, all these algorithms must be combined in a precise way. Chapter 9, "Application Design," provides an overview of the possible sequencing of the processes you can use to create an image. This last chapter also discusses general approaches to building 3D applications—video games in particular. The implementation strategy selected depends on the properties of the virtual scenes you want to model, the available tools and libraries, hardware assistance, and the requirements of the applications. Several libraries (OpenGL and Direct3D) and examples of special hardware are considered. This chapter also presents an overview of how programming paradigms (notably object-oriented programming) can benefit from the structure of 3D graphics applications.

Although 3D graphics is very important for many video games, it's far from being the only component. Besides pure software engineering issues, such disciplines as animation, artificial intelligence, and simulation of physics are also of increasing importance. This book considers 3D graphics only; that is, the process of drawing an image of a constructed (and thus momentarily static) virtual object on the screen. Even the discussion of 3D graphics concentrates primarily (although not exclusively) on the fast techniques suitable for video games. Object animation and their realistic or intelligent behavior are extensive topics in their own right and won't be discussed here (with a few minor exceptions).

Throughout the book, you will encounter many algorithms that allow you to perform particular operations. Very often, the constraints of the hardware will force you to trade off between various factors, such as the quality of the image versus the rendering speed. Also, you're often forced to resort to approximate or even completely heuristic solutions to compute results in a reasonable time.

Computer graphics is a very practical subject whose main purpose is to produce recognizable images under existing constraints. As such, it draws upon many other fields, from geometry and linear algebra to optics and psychology, and adapts their techniques for computation using currently available hardware. Because hardware is bound to change in the future, computer graphics will also adapt to the changing environment.

Conventions Used in This Book

The following typographic conventions are used in this book:

- Code lines, commands, functions, and variables appear in a `computer` typeface.

- *Italics* highlight technical terms when they first appear in the text and are being defined.

CD-ROM

Because computer graphics is such a practical subject, this book includes a CD with a sample graphics library called 3Dgpl to illustrate algorithms discussed in the book. It's written in C and it works on several different platforms. In particular, the enclosed version provides makefiles for MS Windows and UNIX/X11. The makefile for MS Windows is tuned for Microsoft's Visual C++ Version 4 and higher. If you are using another compiler, it may be necessary to change this makefile.

The library is meant to be a working sample that's also practical enough for some application development. Because it is available under the terms of the GNU Library Public License, it can be freely distributed or used for any purposes including commercial ones.

Some small code examples from the 3Dgpl library are presented in the book. Also, there are pointers to relevant sample applications and modules on the accompanying CD. Although the code printed in the book always has a soft copy counterpart, the former may be somewhat simplified to illustrate a particular point and avoid confusion with unnecessary details. The version on the CD should be used for all practical purposes and not the printed version represented in the book.

The library was specifically written to be small and structured, so it's advisable to at least browse through parts of the source code indicated in the examples.

The CD also includes additional material for the book (such as color images and links to additional reading) as well as a collection of free and shareware software.

You can use the enclosed CD in two different ways: 3Dgpl library and other packages can be installed on your hard drive, or you can browse the source code of the library, color images from the book, and pointers to additional material directly on the CD.

If you are running some variation of UNIX, you can unpack the file 3dgpl3.tgz, located in the directory /archives on the CD, to install the 3Dgpl library.

If you are running MS Windows, 3dgpl3.zip is located in the directory /archives so that you can unpack it manually.

To start browsing the material related to the book, navigate to start.htm on the CD-ROM. This material is organized as several HTML documents and you will need a Web browser to view these. Material for each chapter includes the following:

- Color versions of images printed in the book.
- Links to the source code files of 3Dgpl related to the chapter.
- External links to additional reading on the World Wide Web.

When you install the 3Dgpl library, refer to Appendix A for information on how sample applications can be compiled. Refer to the appropriate readme files of additional packages for more information.

CHAPTER 1

Hardware Interface

Computer graphics exists as a discipline only because of the existence of computer hardware. Methods, algorithms, and techniques developed for computer visualization of synthetic scenes are therefore based on and limited by what is achievable with currently available hardware. However, it is also true that computer hardware is often built specifically for the purposes and needs of computer graphics.

This chapter briefly talks about the history of computer graphics and discusses the basic methodology of interactions with the hardware. You will see how the software layer between hardware and graphics applications can be designed. The specifics and particularities of existing computer platforms and operating systems, which manage an application's execution, are introduced. The later sections examine some basic details related to implementing such interfaces for several popular platforms and operating systems.

History of Computer Graphics and Video Games

One of the earliest electronic computers, the ENIAC (Electronic Numerical Integrator And Computer), was built at the University of Pennsylvania's Moore School of Engineers in 1945. Although early computer hardware was hardly up to the task of generating graphics, by the mid-'50s, computers were resourceful enough to deal with the task (albeit quite poorly at first). Special vector display devices were employed in the beginning. They used line segments as the elementary drawing primitives, and the display device was capable of drawing a list of these segments. Vector display can reproduce a wireframe image. Wireframes are very economical and thus vector displays needed only a minimal amount of storage. (Storage was very expensive in the early days, of course.) In 1959, General Motors and IBM created the first industrial drawing system, DAC-1 (Design Augmented by Computer). The system allowed the user to enter a geometric specification of a wireframe car and view it from different angles.

The first video game to use vector display appeared at roughly the same time. Digital Equipment Corporation (DEC) was founded in 1957, and in 1960 it produced the legendary PDP-1 computer. One of the first PDP-1s was sent to MIT, where a group of students led by Steve Russell seized the opportunity and created the first video game—Spacewars. In this game, two opponents controlled two spacecraft, named the Wedge and the Needle because of their shapes. The goal was to shoot your opponent without getting drawn into a star in the middle of the display. The game was tremendously popular and soon accounted for more than half of all computing time on that PDP-1. DEC engineers started to use this game to test new computers (conveniently combining business with pleasure) and to demonstrate the PDP-1's capabilities to potential customers. Spacewars was never copyrighted (at the time, very few people could have afforded the hardware to run it), and the concept has been copied numerous times.

At the same time the first video game was built, another MIT student, Ivan Sutherland, started a long chain of contribution to the field of computer graphics. While still studying at MIT he built the first drawing program, called the Sketchpad. Later on, in 1966, he designed and built the first *head mounted display*. The device was capable of displaying two separate wireframe images, one for each eye. The images were computed from slightly different angles of view corresponding to the different positions of the eyes, thus creating a stereoscopic effect of depth. After receiving his Ph.D., Sutherland went on to work for the Advanced Research Projects Agency, and later taught at Harvard and finally at the University of Utah. In the late '60s and throughout the '70s, the University of Utah was *the* place for graphics research thanks to Dave Evans, who was recruited to direct the computer science program there and made graphics his first priority. Evans and Sutherland soon founded a company of their own to produce graphics systems.

In 1967, General Electric developed the first real-time flight simulator for NASA. Flight simulators today still use some of the most sophisticated computer graphics hardware.

By the early '70s, the speed of computers had increased and the price of circuitry had decreased significantly, which allowed for *raster display* devices to become practical and common. Raster display devices represent an image as a regular mosaic of dots, each with a different color (or shade of gray, in the case of cheaper devices). These devices allow us to display solid bodies with polygonal surfaces as opposed to just wireframes. Raster representation of an image, although more flexible, is also much more expensive in terms of storage. At the time, the color displays and color frame buffers—memory and circuitry to keep color data—were also more accessible, even though they were very expensive at first. Even as late as 1977, a 512-by-512 color frame buffer acquired by the National Institute of Health cost as much as $65,000. A similar device today can be bought for well under $50. This advance in the underlying hardware led to considerable research in the '70s that explored how to model solid objects and display them with correct visibility of individual primitives, as well as how to model the interaction of surfaces with light sources. In 1971, Henri Gouraud proposed a simple algorithm to interpolate a polygon's color and thus to model reflection of a continuous matte surface approximated by planar polygons. Later on, Phong Bui-Toung (while a Ph.D. student at, not surprisingly, the University of Utah) proposed a similar interpolation scheme. He aimed to model shiny surfaces approximated by polygons. Bui-Toung went on to teach at Stanford, but tragically died from cancer only a few years later. In 1974 another student, Ed Catmull, submitted his Ph.D. thesis proposing multiple interesting methods including *texture mapping*, *Z-buffer* hidden surface removal, and modeling with curved surfaces. Catmull later led the graphics division of Lucasfilm. In 1976, Jim Blinn (also at the University of Utah) developed *environmental reflection mapping* and soon after developed *bump mapping*, the techniques for extending visual realism that are commonly used today in higher-end computer graphics.

By the 1970s, the stage was set for mass-market video games. While still a student, Nolan Bushnell spent a lot of time playing Steve Russell's Spacewars on a PDP-1. When he graduated he became certain that computer games of the Spacewars kind could be successful commercially. Together with Ted Dabney, he built the first coin-operated arcade video game, called Computer Space, which was a close reincarnation of Russell's Spacewars. Although not immediately successful, Bushnell went on to create the Pong video game and establish the Atari company. Interestingly enough, Steve Jobs, the future founder of Apple, was an employee at Atari, where he was soon joined by a schoolmate, Steve Wozniak. Soon the two started to work on their own project—a prototype of the Apple personal computer.

Most early arcade video games used special circuitry to directly operate a TV's electron gun, and were not based on a microprocessor. In 1975, Chicago-based Midway introduced the Gun Fight, the first video game using a microprocessor (Intel 8080). The system was actually licensed from a Japanese game company called Taito. Five years later Atari licensed the concept of another video game called Space Invaders, also originally designed by Taito. Space Invaders became phenomenally successful on the Atari VCS platform.

While video games were making advances into the mass market, most used only rudimentary graphics due to the modest hardware available to them. By the early '80s, mainstream computer graphics had advanced quite far. The research into local illumination—that is, into interactions between a surface and light sources only—was moving along to consider some global illumination effects. Global illumination effects, notably shadows and environmental reflections, are caused by the presence of multiple surfaces. In 1980, Turner Whitted of Bell Labs published a paper about a rendering method called *ray-tracing* that allowed some global illumination effects to be easily computed. A similar approach was proposed a decade before by A. Appel in his paper "Some Techniques for Shading of Machine Renderings of Solids." Despite the enormous computational demands of the method, some extremely realistic images can be very easily computed with its help. Ray-tracing corresponds to what's known as *screen-to-world* viewing, which is covered in Chapter 5, "Viewing."

In 1984 Cindy Goral, Don Greenberg, and others at Cornell published a paper describing a method called *radiosity*, which permitted the computation of other global illumination effects—those between multiple emissive and reflective matte surfaces. Radiosity can increase the realism dramatically and can be used as a preprocessing step before ray-tracing or projective polygonal rendering.

In 1982, Silicon Graphics was founded by Jim Clark. The company focused its strategy on producing computers with extensive built-in capabilities specifically designed for graphics. Silicon Graphics still remains at the forefront today. Another milestone was reached in the '80s when computer graphics started to be used extensively in the movies. Disney's *Tron*, a movie about a journey inside a computer, used approximately 30 minutes of computer-generated animation. Although this first try was not very successful commercially, the computer graphics that were used then were of remarkable quality and led the way for many future computer-generated special effects.

Among the many companies producing computer-generated effects for movies, Lucasfilm, the company of the legendary *Star Wars* director, and its Industrial Light and Magic division (part of which branched off as Pixar in 1986) gained special distinction. ILM would produce many spectacular effects, from a projection of the Death Star in *Return of the Jedi* to the sophisticated animation of *Jurassic Park*.

In the late '80s, computer graphics matured to the degree that more research was concentrated on applications than on rendering methods. Numerous advances were still being made, such as those related to image quality and *antialiasing*.

In the '80s, personal computers were making a splash in the market. After the considerable success of startup companies such as Apple, big companies started to take notice. Shortly after, in 1981, IBM decided to move into the new market by introducing its IBM-PC. Owning a personal computer had been possible only for the true hobbyist. In the '80s, owning a PC started to become more and more common and affordable. Not surprisingly, this led to an explosion of game development aimed at personal computers. Many such efforts were home-grown in the beginning, yet turned into successful commercial enterprises. In 1991 John Carmack, Adrian Carmack, and John Romero, having released several shareware games, began id Software. In 1992, id's first huge hit, Wolfenstein 3D, was released.

The game, which used a much simplified ray-tracing and texture mapping technique, brought worldwide attention to id and considerably raised the expectations for computer games. id went on to produce Doom and later Quake, the most anticipated game of recent times.

It is not hard to appreciate the depth of the advances. Although only about five years separate Wolfenstein 3D from Quake, it is interesting to observe how the unsophisticated lighting and low-resolution characters of the former were replaced by the geometrically correct and extensive lighting and detailed character models of the latter. The richness of the environment has also improved dramatically.

Although the personal computer video game market has grown significantly, it has never eclipsed that of dedicated game platforms. The recent iteration of advanced game hardware began in 1990 when the 3DO company was established. The game console 3DO built was the first to use a CD-ROM. Although it flopped commercially, it was succeeded by Sony's PlayStation and advanced designs from Nintendo and Sega.

More recently, special cards for graphics that implement some common algorithms in hardware became affordable enough for personal computers. These were originally possible only for specialized workstations (such as those produced by Silicon Graphics). Multiple manufacturers, such as 3Dfx, nVidia, and Matrox are currently battling for the marketplace and for leadership in standards. These recent developments also underline the need for some common software support for graphics capabilities to allow application programs to take advantage of different brands of graphics hardware. This, together with the significance and the size of the combined video game and graphics market on personal computers, caused manufacturers of operating systems to act. Not that long ago, Microsoft introduced a set of libraries named DirectX, which provide services including 3D graphics to application programs. It competes with the OpenGL library originally ported over from Silicon Graphics workstations. OpenGL is designed for graphics only, whereas DirectX also contains functionality for multimedia, sound, and various input devices.

The foreseeable future promises more advanced and specialized hardware and bigger and faster storage, thus more and more complex areas in computer graphics will undoubtedly be addressed. Some current approaches may perhaps lose their relevance in favor of new ones, but what is certain is that the interest in both computer graphics and video games will remain for many years to come.

Interactions of 3D Applications with the Hardware

As you saw in the previous section, the advances in the field of computer graphics depended heavily on the evolution of computer hardware.

The remaining sections of this chapter discuss the basic principles of interactive 3D applications. In particular, they look at how a typical computer system affects the structure of such application programs. As the very term *interactive 3D graphics* suggests, there are two components worth considering: *graphics* (representing images on a display device) and *interactive* (reacting to a user's input in the course of an application's execution).

Other components of 3D graphics applications such as representation of virtual worlds, rendering of primitives, hidden surface removal, lighting, and so on may not immediately depend on the specifics of computer equipment (except in those cases where some basic algorithms, such as rasterization or geometric transformations, are directly implemented in hardware). Interfacing a particular display or input device, however, always depends on particularities of hardware and the systems software accompanying it.

The prime goal of graphics applications is to represent synthetically created images on a display device. Of the variety of display devices, we are primarily interested in the monitors, because they allow for a fast update of an image, something an interactive application requires. The dominating technology today is *raster* graphics. The idea behind it is that an image is subdivided into a regular mosaic of small, usually rectangular cells called *pixels* (pictorial elements), each having a particular color (see Figure 1.1). An image with small enough spacing of pixels is interpreted by human eyes as a smooth and continuous one. In terms of computer hardware, this technology demands using some memory (referred to as a *frame buffer*) to store an array of values, which are interpreted by the dedicated circuitry of a display device as colors of screen pixels. Changing these values triggers changes on the screen. If you want to draw a geometric primitive, such as a line or a triangle, you must have a function that changes the values responsible for the colors of some neighboring pixels in a coordinated manner.

FIGURE 1.1
A raster image.

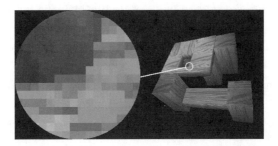

In 1969, Bell Labs developed the first frame buffer to store raster images. Only three bits of storage were allocated for each pixel. Since three bits of storage can describe eight different values, only eight different colors could be used at any moment. Since there are tens of thousands of pixels in any practical frame buffer, combined storage demand was very significant for the time.

Earlier technology, such as vector displays, represented an image as a list of line segments. Since a line can be described in a very compact manner (four numbers describing the two endpoints), the memory demand even for a drawing consisting of many lines was quite reasonable.

Yet it was practically impossible to draw any decent resemblance of a solid object using vector graphics. You could draw only its wireframe. The greater flexibility of the raster image technology, despite some drawbacks, have made vector graphics quite obsolete.

Of the variety of applications for computer graphics, those that require constant interaction with a user are of particular interest. Most video games belong to this category. Such interactive computer graphics programs must often depict movements in synthetic scenes, either of the viewer moving through the scene or movements of the scene itself, or even both. This is achieved by displaying a sequence of images (often called *frames*). Each frame depicts the scene in a slightly more progressive state. When a sufficient amount of frames is sequentially displayed during a short period of time, it creates an impression of smooth movement.

The frames must be completely drawn when they are displayed. In most instances, you don't want to see the process of polygons or lines appearing on the screen one after another as they build a single frame. A common solution is to render a new frame into an *offscreen buffer* while a previously drawn frame is stored in the frame buffer of the display device and thus is displayed. Once a new frame has been drawn, the contents of the offscreen buffer are transferred (or *blitted*, from *bit-block transfer*) into the frame buffer of the display device and the process is repeated for a consecutive frame. A more sophisticated and modern display device may have two frame buffers, one currently displayed and the other one used as an offscreen buffer. Once the image is created in the offscreen buffer, the roles of the buffers can be switched (the offscreen buffer becomes the front buffer, and what previously was used as a front buffer becomes the offscreen buffer) and the process is repeated for the next frame. This strategy is commonly referred to as *double buffering*.

Not surprisingly, the way in which different systems handle access to the frame buffer memory does indeed vary. In older operating systems such as MS-DOS, the memory of the display device could be accessed directly. However, when programming under more advanced operating systems, from any version of Microsoft Windows to any version of UNIX, writing directly into the screen memory is generally prohibited. The memory protection mechanism of the operating system prevents you from doing that. Therefore, developers must invoke different operating system resources and thus delegate some of the low-level work related to interfacing with the display hardware.

An interactive graphics application, in addition to being able to display frames on the screen, must also react to external events such as keyboard presses, mouse clicks, or joystick moves. It has to further use the information about those events to introduce changes in the future frames. For instance, pressing an arrow key may change the angle at which the scene is being viewed. Dealing with external events often depends on the supported *execution flow*—the order in which different fragments of the code composing a computer program are executed by a particular operating system. The flow of execution and even the structure of applications depend on the operating system.

Event-based systems often presume that the code must be executed as a function of occurred events. In other words, if a button is pressed, the code associated with that button is executed. This approach is used in Microsoft Windows. On the other hand, MS-DOS and UNIX applications don't have the event mechanism available unless you implement it yourself or use some event-based system running on top of these operating systems (such as X Windows). Thus, the code there is just executed from the entry point until it exits or until the operating system won't stand the humiliation anymore and dumps the core (as is the case with UNIX) or freezes speechless (as used to be the case with MS-DOS).

Thus, depending on the platform, the handling of external events may have to be implemented differently. You may either use various provisions of a particular operating system or, perhaps, directly access the hardware, if that is allowed.

The different aspects of graphics applications needing exposure to hardware and the nature of the involved interactions are the next topics of this chapter. How these interactions can be implemented on actual platforms and operating systems is discussed later in the chapter.

Note

For the next sections you will find the sample 3Dgpl program `window.c` on the accompanying CD useful. Compile it for your platform using an appropriate makefile. Examine the implementation of the hardware interface module located in the HARDWARE subdirectory of 3Dgpl's source. Examine implementations for other platforms.

Refer to Appendix A, "3Dgpl Graphics Library," for more instructions about 3Dgpl and sample programs.

Displaying Images on the Computer Screen

As mentioned, an image shown in a raster display device is stored in the computer's memory. The technology used by a monitor to display images is not unlike that used in a TV. The ray from the electron gun is deflected by coils in such a way as to go from left to right and from top to bottom, covering all pixels in a sequential manner. The intensity of the ray changes in a way that corresponds to the values in a frame buffer and, thus, pixels appear in different colors. The technology used by the laptop panels is different but leads to the same result.

A platform that provides a *graphical user interface* (GUI) allocates some portion of the physical screen (a window) for an application program. A graphics application must communicate with the operating system in order to create a window and later to display images there. A platform that doesn't have a GUI demands that an application communicate with the display hardware directly, but provides little or no help in doing that. In those cases, an application must switch the display device into the proper mode, perform the required initialization tasks, and later keep moving the contents of the offscreen buffer into the frame buffer of the display device or keep switching the buffers in order to display generated images.

The offscreen buffer contains what is often called a *bitmap* of the image—an array of values that represents colors of individual pixels. There are many ways to associate a value to every pixel in the bitmap. The color value can be comprised of bits that are located in different parts (*planes*) of the bitmap (the so-called *planar* format) or united into bytes or words, each containing a color specification for a single pixel (the so-called *flat* or *linear* format). Figure 1.2 illustrates which bits contribute to the specification of a single pixel in bitmaps of these two formats.

Different display devices maintain different formats for representing bitmaps in the frame buffer. Some devices may support several formats. Flat formats are generally more convenient because only a single memory access is required to set one pixel. However, on a deeper hardware level, this access may translate into several memory accesses performed by the video card of the display device. The video card eventually works with color channels, and thus might internally support planar representation of the image. This discussion concentrates on the flat formats because modern graphics devices seem to favor them for all external interactions.

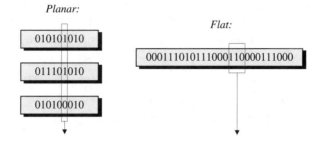

FIGURE 1.2

Planar verses flat formats of bitmaps.

The color of a pixel is commonly described as a combination of intensity values for pure red, green, and blue (an *RGB* representation). The physical reasons for this fact are discussed in Chapter 8, "Lighting." Thus, to describe a color, a certain number of bits has to be assigned to represent the intensity of each of the three components. If it takes five bits per component, 32 intensity levels for each pure color and at least 15 bits are required to describe a single pixel. An array of color values composed in this manner forms a flat bitmap. The first value in the bitmap is usually responsible for the upper leftmost pixel of the image, the value in the next cell represents the second pixel in the first line, and so on, covering all pixels line by line (see Figure 1.3).

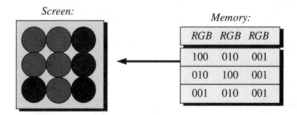

FIGURE 1.3

Screen memory storing RGB values.

There is one practical disadvantage: the space requirement. A small screen of 320-by-200 pixels requiring two bytes per pixel (the smaller number of bytes able to contain 15 bits) demands 128K of memory. The higher the resolution of the display device, the greater the space requirement. Whenever memory is at a premium in hardware, similar space problems are often solved through some form of virtualization. Rather than store a complete RGB value, you can store an index in a table (called a *palette* in this context) where the actual, longer color value will be kept.

Of course, it is assumed that the index placed into the bitmap takes fewer bits than the entire RGB value—for instance, 8 bits instead of 16. As a result, the memory requirement is reduced—at a certain cost, however. Since only 256 entries can be addressed by an 8-bit index, at any single moment you can have only this number of different colors available out of tens of thousands of possible combinations of the intensity values. Space versus flexibility is a usual trade-off (see Figure 1.4).

FIGURE 1.4
Screen memory storing palette indices.

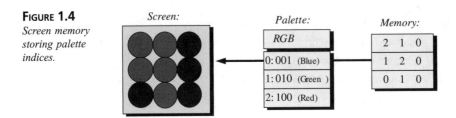

The RGB scheme and the palette scheme require somewhat different handling on the application's part. The lighting computations are particularly affected. It should also be noted that since the palette is likely to be implemented in hardware, the bit size of the color components may differ from one platform to another. This will require the application to adjust the intensities before storing them into the palette.

These days, since the amount of available memory is constantly increasing, palette-based modes are used less and less. Similar approaches are nevertheless employed in other situations, for instance to reduce the size of textures. The *textures* are images applied to the surfaces of polygons during rendering in order to increase visual realism. Chapter 3, "Rasterization," covers texture mapping in more detail.

It is increasingly common to encounter a video card with some graphics algorithms implemented in hardware. Most commonly, this encompasses drawing primitives such as triangles. There could also be an additional memory store to provide hardware support for hidden surface removal (which is discussed at length in Chapter 7). Video cards with these features are known as *graphics accelerators*.

The first task in implementing an interactive graphics application is to analyze all the available resources of both the operating system and display hardware and to design the appropriate interface between the application and the display device. Such an interface will abstract the application from the low-level issues and thus potentially improve the clarity. It can also aid portability of the remaining code since all aspects of dealing with the display hardware will be concentrated in a single choke point, making it much easier to port to a different platform. The ability to introduce the same product on different platforms simultaneously is increasingly important these days.

The presence of additional graphics capabilities, such as hardware-accelerated drawing of primitives, will affect the structure of the interface between the application and the display device. Similarly, provisions of the targeted operating systems such as presence or absence of a GUI will be an important factor to consider. You may also decide to build on top of a library where some functionality is already implemented.

Following are several hypothetical scenarios. They are only to illustrate general approaches and aren't necessarily meant as practical examples to follow.

Consider a very simple situation where only one frame buffer exists and the bitmap it stores keeps RGB color values. Assume that no hardware support is present for graphics algorithms. If that is the situation, a compact hardware interface may have the following functionality described by function prototypes (see Listing 1.1).

LISTING 1.1

Prototypes for Display Device Interfacing Functions

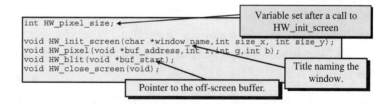

```
int HW_pixel_size;

void HW_init_screen(char *window_name,int size_x, int size_y);
void HW_pixel(void *buf_address,int r,int g,int b);
void HW_blit(void *buf_start);
void HW_close_screen(void);
```

Variable set after a call to HW_init_screen

Title naming the window.

Pointer to the off-screen buffer.

The first function in the set, HW_init_screen, should allocate a window with the given title and size. For platforms lacking a graphical user interface, these parameters will not be useful since only the entire screen can be claimed. The second function, HW_pixel, packs the color values specified and stores the result at the given address.

It knows how many bits each color component occupies and how to pack these bits together. You will see in Chapter 3 why passing the address of a pixel is more appropriate than passing its coordinates for HW_pixel. Note that a global integer HW_pixel_size in this hypothetical interface is provided and should be set internally by HW_init_screen to indicate how many bytes each pixel in the bitmap occupies. This information is necessary for the drawing algorithms to properly advance in the bitmap while drawing primitives and to specify correct addresses to HW_pixel.

Note

Having a global variable in the interface can be considered a questionable programming practice. The interface can be rearranged so that HW_init_screen returns this value, or so that the variable itself is internal and can be read by a provided accessor function.

The HW_blit function is provided to move the contents of the offscreen buffer into the frame buffer of the display device. Since only one frame buffer exists, the offscreen buffer will have to be allocated in the main memory. HW_close_screen performs all the necessary clean-up, such as deallocating a window or, perhaps, restoring the original screen mode.

In this example it is assumed that the bitmap is storing color values directly. If you have to support palette-based modes, the preceding interface should be somewhat different. Particularly, there should be a provision for setting a color of a palette entry and the HW_pixel function should expect an index of an appropriate palette entry instead of color values.

Consider another situation. Suppose that the video card has enough memory for two buffers and the mechanism to indicate which buffer is currently displayed. Suppose also that the memory of the display device is not accessible for the application programs and the only way of drawing primitives is by the provided functionality of the display device itself. Such a situation is not unlike what takes place with many dedicated game platforms. For this situation, the following interface may be appropriate (see Listing 1.2).

```
void HW_init_screen(void);
void HW_triangle(void *tiangle_data);
void HW_quad(void *quad_data);
void HW_swap_buffers(void);
void HW_close_screen(void);
```

Functions to draw
the primitives.

This interface is similar to the one outlined in Listing 1.1. The noticeable differences, of course, are the presence of functions that draw the primitives and the lack of handles to the offscreen buffer since it is no longer in the main memory. The question of what data should be passed to specify the primitives is addressed in Chapter 3.

There are many variations and extensions possible for such sets of interfacing functions. For instance, some applications may need multiple windows or require access to GUI functionality such as menus or buttons. However, the fundamental approach for building sets of interface functions should remain the same. You first need to identify what the planned graphics application requires from the hardware, and then attempt to isolate hardware-related aspects within a module. You may also want to target several platforms, in which case you would have to find some common denominator for the interface and implement it differently for each distinct platform.

Reacting to Events

An interactive application communicates with the user by displaying sequences of generated frames. The user communicates back to the application by acting on the input devices. This section identifies what these interactions entail for the structure of the interactive graphics applications.

Consider first how different applications work. In an interactive game, events on the screen are happening continuously. Whether acting on the input devices or not, the player may still see the ground approaching with an increasing speed in a flying game, for instance. This is an indication that such an application is rendering frames all the time. Actions on the input devices performed by the user only introduce changes to some internal variables describing the state of the 3D world and the parameters of viewing the scene. Such changes cause the application to take different paths and render different frames in the future. However, the application is constantly changing the state of variables by itself. For instance, the flying model function that simulates the physics of aircraft movement changes the position and the orientation of the aircraft.

Other 3D applications don't involve constant motion. These may render a new frame only in response to an event arriving from an input device and be idle otherwise. For example, in the visualization of an object built with a CAD tool, pressing an arrow key to turn the object will cause the application (otherwise idle) to act and draw the scene as viewed at a changed angle.

The apparent difference between the two kinds of applications is that in the first case the state of the 3D world and its viewing parameters can be changed by both the viewer and the application itself, thus requiring the constant generation of frames. In the second case, only the viewer can change the state, and the display needs to be updated only when that happens.

A common paradigm to achieve these interactions is an *event loop* (see Figure 1.5). An event loop is just a sequence of code executed continuously. In this code, you first check if there are new events to be processed. If there are, they are handled in some way. If a special "exit" event is received, the event loop exits. Later on you draw a frame and repeat the process. As a practical consideration, it is often important to attempt to maintain a stable frame rate; that is, a constant number of frames drawn per unit time. This is important because some frames may be much easier to draw than others. If the event loop is allowed to run at its own pace, the resulting behavior may be discontinuous. The program will be slow in some cases and too fast in other cases. To deal with this problem, it is common to attempt to synchronize the frame rate with the computer's internal timer. Thus, if a previous frame took less time to draw, you wait until it is time to draw the next frame. The middle box in Figure 1.5 illustrates this mechanism.

FIGURE 1.5
Non-blocking event loop.

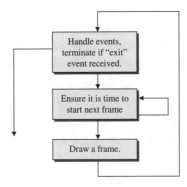

For the second kind of graphics application discussed, the event loop may be altered to block and wait until an event has occurred (see Figure 1.6). Once an event has been received, the application handles it, draws a frame, and blocks until the next event. The advantage of this approach is that the CPU's resources are free to do other things while the program has blocked waiting for an event.

FIGURE 1.6
Blocking event loop.

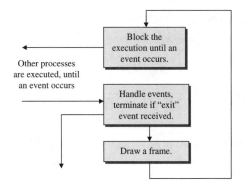

Consider a possible interface that implements the functionality of the event loop for interactive applications (see Listing 1.3).

LISTING 1.3
Prototypes for Control Flow Interface

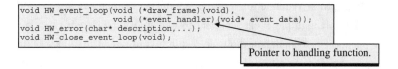

```
void HW_event_loop(void (*draw_frame)(void),
                   void (*event_handler)(void* event_data));
void HW_error(char* description,...);
void HW_close_event_loop(void);
```
Pointer to handling function.

The first function, `HW_event_loop`, implements the event loop and it must call a particular event handler and a particular function drawing frames in the case of every application using this interface. Thus, it is convenient to parameterize it with function pointers that indicate which event handler and which drawing function to call.

The second function is provided so that an error can be reported from either function called from inside the event loop. Good error handling is extremely important. The last function, HW_close_event_loop, provides a way for HW_event_loop to terminate. It is called from either the event handler or the drawing function and perhaps modifies some variable that will indicate that the event loop must exit at the next iteration.

For a blocking event loop, you can extend this interface and perhaps provide an additional function pointer to HW_event_loop that specifies a function which should be continuously executed while waiting for an event (see Listing 1.4).

LISTING 1.4

Prototypes for Blocking Control Flow Interface

```
void HW_event_loop(void (*draw_frame)(void),
                   void (*event_handler)(void* event_data),
                   void (*idle)(void));
void HW_error(char* description,...);
void HW_close_event_loop(void);
```

Pointer to handling function.

Note that the second of the proposed interfaces subsumes the first one. Indeed, if you want to emulate a non-blocking event loop with the functions from the blocking interface, it suffices to ensure that the draw_frame function is also called from inside the idle function. That will ensure that frames are rendered even if you are waiting for an event.

The proposed sets of the interface functions are, of course, quite minimalistic. They could be extended in a number of ways depending on the planned applications. For instance, you can support multiple event handlers responsible for different types of events. If the application is to maintain multiple display windows, it may also be necessary to assign a separate set of event handlers for each and, perhaps, provide facilities for communication between the code responsible for different windows.

These interface functions, similarly to the display device interface functions, shield the application from the details of the particular operating system and the hardware by providing the functionality that graphics applications conceptually need. The implementation of the functionality will differ, of course, from one system to another. For instance, event-based graphical user interfaces already provide most of the functionality you need. Thus, you can use an already existing interface without much need to make your own insulating layer. If the goal is portability and clarity, insulating may still be a good idea, however.

The following sections look at examples of actual operating systems and how display and input devices could be accessed.

Using Different Architectures

The previous sections discussed the aspects of graphics applications that are directly exposed to hardware or operating systems. The necessary types of interactions required by most graphics applications have been defined.

It has been noted that the interface functions must be implemented differently depending on the targeted platform. This section discusses some particularities of the implementation for several existing platforms.

The differences you will encounter relate to the presence or absence of a graphical user interface, the type of the execution flow supported by the system, and the accessibility of the input/output devices to application programs. Some of the complications also stem from the compiler differences. Many compilers have specific features that help programming in some way, yet aren't part of the standard specification of the language. Often there are also minor differences caused by a slightly different interpretation of the standard.

The most significant difference in C compilers is caused by the differences in the processors. The bit size of fundamental data types often differs from one compiler to another primarily due to the variation in the bit size of the processors' register storage. For example, some compilers assume that a value of type int must be stored using 32 bits, whereas other older compilers allocate only 16 bits for this purpose. It is important in a number of situations (for instance, during manipulation with bitmaps) to precisely know the bit size of the data type (after all, the format of the bitmap is fixed by the hardware). Thus, for your code to stay portable, some measures have to be taken to introduce the data types of precisely known bit length.

This section considers several different operating systems, some of their features, and the particularities related to the two areas we are interested in the most: displaying images and handling some external events. Of course, other aspects of interaction with the hardware not discussed here will also be important for graphics applications and video games in particular. For instance, sound and networking capabilities are very much expected these days. It should also be noted that long manuals have been written about each of the systems discussed, whereas the discussions that follow provide only a rudimentary overview. Additional reference literature is listed in Appendix C, "Additional Reading."

UNIX and X Windows

The first version of UNIX was created by Ken Thompson, Dennis Ritchie (who is also the *R* in *K&R C*), and others at Bell Labs, including Brian Kernighan (the *K* in *K&R C*), who has given the system at the very least its name. Curiously enough, it is rumored that one of the motivations behind Ken Thompson's work was to improve his video game called Space Travel, which was written in FORTRAN for a General Electric mainframe. He found a little-used PDP-7 with a good graphics display. Since the development tools for PDP-7 were on a GE mainframe running the GECOS operating system, the development process was quite clumsy, requiring him to constantly take perforated tape from one computer to another. To improve the development environment, Thompson and Ritchie coded a kernel of an operating system they had previously discussed and, eventually, PDP-7 did not require support from the GECOS anymore. The new system was named UNIX, paraphrasing MULTICS, the name of an ill-fated operating system project Bell Labs withdrew from a short time prior to that.

In 1971, UNIX was ported to PDP-11. Thompson wanted to build a Fortran compiler for the new system but instead got interested in a language called B. B was an interpreting language. The source code of a B program was executed on-the-fly by an interpreter program instead of being compiled into machine code for direct execution by the CPU. Ritchie soon produced a compiled variation of the language, which was named C. In 1973, UNIX was rewritten in C, an unheard of occurrence at the time when all systems software was written in low-level assembly because of efficiency considerations.

In 1977, there were about 500 computers running UNIX, many of them with quite different hardware. The operating system's popularity has been growing ever since. Workstations from IBM, Sun Microsystems, and Silicon Graphics use various brands of UNIX, with Linux becoming increasingly popular on a PC platform. The C language, a spin-off from the same effort, long ago crossed operating system boundaries and is *the* development language of many (if not all) modern platforms.

X Windows is a GUI system commonly placed on top of UNIX. It was developed at MIT with some industry input. Subsequent standardization was maintained by a specially created X-Consortium, which united multiple business institutions. The current version of X Windows is named X11R6. Most workstation manufacturers license X Windows and implement it for their platforms, adding some customized extensions.

Thus, X Windows is available for overwhelmingly diverse platforms, from personal computers to supercomputers. Similar to some other windowing systems, X Windows is not an operating system, but a graphical user interface functioning on top of other operating systems, most commonly UNIX.

An important feature of X Windows is its networked nature. An application written for this system, often referred to as an *X client*, sends requests to an X Windows server running on either a local or remote computer connected via the network. The server interprets the requests and performs the required actions. It also maintains on the queues the information about the events received from the local input devices. Applications can request this information and handle the situation accordingly. Thus, it is possible to have an X server on an inexpensive workstation controlling local display but running applications remotely, perhaps even on a supercomputer. The remote X-client sends requests to the local X server and receives its input back.

The requests to the server are generated when the application calls one of the X library functions. The library covers the necessary functionality to create and change the shape of windows and display text of different fonts and graphics primitives in the windows. The functions to manage events from the input devices are also provided. By convention, all the functions from this library are prefixed with an X.

Displaying images in a window can be done by calling the XPutImage function. Thus, a usual X application will first open the access to a certain display device by calling a dedicated function XOpenDisplay, then it will allocate the necessary interface components, such as windows, and later enter an event loop fetching messages from the queue and responding to events by specific actions. The code in Listing 1.5 demonstrates an event loop.

LISTING 1.5
Fragment of an X Windows Event Loop

```
                          . . .
if(XCheckWindowEvent(HW_display,HW_window,KeyPressMask,&report)==1)
{
  key=XKeycodeToKeysym(HW_display,((XKeyEvent*)&report)->keycode,0);
  if(key) event_handler(key);
}
draw_frame()                                        Handle keyboard events.
                          . . .
                                        Redraw the scene.
```

Only those events that the application specified as capable of handling the call to XSelectInput will appear on the queue. It should be noted that basic X Windows has only fundamental interface components available. However, there is a special provision for extensions that are used by particular manufacturers to introduce helpful features. Additional libraries also exist that provide both more advanced interface components and a template to write X applications using an *object-oriented* paradigm. Generally, the conventions and fundamental concepts used in X Windows are very intuitive and flexible, allowing multiple manufacturers to re-adapt the system for their hardware while maintaining a considerable level of compatibility across different implementations.

Mac OS

In 1976, Steve Jobs and Steve Wozniak founded Apple computer. As a popular story has it, the first Apple IIs were assembled in a garage belonging to Jobs' family. Right before going on their own, both Jobs and Wozniak worked at Atari for a short time developing video games. Taking advantage of a favorable climate, Apple was very soon growing at a tremendous speed. Many new technologies were emerging at that time. At a nearby Xerox Palo-Alto Research Center, advances were being made in graphical user interface design. Jobs was particularly impressed and inspired by this work and guided Apple in the direction of a platform having an operating system with an easy-to-use graphical user interface. The first try, called Lisa, was introduced in the early '80s. This attempt was largely unsuccessful, but it opened new ground for the introduction of Macintosh in 1984.

Apple had many ups and downs over the years. Both of the original founders left the company at one point. In 1986, Steve Jobs departed Apple and founded NeXT computer, which in 1989 unveiled its product of the same name. NeXT was a pioneering product in many respects. Built on top of the Mach brand of UNIX from Carnegie Mellon, it had an excellent user interface named NeXTStep. Despite numerous innovations, the project flopped and Jobs was forced to sell the hardware part of the business. The company attempted to concentrate on software but eventually was acquired by, of all companies, Apple, with Jobs taking the position of an interim CEO of his original (and as of that moment troubled) company. A new version of the Macintosh operating system, Mac OS X, inherited a significant number of approaches introduced in NeXTStep. In particular, it inherited the UNIX core and the use of object-oriented libraries with convenient functionality for development of application programs.

The traditional Macintosh operating system, understandably named Mac OS, consists of a number of modules called *managers,* which handle basic functionality. For example, the *File Manager* is used to access the file system, the *Virtual Memory Manager* provides services related to the address space, the *Device Manager* services the attached devices, and so on. The managers of the operating systems are accompanied by sets of interface functions from the *Toolbox* that provide somewhat higher-level functionality for the application programs. For instance, *QuickDraw* performs all display operations including the drawing of graphics primitives; the *Windows Manager* allows the creation and managing of windows; and the *Event Manager* gives access to the event queue.

On its start-up, a Macintosh application is responsible for initializing the managers it is planning to use. The sequence of instructions in Listing 1.6 illustrates this process.

LISTING 1.6
Initializing
Managers

```
             . . .
InitGraf(&qd.thePort);
FlushEvents(everyEvent, 0);
InitWindows();
             . . .
```

Initialize *QuickDraw*.

Initialize Windows Manager.

Once the managers are initialized, an application can create a window through, for example, a call to the `NewWindow` function. This function will allocate the necessary structure and pass to the application a pointer that can be further used to identify the created window to other interface functions.

Due to its early support of GUI, the Macintosh always had better-than-average display hardware. For the purposes of graphics applications, this hardware can be accessed through the services provided by the QuickDraw library. These services include support for bitmaps. Handling for offscreen buffers is encapsulated within the `GWorld` structure and associated routines. The `GWorld` structure contains all the necessary information on the layout and geometry of an image and keeps a pointer to the actual bitmap. Blitting is achieved by copying this array into the frame buffer of the destination window by calling the `CopyBits` function.

The handling of events under Mac OS is quite similar to that in other windowing systems. An event can be fetched from the queue with a call to the `GetNextEvent` function, which can also filter the events and send only the necessary ones to the application (see Listing 1.7).

LISTING 1.7

A fragment of Mac OS's event loop.

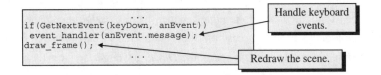

```
            . . .
if(GetNextEvent(keyDown, anEvent))
  event_handler(anEvent.message);
draw_frame();
            . . .
```

Handle keyboard events.

Redraw the scene.

Generally, Macintosh provides a pleasant environment for both developers and users. Despite its excellent user interface, Mac OS suffers from unsophisticated multitasking and lack of memory protection. Thus, a crashing program can very often take down the entire system.

A recent version of the operating system, named Mac OS X, is a radical departure from earlier versions, however. While it provides backward compatibility, there are also some considerable changes. Most importantly, the underlying UNIX kernel solves many of the multitasking and memory management problems that plagued its predecessors. Multiple software development kits and libraries are provided, which allow you to develop in various languages from Java to Objective-C. The latter was inherited from NeXTStep, where Objective-C was essentially the prime development language. You will see how this language is different from C++, another object-oriented extension of C, in Chapter 9, "Application Design." That chapter also discusses why object-oriented development can help in building graphics applications.

Apple appears to recognize the importance of video games for the success of its product line. Several libraries were recently introduced to help game development under Mac OS. There is also support for OpenGL, a popular graphics API (OpenGL is discussed in Chapter 9).

MS-DOS and MS Windows

Microsoft was founded in the mid-'70s by Bill Gates and Paul Allen. Gates even dropped out of Harvard to concentrate on building the company. Their first product was a version of BASIC for ALTAIR 8800, the first microcomputer. In 1980, IBM was shopping around for an operating system for its soon-to-be-released personal computer. Gates seized the opportunity. For $50,000, he bought an operating system for Intel 8086–based computers from Seattle Computer Products. The system was rewritten, renamed MS-DOS, and licensed to IBM. This was perhaps the turning point in the history of the company that has become the biggest software manufacturer today.

Although MS-DOS controlled very little and was allowed to override itself in an astonishing number of ways, as surprising as it sounds, it gave a certain boost to the development of fast game graphics and became a targeted platform for many developers (although not necessarily a favorite platform). MS-DOS provides only rudimentary support for display and input devices, leaving most hardware interface tasks to the application.

Realizing the benefits of graphical user interfaces, Microsoft started to work on possible ways to extend MS-DOS in this direction. There was some initial collaboration with IBM, but the parties soon went their separate ways. IBM released its OS/2, which eventually flopped, and Microsoft introduced MS Windows. The first version of Windows was officially marketed as an "application suite" rather than an operating system.

Although early versions of MS Windows did not win many followers, the situation changed in 1990 with the introduction of version 3.0. Due to various marketing and technical reasons, eventually several brands of Windows started to be marketed. Windows NT was aimed at the higher end. Windows 95/98 updated the mass-market version introduced in 1990, and more recently Windows CE appeared, aimed at the palmtop market.

With all of its current incarnations, MS Windows dominates in office and home environments today. Originally, developing fast graphics applications under Windows was next to impossible due to the constraints of the system. In its attempt to make Windows more attractive for fast interactive graphics applications such as 3D games, Microsoft first created a library called WinG that provided a shortcut to blitting of bitmaps. Eventually, DirectX was introduced, which was a set of different libraries designed to address various needs, from fast 3D graphics to input handling and sound. Such a library is quite timely for PCs, which a long time ago started to diverge as a single platform. Ever since IBM allowed its design to be cloned, multiple manufacturers started to produce PC hardware. This led to an array of often incompatible devices, leaving it to the operating system to provide particular drivers so that application programs could work through the driver layer and didn't have to know how to communicate to hundreds of different sound or video cards. DirectX provides such a driver layer to new graphics accelerators. Hardware acceleration is a must for new games on a PC platform. We will return to the issues of accelerated graphics and DirectX in Chapter 9.

Generally, the programs designed to run under MS Windows have a very different structure than the ones designed for MS-DOS. For instance, there must be special provisions for the event messages received from the windowing system. Accessing resources, including allocating windows and displaying images, must be done via a set of API (Application Program Interface) calls. For example, in order to display an image, you must first ask the operating system to allocate a window and then, through another sequence of API calls, request displaying a bitmap in this window. The sequence of instructions in Listing 1.8 performs the latter task.

LISTING 1.8

Displaying Image Bitmaps in MS Windows

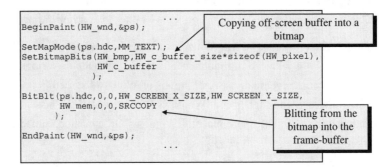

```
                          . . .
BeginPaint(HW_wnd,&ps);

SetMapMode(ps.hdc,MM_TEXT);
SetBitmapBits(HW_bmp,HW_c_buffer_size*sizeof(HW_pixel),
              HW_c_buffer
              );

BitBlt(ps.hdc,0,0,HW_SCREEN_X_SIZE,HW_SCREEN_Y_SIZE,
       HW_mem,0,0,SRCCOPY
       );

EndPaint(HW_wnd,&ps);
                          . . .
```

Copying off-screen buffer into a bitmap

Blitting from the bitmap into the frame-buffer

The code in Listing 1.8 uses functions provided by the operating system. The DirectX library that gives access to hardware accelerators provides a separate set of functions. Thus, the code to display a bitmap will look different if DirectX is used. Chapter 9 examines how this is done.

There is also a collection of API functions responsible for maintaining palettes. Palette-based modes are at times fairly complex for the windowing system to handle. There may be many color-intensive applications running at the same time, each demanding a different set of colors to be placed into the master palette, which only has a finite, and usually small, number of locations. To offset this complication, Windows provides API functions for color matching and has a mechanism for messages signaling changes in the palette's state.

When there are no available entries in the palette, you can, at the very least, find a close color via the matching routine. When some application radically changes the palette, other applications are notified and may rematch their colors accordingly. The master palette also contains a set of reserved colors used to draw visual interface components such as menus, borders, and so on. The reserved colors can be changed also, except for two—pure black and pure white. Luckily, palette-based modes are used less and less due to advances in hardware, making the modes where the color value is stored directly much more common.

Execution flow in Windows follows the event-driven paradigm. Certain fragments of code are executed in response to specific events. A usual application would first allocate a window or windows and then enter an event loop that would be responsible for fetching event messages from the queue and forwarding them to specific responding functions. These are usually associated with a specific window and describe actions that must be taken in response to events.

The code in Listing 1.9 demonstrates an event loop.

LISTING 1.9
An MS Windows Event Loop

```
            . . .
while(1)
{
 if(PeekMessage(&msg,NULL,0,0,PM_REMOVE))
 {
  if(msg.message == WM_QUIT) break;
  TranslateMessage(&msg);
  DispatchMessage(&msg);
 }
 else
 {
  InvalidateRect(HW_wnd,&HW_rect,TRUE);
  UpdateWindow(HW_wnd);
 }
}
            . . .
```

Events await to be handled, thus, forward them.

No events, redraw the window.

In the example in Listing 1.9, a message is fetched in the loop by means of the PeekMessage routine. It is processed and then dispatched to some responding function. A msg structure, filled during the call, carries the information describing the event. The field message in this structure specifies the type of the event. For instance, the key presses are identified as WM_KEYDOWN. There are two routines designed for accessing information on the event queue. GetMessage fetches a message or, if none is present, blocks and waits till a message appears on the queue. PeekMessage is a non-blocking version.

If there are no messages, it returns a zero value. This is important for an interactive application that must constantly generate and display new frames, and thus has to perform some useful work even when there are no events to process. Whenever the `PeekMessage` function returns a zero, the particular implementation of an event loop presented in Listing 1.9 starts sending messages to the handling function. The calls to `InvalidateRect` and later to `UpdateWindow` cause sending of `WM_ERASEBKGND` and `WM_PAINT` messages, respectively. These two messages are forwarded to the handling function, which must erase the window's background in response to the first message and repaint the window in response to the second one.

Since Windows tries to minimize expensive manipulation with the memory of the display device, an application must advise the operating system which parts of its windows were updated (and thus require refreshing) through a call to `InvalidateRect`. Only the memory locations responsible for the specified area will be changed in the frame buffer of the display device. Thus, although you don't have to explicitly erase the frame buffer in between the frames (each consecutive frame is simply written over the previous one), in this case you must nevertheless call the `InvalidateRect` function to advise the operating system and later simply ignore the `WM_ERASEBKGND` message instead of physically erasing the background.

The code in Listing 1.10 illustrates a handling function.

LISTING 1.10
An MS Windows Event Handler

```
long FAR PASCAL WndProc(HWND hWnd,UINT message,WPARAM wParam,
                        LPARAM lParam
                       )
{
  switch(message)
  {
    case WM_PAINT:       draw_frame();
                         break;
    case WM_ERASEBKGND:  return(1L);            /* don't erase background */
    case WM_DESTROY:     PostQuitMessage(0);
                         break;
    case WM_KEYDOWN:     event_handler(wParam);
                         break;
    default:             return(DefWindowProc(hWnd,message,wParam,lParam));
  }
  return(0L);
}
```

Redraw the scene.

Handle keyboard events.

As the code in Listing 1.10 demonstrates, unprocessed messages are re-routed to a special API function that ensures some default handling.

All the machinery and conventions of programming for MS Windows may seem overwhelming. However, an attractive side to Windows or, for that matter, any other modern operating system, is in the abstraction from the physical hardware that applications enjoy. The tradeoff is a probable loss of performance, which results from using an extra layer of code as opposed to accessing the hardware directly. With the introduction of DirectX, which can route data directly to a graphics accelerator, this is becoming less important and it is an acceptable price to pay for simpler programming.

Console Game Platforms

From products of Nolan Bushnell's Atari and Magnavox Odyssey to today's advanced designs, game platforms have come a long way. Early platforms were not even microprocessor-based, but this soon changed and the development of microcomputers and game platforms proceeded mostly in parallel.

What distinguishes game platforms from microcomputers is of course their extreme focus on one type of application. Very often, some special hardware is provided to speed up and simplify some aspects of video games such as graphics and sound. Secondly, since low price is the key to mass market, designs tend to be very Spartan, which presents some challenge for the developers. In addition, a TV is used as a display device and a small game pad is used for input. These devices are sufficient for the user but, of course, not nearly enough for a developer. A separate computer connected to the game console is normally used to write code.

The most recent iteration of advanced video game platforms started when Trip Hawkins, former first marketing executive at Apple, established the 3DO company. The 3DO platform was supposed to be the third revolution in the entertainment industry, hence the name, which is to fit into the line audio, video, threedeo (3DO). Although this particular product was not that successful, other companies came up with new, advanced designs such as Sony's PlayStation, which also used a CD-ROM drive for storage just like the original 3DO console.

The most recent platforms, such as Sega Dreamcast, PlayStation2, and Nintendo 2000 (project Dolphin), contain a lot of advanced hardware and surpass the graphics performance of many (if not most) personal computers even with graphics accelerators. The lifespan of a game console is relatively long, however. By the time it is nearing its end and the hardware manufacturer is preparing to introduce a new design, the performance level of the previous model has been long surpassed by personal computers and workstations.

A fast, reduced instruction set CPU is used in all new game platforms. This is supported by an array of co-processors, added for handling geometric transformations, drawing primitives, and processing sound. It is the presence of these specialized processors that adds so much power.

Game development for console platforms is constrained by the fact that they don't have any operating system. Thus, the development tools are provided on a different computer. Cross-compilers work on a certain computer to produce code for another platform. This is what is done in this situation. Some special interface hardware is provided (cables, interface boards) to allow downloading generated code into the game console.

Console manufacturers recognize the importance of a good development environment and provide special editions of their platforms for game programmers. For instance, the TOOL edition of PlayStation2 adds another Intel Pentium CPU, an internal hard-drive, and a LINUX-based operating system kernel to support game development. Similarly, Sega Dreamcast has a Windows CE–based solution.

Here's a brief overview of the internals of the original Sony PlayStation, which was introduced in 1995. The heart of the console is a MIPS R3000 CPU running at 33 MHz clock speed (PlayStation2 will have a CPU running roughly 10 times faster). There are 4K instruction and 1K data caches, 32 general-purpose registers and 2 co-processors. There is a system control co-processor and a co-processor named GTE (Geometry Transfer Engine) to support geometric transformations. A separate processor, GPU (Graphics Processor Unit), is provided for rasterization of primitives. It controls a 1M frame buffer that is not accessible by the CPU. Thus, the only way to draw any graphics is by asking the GPU to draw some primitives, particularly triangles and quads. Two megabytes of main memory is present as well as additional memory to buffer sound and CD input.

The GTE unit allows you to perform matrix arithmetic (which is discussed in the following chapter). In particular, it can multiply a vector by a scalar value, multiply a vector by a matrix, and multiply two matrices. These operations are used to implement geometric transformations and some lighting calculations.

There is no floating point coprocessor in the PlayStation. Thus all arithmetic has to be done in fixed point. Fixed-point arithmetic is discussed at the end of the next chapter.

Various development tools exist to facilitate PlayStation game programming. They include several different cross-compilers and even emulators, allowing you to simulate PlayStation on Windows- or LINUX-based machines.

The newer generation of game consoles, such as PlayStation2, pack even more power and specialized hardware. In fact, it is rumored that Sony plans to use a design similar to that of PlayStation2 to also produce a line of graphics workstations.

Although game development for the console platform is quite difficult and often requires resources that only big companies can afford (the TOOL version of PlayStation2 costs around $18,000) it is still a very promising direction for video games and will probably become even stronger in the future.

Summary

Various graphics applications use different methods to interface with the hardware and communicate with the user. Implementations of the strategy differ depending on the particular operating system and the hardware. For the purposes of interactive graphics applications, we concentrate on displaying images on the screen and handling user responses.

The following chapters discuss the algorithms that allow us to create images of the virtual worlds. These algorithms may not be exposed to the hardware, yet they depend on our ability to access the display device.

CHAPTER 2

Geometric Transformations

True reality is composed of matter. Matter can reflect light and make itself visible to humans who can detect the light. Virtual reality, in a computer graphics sense, doesn't exist as matter. Rather, it is an analytical description of certain abstract entities which, with the help of visualization algorithms and computer hardware, resemble matter and true reality when drawn on a display device and viewed by humans.

The very first challenge in computer graphics is to find a way to analytically describe objects. The next challenge is to find a mathematical apparatus to support visualization algorithms. Geometry and linear algebra lend their methods to both purposes because computer graphics deals with the problems typical of geometry and linear algebra.

This chapter discusses these mathematical methods, concentrating primarily on different transformations of coordinates. A *transformation* is a function that maps points from one *coordinate system* (or *space*) to another. Movements of objects in the virtual world (one space) and their projections onto the screen (another space) are computed using various transformations of coordinates. This chapter also considers techniques to represent the transformations and methods for their efficient computation.

> **Note**
>
> For the following sections, examine the source code of the module implementing the geometric transformations. It is located in the /3DGPL3/TRANS subdirectory on the enclosed CD.
>
> Refer to Appendix A, "3Dgpl Graphics Library," for more instructions about the 3Dgpl library.

Euclidean Spaces, Scalars, Points, and Vectors

In geometry, the shapes of entities can be described by the positions of some of their *points* (also called *vertices*) in space. The way we perceive the surrounding world on the local scale corresponds to what is known in mathematics as *Euclidean* space.

The position of a single point in a plane, which is Euclidean space, can be unambiguously specified through its coordinates: x and y (see Figure 2.1(a)). These coordinates (known as *Cartesian* coordinates) describe how far the point is from the origin of the space (also called the *beginning of the coordinates*) along two perpendicular directions, or *axes*. This is not the only approach, although it is perhaps the most common one. Distance from the origin together with the angle between a fixed axis and the line passing through the origin and the given point can equally well describe this point. These are known as *polar* coordinates. This book works mostly with the *Cartesian* coordinates, although polar coordinates will also be referred to at times (see Figure 2.1(b)).

FIGURE 2.1
Plane with Cartesian and polar coordinate systems.

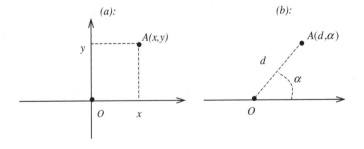

In the notation used from this point on, the axes will be denoted in capital letters and coordinates will be denoted in lowercase letters.

The world around us, which for one reason or another has three dimensions, can be modeled by Euclidean three-dimensional space, which is generally referred to as just *3D space*.

The following chapters consider many methods of representing virtual objects. These methods essentially provide a way to compute the coordinates of all points in 3D space that belong to the described object. Most representation methods also explicitly refer to some key points of objects such as the vertices of polygonal meshes.

Points are used to represent positions in the virtual world. Describing a single point in 3D requires three scalar values: the coordinates x, y, and z (thus, a point A will be denoted as $A(x,y,z)$). A *scalar* is a value that describes only magnitude—in this case, the magnitude of how far the point is from the origin along one of three perpendicular directions. There are some other entities that need to be represented that have only a magnitude. These will be described by scalars. For instance, the magnitude of a constant level of illumination, which is the same in every direction throughout a virtual scene, can be described by a single scalar.

Other entities have a direction in addition to a magnitude or a position. A traditional example from physics is the velocity of an object. This entity clearly has a direction and a magnitude. Vectors are used to represent these. A vector can be represented as a directed line segment where the vector's magnitude is equal to the length of the segment. Clearly, infinitely many equally directed and parallel line segments whose length is the same describe the same vector (since position doesn't matter). However, of these only one will originate in the beginning of the coordinates and, thus, any vector can be described by specifying one end-point assuming that vectors always originate in the beginning of the coordinates. A vector in a plane is denoted as $\overline{V}(x, y)$.

The components *(x,y)* specify the position of the end-point (see Figure 2.2).

FIGURE 2.2
A vector.

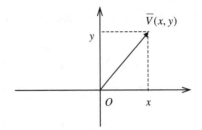

Similar to the operations defined for scalar values, such as addition and subtraction for real values or integers, there is also a set of operations defined for vectors. Vector addition and multiplication by a scalar are two basic operations.

The sum of two vectors is defined as a vector whose components are the sums of the respective components of the two given vectors:

$$\overline{A}(x_a, y_a, z_a) + \overline{B}(x_b, y_b, z_b) = \overline{C}(x_a + x_b, y_a + y_b, z_a + z_b)$$

A vector can be multiplied by a scalar value to produce another vector whose components are obtained by multiplying the components of the given vector by the given scalar:

$$a\overline{A}(x, y, z) = \overline{B}(ax, ay, az)$$

Vector addition allows for expressing the combined effect of several vector entities. For instance, if two force vectors act on the same body, the vector denoting the sum of the two vectors describes the combined effect. Multiplication by a scalar permits changing the magnitude or the direction of the vector entity leaving the orientation unchanged. For instance, by multiplying a vector by a scalar *-2*, the direction is reversed and the length is doubled. Figure 2.3 illustrates the geometric sense of these operations.

FIGURE 2.3
Operations on vectors.

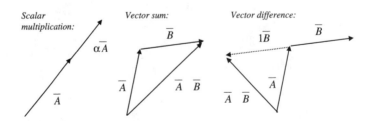

Other operations on vectors can be defined as well. For instance, subtraction of two vectors $\overline{A}$ and $\overline{B}$ can be defined as addition of $\overline{A}$ and $-1\overline{B}$ (see Figure 2.3). That is,

$$\overline{A} - \overline{B} = \overline{A} + (-1\overline{B})$$

Two other operations on vectors, a *scalar* (or *dot*) *product* and a *vector* (or *cross*) *product* will also appear in the forthcoming chapters.

Rigid Transformations

Points, scalar values, and vectors allow for construction of virtual worlds. Objects in these worlds move and change their orientation. If a restriction is placed on a body requiring the distances between all of its points to never change, such a *rigid body* possesses three degrees of freedom in a plane and six degrees of freedom in 3D space. A single *degree of freedom* is a scalar parameter. When altered, it induces changes in the state of the system being described. For instance, a point on a line has a single degree of freedom since any state (the position of this point) can be specified through variation of a single parameter—the linear coordinate. In the case of a rigid body in 2D space, degrees of freedom are displacements along the two axes (*translations*) and the *rotation* around a point. Changing any of these parameters will take a body into a new, distinct state. Also, any transformation of a rigid body from some initial position in space to any other position can be expressed through variation of those three parameters.

In the case of 3D space, there are three different independent translations possible: one along each of the three axes as well as three different rotations about axes, which are parallel to the three reference axes of the coordinate system. Thus there are six degrees of freedom altogether.

To summarize, any transformation of a rigid body can be expressed through two different types of transformations: the translations and the rotations. For many computer graphics applications, synthetic objects keep their shape and size unchanged.

In such applications, only rigid transformations are required. However, if the shape of objects (distances between points) does change, other transformations need to be used as well. Such a situation may occur, for instance, during modeling. Perhaps the most common of the non-rigid or *structure deforming* transformations are *scaling* and *shearing*. These transformations affect the size and the shape of objects.

It is possible to consider all 3D transformations either as a transformation of a set of points in a static coordinate system or as a transformation of the space; in other words, a change in the coordinate systems. As you will see, the first way of thinking is more productive for some transformations, whereas the second way is more productive for others.

Translation

Translation transformation moves the points of an object to a new specified position (see Figure 2.4(a)). It is also possible to think of this transformation as moving the coordinate system (the space) into the opposite direction (see Figure 2.4(b)).

FIGURE 2.4

Translation of a set of points versus translation of space.

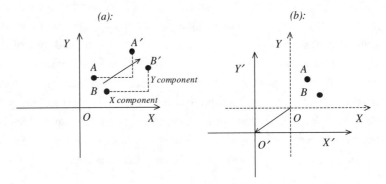

As Figure 2.4 illustrates, if a set of points is translated, distances between these points will not change. Any move across 2D space separates into two independent components—the move along the X axis and the move along the Y axis. It will take three components in 3D space—along the X, Y, and Z axes. A translation transformation of a point $A(x,y,z)$ into $A'(x',y',z')$ can be described as

$$x' = x + t_x$$
$$y' = y + t_y$$
$$z' = z + t_z$$

where t_x, t_y, t_z are translation displacements for each axis. An important use of the translation transformation is when you need to move the beginning of the coordinates of the virtual screen to the center of the physical screen, which often has a system of references originating in the upper-left corner and not the physical center of the screen.

Another use of translation helps to specify vector components. Vectors are described using a special point and the assumption that the vector's origin is in the beginning of the coordinates. Very often a vector must be constructed given its two endpoints. To find a vector's components, these two points can be translated to the origin of the space. The negated coordinates of the point that is to travel into the beginning of the coordinates gives the parameters of the translation to perform. This results in a familiar algorithm where it is necessary to subtract coordinates of the origin-point from the endpoint to obtain the vector's components.

A possible implementation for the translation routine is presented in Listing 2.1.

LISTING 2.1
Translation
Transformation
(see /3DGPL3/
TRANS/
trans-bs.c
on the CD)

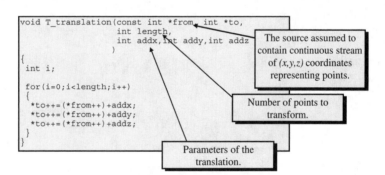

```
void T_translation(const int *from, int *to,
                   int length,
                   int addx, int addy, int addz
                   )
{
  int i;

  for(i=0;i<length;i++)
  {
    *to++=(*from++)+addx;
    *to++=(*from++)+addy;
    *to++=(*from++)+addz;
  }
}
```

The source assumed to contain continuous stream of *(x,y,z)* coordinates representing points.

Number of points to transform.

Parameters of the translation.

Note that the function in Listing 2.1 operates on a stream of coordinates that represents a set of points of some object. Of course, in practice a more sophisticated data structure can be created to store the coordinates of points. For the moment, however, the simplest possible representation was used.

Rotation in 2D

Of all the transformations this chapter discusses, the rotation is perhaps the most complex. Consider a planar, 2D case of the rotation transformation. There is some trigonometry involved, notably *sin* and *cos* functions. These functions for a right-angle triangle in Figure 2.5 are defined as:

$$\cos(\alpha) = \frac{x}{l}$$

$$\sin(\alpha) = \frac{y}{l}$$

Knowing *sin* or *cos* functions makes it easy to compute the segments x and y given the length of l:

$$x = l\cos(\alpha)$$

$$y = l\sin(\alpha)$$

FIGURE 2.5
Right angle triangle.

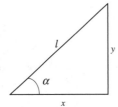

This can be considered as seeking the projections onto two orthogonal axes of the point for which the distance from the beginning of the coordinates is known (see Figure 2.6).

Such an operation, in addition to being useful for transforming polar coordinates of a point (distance from the origin and an angle) into Cartesian coordinates, also helps to obtain formulas for the rotation transformation. Consider the situation in Figure 2.7, where the system of references rotates counterclockwise by some angle α. It is necessary to find the coordinates of the point A in the transformed system of references $X'Y'$ assuming that its coordinates in the original system XY were *(x,y)*.

FIGURE 2.6
*Projection of a
point onto the
axes.*

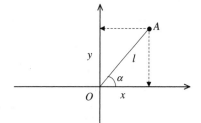

FIGURE 2.7
*Rotating the
coordinate
system.*

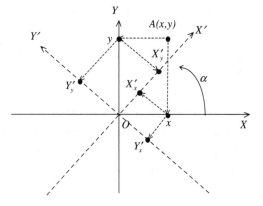

Using the *sin(x)*, *cos(x)* formulas mentioned earlier, the projections of *x* and *y* (that is, of the coordinates of the point in the original system of references) onto the new axes *X'* and *Y'* are found. To do that, sum the projections of *x* and *y* onto the *X'* axis and do the same with the projections of *x* and *y* onto the *Y'* axis:

$$x' = Y'_x + X'_x = y\sin(\alpha) + x\cos(\alpha)$$

$$y' = Y'_y + X'_y = y\cos(\alpha) + (-x\sin(\alpha))$$

These sums represent the coordinates of the point *A* in the rotated system of references *X'Y'*. Note the sign of X'_y.

Simply by examining Figure 2.7, you can see that in this case *x* is projected onto the negative side of the axis *Y'*. That's the reason for the negative sign.

Alternatively, this rotation transformation represents the situation of the point *A* rotating clockwise around zero with the system of references being stationary.

Thus, the only parameter of planar rotation transformation is its angle. The rotation is performed around the beginning of the coordinates. If it's necessary to rotate around some arbitrary point, it is not hard to do that by first moving this point into the origin of the space, performing the rotation there, and then translating back to the original position.

In the computation of this transformation, trigonometric functions are important. Although considerable software and hardware support exists for these functions, sometimes none is available. The section "Evaluating Trigonometric Functions," later in the chapter, discusses how to compute these from scratch.

Rotation in 3D

The previous section described the formulas for performing planar rotation transformation. Brought into 3D, that transformation will have a sense of rotation around the newly added axis *Z* rather than just around a point. That is because the coordinate *z* isn't influenced by the formulas and remains the same after their application. By applying the formulas to different pairs of coordinates and leaving the third unchanged, there are three different rotations around three different axes.

If one point of some object is fixed and designated to be the beginning of the coordinates, any orientation of that object around that point can be described in terms of the three rotations around the axes of the coordinate system. In other words, 3D rotation around a point can be achieved by sequential application of three rotations around different axes, so that each consecutive rotation transforms the coordinates obtained from the previous rotation.

There are a few important factors influencing the form of the 3D rotation formulas:

- The kind of reference system
- Directions of positive rotations
- The order in which rotations are applied

Generally, there are no particular constraints on the geometry of the reference system and there is a freedom to choose the directions of the axes. Different branches of science and engineering have certain more or less developed conventions and customs on the usual system of references. In most cases, the system of references is either left-handed or right-handed (see Figure 2.8). For the purposes of this book, we will mostly rely on the left-handed notation, although the difference is quite trivial.

FIGURE 2.8
Right-handed and left-handed coordinate systems.

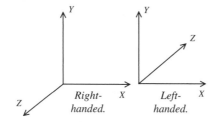

Tip

In certain applications, there may be reasons to choose a particular system of references. It is customary, for example, to have the positive direction of the Y axis pointing upward. However, remembering that in the most typical bitmap the Y axis points downward (which is dictated by the memory layout for the display hardware), this might be a semi-valid reason to choose the corresponding system of references in 3D space. The counter argument is that it is more natural to have it pointing upward, measuring height in such applications as flight simulators, for instance. Choosing the direction that is more natural for human perception might help to prevent misunderstandings at the debugging stage in the future, actually saving some development time.

The rotation angles must also be defined. It is customary to refer to the angle to turn the *XY* plane around the *Z* axis as the *roll*, *ZY* around *X* as the *pitch*, and *ZX* around *Y* as the *yaw*. In Figure 2.9, the roll is denoted as α, the pitch as β, and the yaw as γ.

FIGURE 2.9
*Positive direction
of rotation
angles.*

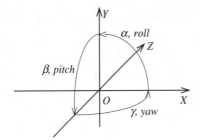

It is convenient to define a positive direction of the angles as shown in Figure 2.9.

Defining the order in which to apply the rotation transformations is very important. A point consequently turned by the angles γ-β-α won't necessarily be at the same position in space where it may be placed if turned by the same angles α-β-γ but taken in a different order. Consecutive applications of rotation don't *commute*. The reason is in the original assumption that each subsequent transformation works on a point already transformed by the previous axis rotations. In other words, angles are given with respect to moving axes. In Figure 2.10, rotations α-β take the object to a different location compared with the same rotations but in the opposite order—β-α.

FIGURE 2.10
*Consecutive
rotations.*

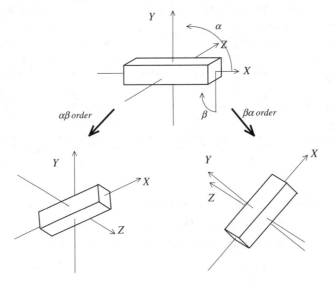

Think about how you normally coordinate the surrounding world. First you think of the direction. Then you can tilt your head up or down, and from that position you can move it left or right. You have already chosen the direction when you tilt your head. If you tilted your head first, the directional rotation would not be in the plane parallel to the ground. Rather, it would be in the plane perpendicular to the imaginary line extending from your tilted neck. (No responsibility is hereby assumed for any direct or consequential damages or injury resulting from experimenting in the aforementioned fashion.) In terms of the defined system of references, it all comes down to the directional rotation: *yaw* first (γ), *pitch* second (β), and *roll* last (α).

This sequence describes, of course, the order of individual rotations applied to the world with respect to the viewer, whose orientation changes. In other words, rotation axes are centered in the viewer's eye. If an object is coordinated in the world with the rotation axes being local to the object, the convenient order is often different—pitch is done with respect to where the object was turned by roll, and yaw is applied last.

Derivation of combined rotation formulas is similar, of course. Consider the first case in Figure 2.11.

FIGURE 2.11
Three consecutive rotations.

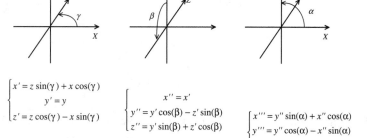

$$\begin{cases} x' = z\sin(\gamma) + x\cos(\gamma) \\ y' = y \\ z' = z\cos(\gamma) - x\sin(\gamma) \end{cases}$$

$$\begin{cases} x'' = x' \\ y'' = y'\cos(\beta) - z'\sin(\beta) \\ z'' = y'\sin(\beta) + z'\cos(\beta) \end{cases}$$

$$\begin{cases} x''' = y''\sin(\alpha) + x''\cos(\alpha) \\ y''' = y''\cos(\alpha) - x''\sin(\alpha) \\ z''' = z'' \end{cases}$$

The nine formulas in Figure 2.11 describe the 3D rotation. They can be applied to the coordinates *(x,y,z)* and eventually produce transformed coordinates *(x''',y''',z''')*, representing the position where the original point must go under the 3D rotation. There are 12 multiplications involved.

Since multiplications are expansive, the first obvious optimization effort for graphics applications is to attempt to reduce their number.

You can get rid of temporary points *(x',y',z')* and *(x",y",z")* by substituting their occurrences with the expressions describing their meanings.

First, obtain *(x",y",z")* expressed directly via *(x,y,z)*:

$$x'' = z\sin(\gamma) + x\cos(\gamma)$$

$$y'' = x\cos(\beta) - z\cos(\gamma)\sin(\beta) - x\sin(\gamma)\sin(\beta)$$

$$z'' = y\sin(\beta) + z\cos(\gamma)\cos(\beta) - x\sin(\gamma)\cos(\beta)$$

Further, using the preceding expressions, *(x''',y''',z''')* can be directly represented as a function of *(x,y,z)*:

$$x''' = x[\sin(\gamma)\sin(\beta)\sin(\alpha) + \cos(\gamma)\cos(\alpha)] + y[\cos(\beta)\sin(\alpha)]$$

$$+z[\sin(\gamma)\cos(\alpha) - \cos(\gamma)\sin(\beta)\sin(\alpha)]$$

$$y''' = x[\sin(\gamma)\sin(\beta)\cos(\alpha) - \cos(\gamma)\sin(\alpha)] + y[\cos(\beta)\cos(\alpha)]$$

$$+z[-\cos(\gamma)\sin(\beta)\cos(\alpha) - \sin(\gamma)\sin(\alpha)]$$

$$z''' = x[-\sin(\gamma)\cos(\beta)] + y[\sin(\beta)] + z[\cos(\gamma)\cos(\beta)]$$

This set of formulas appears to be more complex than the original. It has many more multiplications. However, by looking closely at the resulting formulas you can see that all the coefficients in the square brackets can be computed just once so that the transformation of a point will look like this:

$$x''' = x \cdot m_{x1} + y \cdot m_{y1} + z \cdot m_{z1}$$

$$y''' = x \cdot m_{x2} + y \cdot m_{y2} + z \cdot m_{z2}$$

$$z''' = x \cdot m_{x3} + y \cdot m_{y3} + z \cdot m_{z3}$$

This computation takes nine multiplications. Of course, finding all the coefficients takes another 16 multiplications:

$$m_{x1} = \sin(\gamma)\sin(\beta)\sin(\alpha) + \cos(\gamma)\cos(\alpha)$$

$$m_{y1} = \cos(\beta)\sin(\alpha)$$

$$m_{z1} = \sin(\gamma)\cos(\alpha) - \cos(\gamma)\sin(\beta)\sin(\alpha)$$

$$m_{x2} = \sin(\gamma)\sin(\beta)\cos(\alpha) - \cos(\gamma)\sin(\alpha)$$

$$m_{y2} = \cos(\beta)\cos(\alpha)$$

$$m_{z2} = -\cos(\gamma)\sin(\beta)\cos(\alpha) - \sin(\gamma)\sin(\alpha)$$

$$m_{x3} = -\sin(\gamma)\cos(\beta)$$

$$m_{y3} = \sin(\beta)$$

$$m_{x3} = \cos(\gamma)\cos(\beta)$$

However, if there are 100 points to rotate, the original method will require 12×100, or 1200 multiplications. The new technique will only take 9×100 plus 16, or 916 multiplications because the coefficients are computed only once for any number of points to transform.

Coding the 3D rotation transformation is quite straightforward given the formulas. The function in the implementation in Listing 2.2 builds a set of rotation coefficients for a predetermined order of rotations. Note that variables T_mx1, T_mx2, and so on are assumed to be global.

LISTING 2.2

Computing Rotation Coefficients (see /3DGPL3/TRANS/ trans-bs.c *on the CD)*

```
void T_set_rotation(float alp,float bet,float game)
{
  float cosalp,sinalp,cosbet,sinbet,cosgam,singam;

  cosalp=cos(alp); sinalp=sin(alp);
  cosbet=cos(bet); sinbet=sin(bet);
  cosgam=cos(gam); singam=sin(gam);

  T_wx1=singam*sinbet*sinalp + cosgam*cosalp;
  T_wy1=cosbet*sinalp;
  T_wz1=singam*cosalp - cosgam*sinbet*sinalp;
  T_wx2=singam*sinbet*cosalp - cosgam*sinalp;
  T_wy2=cosbet*cosalp;
  T_wz2=-cosgam*sinbet*cosalp - singam*sinalp;
  T_wx3=-singam*cosbet;
  T_wy3=sinbet;
  T_wz3=cosgam*cosbet;
}
```

Rotation angles.

Computing the coefficients.

Another function, T_rotation, which is presented in Listing 2.3, uses the coefficients computed in the T_set_rotation function to perform the actual rotation transformation.

LISTING 2.3

Rotation Transformation (see /3DGPL3/ TRANS/ trans-bs.c *on the CD)*

```
void T_world_rotation(int *from,
                      int *to,
                      int length)
{
  register int i,xt,yt,zt;

  for(i=0;i<length;i++)
  {
   xt=*from++;  yt=*from++;  zt=*from++;

   *to++=(int)(T_wx1*xt+T_wy1*yt+T_wz1*zt);
   *to++=(int)(T_wx2*xt+T_wy2*yt+T_wz2*zt);
   *to++=(int)(T_wx3*xt+T_wy3*yt+T_wz3*zt);
  }
}
```

The source assumed to contain continuous stream of points.

Using the coefficients computed previously

The approach implemented in the preceding listings is quite rigid. It is assumed that all three axis rotations are needed, which may not be the case. Also, the sequence of the axis rotations is predetermined and cannot be easily changed. The section "Representing Transformations in a Matrix Form" later in the chapter discusses a more general and flexible framework for geometric transformations.

Evaluating Trigonometric Functions

The key to the rotation transformation is the ability to evaluate trigonometric functions. Most of the time this is taken for granted thanks to available software libraries and at times even hardware assistance. However, there are situations when no assistance is available and developers are forced to compute *sin* or *cos* from scratch. A common approach is to represent these continuous functions by *power series*. A *Taylor power series*, allowing for expressing many functions, has the following form:

$$f(x) = f(a) + \frac{x-a}{1!}f'(a) + \frac{(x-a)^2}{2!}f''(a) + \frac{(x-a)^3}{3!}f'''(a) + ...$$

This expression permits finding the value of *f(x)* for argument *x* in the neighborhood of some argument point *a*. It demands, however, to know the values of derivative functions in the point *a*—that is, $f'(x)$ (the functions describing the rate of change for *f(x)*) as well as $f''(x)$ (the rate of change of the rate of change for *f(x)*) and so on. Computing the derivative functions for an arbitrary *a* is at least as complex a task as the one attempted in the first place. To avoid this problem, a convenient value of zero for *a* can be selected. The resulting series is known as a *Maclaurin power series*:

$$f(x) = f(0) + \frac{x}{1!}f'(0) + \frac{x^2}{2!}f''(0) + \frac{x^3}{3!}f'''(0) + ...$$

Since the values of all derivatives of *sin(a)* and *cos(a)* when *a=0* will be either *0* or *±1*, it is not difficult to obtain the expressions for particular power series computing the trigonometric functions:

$$\sin(x) = x - \frac{x^3}{3!} + \frac{x^5}{5!} - \dots$$

$$\cos(x) = 1 - \frac{x^2}{2!} + \frac{x^4}{4!} - \dots$$

It should be pointed out that these series are infinite in the number of terms, thus in order to obtain a precise value it is necessary to perform an infinite computation. For all practical purposes, approximate values for trigonometric functions are good enough. Computers can store values of only limited precision. Furthermore, fast graphics applications where frames are changing very fast allow for certain imprecisions to go completely unnoticed. Thus, selecting only the first few terms of the power series gives a procedure to find approximate values of trigonometric functions.

$$\sin(x) \approx x - \frac{x^3}{3!}$$

$$\cos(x) \approx 1 - \frac{x^2}{2!}$$

However, the fewer number of terms taken, the faster the computation yet the smaller the precision. In the case where only two first terms are selected, the computation will work reasonably well only in the immediate neighborhood of zero.

Consider Figure 2.12. Note that $x - \frac{x^3}{6}$ appears to approximate *sin(x)* well enough only in a very narrow domain.

FIGURE 2.12
Approximating
sin(x).

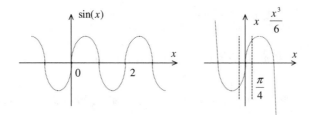

Generally, such an approximation works sufficiently well in the domain from $-\pi/4$ to $\pi/4$ (-45° to 45°). Note that this is also the case with approximation of *cos(x)* with $1 - \frac{x^2}{2}$ (see Figure 2.13).

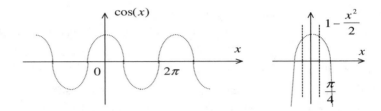

Obviously, it is necessary to know values for trigonometric functions outside of this narrow domain as well. To do that, you can take advantage of the regular nature of both *sin(x)* and *cos(x)*. It is not hard to recognize that trigonometric functions have a repetitive nature. The values of the functions repeat with the period of 2π *(360°)*, and hence it is sufficient to be able to compute the value in the domain from *0* to 2π in order to easily deduce it for the entire infinite range of arguments.

There is also a close relationship between *sin* and *cos* functions. From examining Figures 2.12 and 2.13 it is not hard to see that *sin(x)* looks like a horizontally shifted *cos(x)* and vice versa. Indeed, $\sin(x) = \cos(x - \frac{\pi}{2})$.

Thus, *sin(x)* from $\pi/4$ to $3\pi/4$ (45° to 135°) can be computed as *cos(x-π/2)* allowing for using $1 - \frac{(x-\pi/2)^2}{2}$.

Similarly, the values from $3\pi/4$ to $5\pi/4$ are nothing else but *–sin(x-π)*, that is $-(x - \pi) + \frac{(x-\pi)^3}{6}$ (see Figure 2.13). Proceeding this way, any value in the range from *0* to 2π *(360°)* can be computed.

The preceding formulas work for any fractional value in the neighborhood of zero. However, in some cases it makes sense to consider only integer angles because in many applications it is acceptable to manipulate with fairly rough measures for angles. If that is the case, *sin(x)* and *cos(x)* are not needed for the continuous real number range and can be limited to a discrete domain of 360 integers, one for every degree. The functions could be computed just once for all 360 degrees before any rotations are performed and the results could be stored in arrays. With that done, *sin(x)* or *cos(x)* can be found through a simple array lookup rather than through a relatively expensive evaluation of a power series.

Moreover, in some applications there is no need for 360 degrees. This measure is not very convenient. It is somewhat more efficient to divide the full angle into 256 pseudo degrees. By doing this, just one `unsigned char` (a byte) is needed to store an angle measure. Since a byte consists of eight bits, this allows for representing numbers from 0 to 255. When in the course of some computation a bigger (or smaller) value is obtained, the overflow is ignored and only part of the result is stored. For instance, 256 is stored as a 0 and 257 is stored as 1. This naturally limits the arguments to the range of 0 to 255, and since trigonometric functions are repetitive it permits automatically computing values even for big arguments through the corresponding value from the first period of the function.

Structure Deforming Transformations

Previous sections discussed rigid transformations. These leave the distances between points unchanged. Most algorithms that move objects in the virtual world or compute their images on the screen require only these transformations. There are situations in which the size or shape of objects has to change. This happens, for instance, during modeling or for the purposes of model animation. For that, *structure deforming* transformations are used. This section discusses two basic structure deforming transformations: *scaling* and *shearing*.

Scaling

The scaling transformation results when the distances between points proportionally expand or contract. Alternatively, scaling can be thought of as the contraction or the expansion of the space itself (see Figure 2.14).

One obvious use of this transformation is when trying to fit an object of the size x by x into a window of the size y by y. Evidently, every point of the object will have to be scaled in order to fit the window. In this case, the scaling is performed by multiplying the coordinates by the constant y/x. Alternatively, this transformation can be considered as scaling the window space to enclose the object. In general, separate scaling factors

s_x, s_y, s_z can be introduced for every axis:

$$x' = s_x x$$
$$y' = s_y y$$
$$z' = s_z z$$

This results in non-uniform scaling, as opposed to uniform scaling where the same factor acts in each direction. In both cases, if the factor is greater than zero and less than one, the object contracts. If the factor is greater than one, the object expands.

FIGURE 2.14
Scaling transformation.

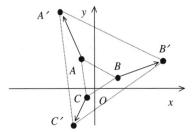

Shearing

The shearing transformation displaces points along the direction of some axis by the length proportional to the point's distance to the origin along another direction (see Figure 2.15).

FIGURE 2.15
Shearing transformation.

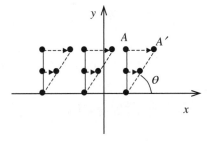

For instance, the transformation in Figure 2.15 moves points along the X axis proportional to their distance to zero along the Y axis. Points with a smaller y coordinate move by a proportionally smaller distance than those with a larger y. This transformation can be described by the following formulas:

$$x' = x + ky$$
$$y' = y$$
$$z' = z$$

In the preceding formulas, the coefficient k represents the parameter of the shear. The physical meaning of k is to describe how far a point with $y=1$ is displaced. If the shear is performed along another axis, the formulas will change accordingly. Note that the coefficient k is equal to $tan(\theta)$ (which is, of course, another trigonometric function such that $tan(x)=sin(x)/cos(x)$) where θ is the angle of the shear (see Figure 2.15). Specifying the angle instead of the displacement may, at times, be more convenient.

Representing Transformations in a Matrix Form

A *matrix* is a table of values:

$$A = \begin{bmatrix} a & b & c \\ d & e & f \\ g & i & j \end{bmatrix}$$

Special cases are matrices where one of the dimensions is equal to one. These are known as *row* and *column vectors*:

$$V = \begin{bmatrix} a & b & c \end{bmatrix}$$

$$C = \begin{bmatrix} x \\ y \\ z \end{bmatrix}$$

Both row and column vectors could be referred to as *tuples*. Thus, a vector with three elements could be called a three-tuple.

Note a slight notational ambiguity. Although *vectors* (meaning directed line segments) are often represented by *row* or *column vectors* (that's the reason for the ambiguity), the latter may also be used to store points or some other unrelated information.

A row can by multiplied by a column to produce a scalar value:

$$[a \quad b \quad c] \begin{bmatrix} x \\ y \\ z \end{bmatrix} = a \cdot x + b \cdot y + c \cdot z$$

Two matrices of the same size can be added. Each entry of the resulting matrix is a sum of the respective entries of the arguments. Matrix subtraction is effected in a similar way.

A matrix can be multiplied by another matrix. Each entry of the resulting matrix is obtained by multiplying respective rows and columns of the arguments. The fact that columns and rows need to have the same length in order for multiplication on them to be defined automatically places restrictions on the dimensions of the matrices that can be multiplied. The row size of the matrix on the left has to be equal to the column size of the matrix on the right, in which case their product can be computed as:

$$\begin{bmatrix} a & b & c \\ d & e & f \\ g & i & j \end{bmatrix} \begin{bmatrix} x & k \\ y & l \\ z & m \end{bmatrix} = \begin{bmatrix} [a \quad b \quad c]\begin{bmatrix} x \\ y \\ z \end{bmatrix} & [a \quad b \quad c]\begin{bmatrix} k \\ l \\ m \end{bmatrix} \\ [d \quad e \quad f]\begin{bmatrix} x \\ y \\ z \end{bmatrix} & [d \quad e \quad f]\begin{bmatrix} k \\ l \\ m \end{bmatrix} \\ [g \quad i \quad j]\begin{bmatrix} x \\ y \\ z \end{bmatrix} & [g \quad i \quad j]\begin{bmatrix} k \\ l \\ m \end{bmatrix} \end{bmatrix}$$

These operations of matrix arithmetic are a convenient framework for vector operations and for geometric transformations.

A point in 3D space has three coordinates. Using the notation of matrix multiplication, you can try to represent geometric transformations as a multiplication of a vector representing a point and a three-by-three matrix to produce another vector storing the transformed point.

$$[x \quad y \quad z] \begin{bmatrix} a & b & c \\ d & e & f \\ g & i & j \end{bmatrix} = [x \cdot a + y \cdot d + z \cdot g \quad x \cdot b + y \cdot e + z \cdot i \quad x \cdot c + y \cdot f + z \cdot j]$$

Looking closely at the preceding expression, you can see that nine rotation coefficients derived for 3D rotation transformation can be conveniently accommodated in a three-by-three matrix. The 3D rotation can then be thought of as just multiplication of a point by a rotation matrix producing the transformed point.

Similarly, other transformations can be expressed in this form as well. For instance, scaling will require the following transformation matrix:

$$\begin{bmatrix} x & y & z \end{bmatrix} \begin{bmatrix} s_x & 0 & 0 \\ 0 & s_y & 0 \\ 0 & 0 & s_z \end{bmatrix} = \begin{bmatrix} x \cdot s_x & y \cdot s_y & z \cdot s_z \end{bmatrix}$$

Shearing along the X axis can be described in this way:

$$\begin{bmatrix} x & y & z \end{bmatrix} \begin{bmatrix} 1 & 0 & 0 \\ k & 1 & 0 \\ 0 & 0 & 1 \end{bmatrix} = \begin{bmatrix} x + ky & y & z \end{bmatrix}$$

Representing the translation transformation in a matrix form is somewhat more difficult. Usual matrix multiplication doesn't allow for additions, which we require in this case. However, it is possible to express this transformation properly by using four-by-four matrices and somewhat adjusted coordinate vectors. A unit constant is inserted as the fourth element into coordinate vectors. Translation is what is called an *affine transformation*, whereas rotation and scaling are *linear transformations*. A general affine transformation can be thought of as a composition of some linear transformation (specified for the case of 3D space by a three-by-three matrix) and some translation (specified by an additional matrix dimension).

The following four-by-four matrix represents the translation transformation:

$$\begin{bmatrix} x & y & z & 1 \end{bmatrix} \begin{bmatrix} 1 & 0 & 0 & 0 \\ 0 & 1 & 0 & 0 \\ 0 & 0 & 1 & 0 \\ t_x & t_y & t_z & 1 \end{bmatrix} = \begin{bmatrix} x + t_x & y + t_y & z + t_z & 1 \end{bmatrix}$$

If matrices are chosen as a formalism to represent transformations and there is a need for translations, other transformations will have to be expressed as four-by-four matrices as well. When adding a new dimension to a rotation or a scaling matrix, in order to preserve the correctness of the operation all newly added entries will equal zero except for the new diagonal entry, which will have to be set to one.

According to the matrix multiplication rule, it is also possible to multiply a matrix by a column vector on the right in the following way:

$$
\begin{bmatrix} a & b & c \\ d & e & f \\ g & i & j \end{bmatrix} \begin{bmatrix} x \\ y \\ z \end{bmatrix} = \begin{bmatrix} x \cdot a + y \cdot b + z \cdot c \\ x \cdot d + y \cdot e + z \cdot f \\ x \cdot g + y \cdot i + z \cdot j \end{bmatrix}
$$

This kind of multiplication is also used as a formalism to express transformations. No particular difference exists between row vector and column vector formalisms. Conventions and personal habits usually determine the choice. Many earlier mathematics and computer graphics books used the row vector formalism since row vectors are easier to fit in a line and typeset for a publication. On the other hand, from a purist perspective, column vector formalism is closer to the notation *y=f(x)* used for scalar functions. This way, in the matrix notation *[Y]=[F][X]*, the transformation matrix *[F]* can be thought of as a transformation function. That is why many (although not all) current computer graphics books stick with the column formalism. As mentioned, there is no particular conceptual difference between the two formalisms. Either one can be used. It is, of course, either one or the other since matrices in the row vector formalism are transposed matrices of the column formalism and vice versa. The *transposition* is a matrix operation where an element at position *(i,j)* of the argument is to be found at the position *(j,i)* of the result:

$$
\begin{bmatrix} a & b & c \\ d & e & f \\ g & i & j \end{bmatrix}^T = \begin{bmatrix} a & d & g \\ b & e & i \\ c & f & j \end{bmatrix}
$$

Besides being mathematically pretty, there are a number of advantages to the matrix approach. It allows a generalized expression of transformations and it gives a computational shortcut for the cases with many consecutive transformations. For instance, suppose that there are several transformations, each represented in matrix form:

$$
[X'] = ([X][A])[B]
$$

where *[A]* and *[B]* are transformation matrices and *[X]* is the argument vector to be transformed. Since matrix multiplication has a property of associativity, which can be stated as:

$$([A][B])[C] = [A]([B][C])$$

the same transformation can then be expressed as:

$$[X'] = [X]([A][B])$$

This allows first finding the *concatenated* transformation matrix *[K]=[A][B]* and thereafter each transformation of some point can be computed as just:

$$[X'] = [X][K]$$

It should be noted that by representing each of the axis rotations in the form of a three-by-three matrix, it is easy to derive the formulas for 3D rotation by computing the concatenated matrix. In some sense, that's what was done when the formulas for the coefficients were derived in the section "Rotation in 3D." Initial expressions represented axis rotations and consecutive derivations mimicked two matrix multiplications:

$$[x'\ \ y'\ \ z'] = [x\ \ y\ \ z] \begin{bmatrix} \cos(\gamma) & 0 & -\sin(\gamma) \\ 0 & 1 & 0 \\ \sin(\gamma) & 0 & \cos(\gamma) \end{bmatrix}$$

$$\begin{bmatrix} 1 & 0 & 0 \\ 0 & \cos(\beta) & \sin(\beta) \\ 0 & -\sin(\beta) & \cos(\beta) \end{bmatrix} \begin{bmatrix} \cos(\alpha) & -\sin(\alpha) & 0 \\ \sin(\alpha) & \cos(\alpha) & 0 \\ 0 & 0 & 1 \end{bmatrix}$$

If you trace the expressions that are formed as the concatenated matrix is constructed, you'll get the same result as before (see "Rotation in 3D").

It was already demonstrated that rotation transformations don't commute. That is, depending on the order in which rotation transformations are applied, different results can be obtained. This has an obvious reflection in matrix multiplication. Unlike conventional integer or real number multiplication, which does commute *(ab=ba)*, matrix multiplication doesn't *([A][B]≠[B][A])*.

Consider the following:

$$\begin{bmatrix} a & b \\ c & d \end{bmatrix} \begin{bmatrix} i & j \\ u & v \end{bmatrix} = \begin{bmatrix} a \cdot i + b \cdot u & a \cdot j + b \cdot v \\ c \cdot i + d \cdot u & c \cdot j + d \cdot v \end{bmatrix}$$

This result is not equal for most *a,b,c,d,i,j,u,v* to:

$$\begin{bmatrix} i & j \\ u & v \end{bmatrix} \begin{bmatrix} a & b \\ c & d \end{bmatrix} = \begin{bmatrix} i \cdot a + j \cdot c & u \cdot a + v \cdot c \\ i \cdot b + j \cdot d & u \cdot b + v \cdot d \end{bmatrix}$$

For example, in the case when *d=1* and *b=1* and the rest are zeros:

$$\begin{bmatrix} 0 & 0 \\ 0 & 1 \end{bmatrix} \begin{bmatrix} 0 & 1 \\ 0 & 0 \end{bmatrix} = \begin{bmatrix} 0 & 0 \\ 0 & 0 \end{bmatrix} \neq \begin{bmatrix} 0 & 1 \\ 0 & 0 \end{bmatrix} \begin{bmatrix} 0 & 0 \\ 0 & 1 \end{bmatrix} = \begin{bmatrix} 0 & 1 \\ 0 & 0 \end{bmatrix}$$

Matrix approaches are very effective when there are a lot of consecutive transformations. For example, for consecutive rotations it makes sense to compute their concatenated matrix and then use it to transform multiple points. (It will save quite a few multiplications; one versus several consecutive matrix multiplications for each point to transform.)

It should be noted, however, that matrix formalism generalizes transformations. Multiplication of a vector by a three-by-three matrix triggers nine scalar multiplications. On the other hand, an individual rotation transformation around one axis that is expressed through two formulas has only four. (Five matrix entries are zeros, but this doesn't prevent a processor from spending some cycles on them). The situation is even worse in the case of scaling where only three multiplications are needed, yet when represented as a matrix, nine multiplications will result.

One implication of this fact is that when the transformations to be performed are known in advance and they can be represented as sparse matrices (matrices with very few nonzero entries), it may be worthwhile to derive the formulas for all coefficients of the concatenated matrix directly instead of obtaining the latter using matrix multiplication. With the example of 3D rotation, calculating coefficients directly cost 16 multiplications, whereas two matrix multiplications cost 54 multiplications (3 multiplications per entry, 9 entries, 2 multiplications), again due to the fact that a lot of matrix entries in this particular case were zeros.

Matrix representation provides a very effective unifying framework to express transformations. When an application needs an arbitrary set of transformations in the runtime, implementation may directly express any transformation as a matrix. This may be the case in model animation, for instance. On the other hand, in the cases where only a limited number of transformations is required and their order is known in advance, it may be worthwhile to take advantage of a more specialized approach, such as precomputing the coefficients directly.

Projection Transformations

The world that we are modeling is three dimensional. Yet the display device where the scene must appear possesses only two dimensions. The process of mapping 3D world coordinates into 2D screen coordinates is performed by *projection* transformations.

Although there are infinitely many imaginable ways to map the 3D space onto a 2D plane, two methods are of particular interest for computer graphics: parallel and perspective projections. The following subsections discuss these two projection transformations.

Parallel Projection

Parallel projection is obtained when one dimension of the space collapses so that all the points belonging to parallel lines in 3D space map into single points on the projection plane. Hence the name, parallel projection (see Figure 2.16).

FIGURE 2.16
*Parallel
projection.*

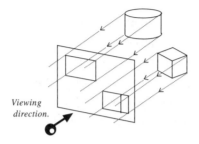

*Viewing
direction.*

The parallel projection can be further differentiated based on the angle at which the projection lines cross the projection plane. If it is the *right* (90 degrees) angle, these projections are called *orthographic*. The rest are called *oblique*.

Representations, which are perhaps familiar from engineering drawings, are often based on a set of multiple orthographic projections (*top view*, *front view*, and *side view*). Interactive computer graphics is concerned primarily with orthographic projections, perhaps because they correspond to how humans see surrounding objects located at some distance away.

If the projection plane is parallel to the plane *XY* of the coordinate system, then, the projection lines will be parallel to the *Z* axis. Hence, the parallel projection transformation will only involve discarding *z* coordinates for all points in space.

Of course, for practical applications it is interesting to obtain a projection corresponding to the position and orientation of the viewer's camera in the virtual world. For most of these cases, the projection plane will not be necessarily parallel to the *XY* plane of the coordinate system.

An arbitrary parallel projection can be represented as a two-step process. In this process, you first perform some affine transformation that will transform the space so that the projection plane is mapped into the *XY* plane, and then in the second step, the parallel projection of the simplified kind discussed above is performed.

Clearly, the affine transformation to apply during the first step will involve translating the viewer into the center of the world space and rotating the world according to the viewer's orientation. Chapter 5, "Viewing," will return to this problem and discuss in detail how to find the affine transformation required during the first step for cameras described in different ways.

As you have just seen, discarding the z coordinate is fundamental to the parallel projection transformation. However, by discarding it, all depth information of the original 3D space is lost. In order to somewhat reduce this effect, perspective projection should be considered. Despite this drawback, the parallel projections are widely used in many areas, such as in CAD applications. For these, the important qualities of the parallel projection to preserve parallel lines in the images and to preserve actual sizes of objects is more important than a realistic view.

Perspective Projection

The *perspective projection* creates an image in which sizes of the projections of objects depend on their distance from the viewer. It is not hard to visualize this effect of perspective transformation. Perhaps the first association a lot of people have is an empty straight street with identical buildings on both sides disappearing into infinity. This example illustrates that objects farthest away have virtually zero size, whereas the objects closest to the viewer are extremely big.

The perspective projection transformation can be modeled by simulating the viewer's eye as the convergence point for all rays reflected from objects in virtual space—not a big stretch from what's happening in reality. Each ray, before being caught by the eye, would intersect the plane located in front of the viewer. By finding the intersection and plotting a point there on the display, the viewer observing it can be deceived into thinking that the ray from the plotted point was actually coming from the original position in space (see Figure 2.17).

FIGURE 2.17
Perspective projection.

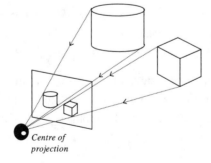

Centre of
projection

Similar to the method used in the previous section, a projection plane can be chosen to coincide with the *XY* plane of the reference system. In such a case, there is some straightforward relationship linking the original point and its image on the projection plane. Let's consider a planar case first (see Figure 2.18).

FIGURE 2.18
Geometry of perspective projection.

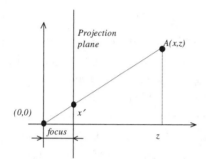

The viewer's eye is located at the origin of the reference system. The distance between the viewer's eye and the projection plane is often called the *focus* distance. The goal is to determine at what point the ray coming from point *A* into the viewer's eye will intersect the projection plane. A point will have to be plotted at the corresponding position on the screen. Clearly, this is a case of some similar triangles whose properties are proportional. Thus, focus distance is proportional to the value of *z* and *x'* is proportional to *x*. The following relationship is derived from the fact that the angle at the beginning of the coordinates is the same for both triangles (the bigger one and the smaller one) and the fact that if two angles are the same, their tangents will be too:

$$\frac{x'}{focus} = \frac{x}{z} \Leftrightarrow x' = \frac{x \cdot focus}{z}$$

The same consideration applies for the dimension *Y*. Together, the two formulas describe the 3D case:

$$x' = focus \cdot x/z$$

$$y' = focus \cdot y/z$$

This situation applies only in the case where the viewer is located at the beginning of the coordinates looking along the axis Z. If that is not the case, the same two-step process can be used as with parallel projection. First some affine transformation is performed that places the viewer into the beginning of the coordinates. This is followed by a simplified perspective projection just described. Which affine transformation needs to be applied will be discussed in Chapter 5.

The situation with the z coordinate requires some clarification. After the perspective transformation, the primitives are rendered onto the screen, which is planar. This requires knowing the x and y coordinates but not z, so z could be discarded. However, when trying to render multi-face objects, it is important to know the depth (z) of all polygons so that it is possible to deduce which are visible and which are obscured. (This will be discussed in detail in Chapter 7, "Hidden Surface Removal.") So the depth information can be preserved for future use by having $z'=z$. However, doing the transformation on x and y and leaving z unaltered may actually allow for the depth relation to change. That is, a polygon obscuring another polygon in the original space, before the projection, can actually come out behind or partially behind the second polygon after the perspective transformation (see Figure 2.19).

FIGURE 2.19
The depth relations before and after perspective transformation.

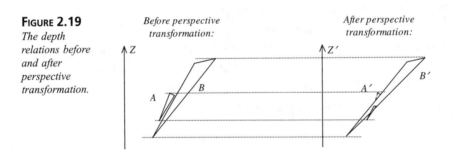

To avoid this undesirable effect, a non-linear transformation should be applied to the z coordinate as well. For instance, $z'=-C/z$, where C is some constant.

The implementation of the perspective transformation is quite straightforward. However, since the computation is parameterized with the focus distance, its physical meaning must be clarified, which will allow for choosing the proper numeric value (see Figure 2.20).

FIGURE 2.20
Meaning of the focus distance.

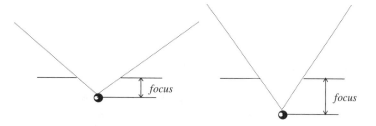

The focus distance determines the field of view angle. When the focus distance is smaller, the angle is wider; when it is bigger, the angle is narrower. It is helpful to think of this distance as measured in screen pixels. For instance, if the chosen focus distance is 160 pixels and the display is 320-by-320 pixels, the resulting view angle is 90 degrees.

The perspective transformation may at first produce poor looking images with some unnatural distortions. Experimentation is usually necessary to improve the realism. Focus distances that give the view angle somewhere between 75 and 85 degrees may be a good place to start, but that, of course, depends on the geometry of a particular scene.

It is more difficult to express the perspective transformation in a matrix form. Actually, the usual matrix multiplication deals with only linear transformations, while perspective projection that involves division is non-linear. Another special convention is needed in order to represent it as a matrix. One smaller convention has been already taken in order to allow for translation. The translation is an affine transformation. The convention was to add an extra dimension to the three-by-three matrices.

The convention that is taken to enable representing the perspective transformation is maintaining *homogeneous* coordinates. A value of 1 that was added after x, y, and z into the coordinate vector should remain as 1. If, in the course of applying a transformation, a different value will be obtained at that place, the vector should be *renormalized*. Every entry should be multiplied by the same constant to make the last entry become 1 again.

Assuming this strategy, the matrix for perspective transformation can be composed as follows:

$$[x \quad y \quad z \quad 1] \begin{bmatrix} 1 & 0 & 0 & 0 \\ 0 & 1 & 0 & 0 \\ 0 & 0 & 0 & 1/focus \\ 0 & 0 & -1 & 0 \end{bmatrix} = [x \quad y \quad -1 \quad z/focus]$$

Because the last entry in the result vector is not 1, normalization has to be performed by multiplying each entry by its reciprocal *focus/z*.

$$[x \quad y \quad -1 \quad z/focus] = [x \cdot focus/z \quad y \cdot focus/z \quad -focus/z \quad 1]$$

Depending on the requirement for the *z* coordinate, which may even be discarded when the depth information is not required any further, the preceding matrix will have a somewhat different form:

$$\begin{bmatrix} 1 & 0 & 0 & 0 \\ 0 & 1 & 0 & 0 \\ 0 & 0 & 0 & 1/focus \\ 0 & 0 & 0 & 0 \end{bmatrix}$$

Moreover, if the viewer's position were not conveniently chosen to be at the beginning of the coordinates but at some location with negative *z*, for instance, the transformation formulas and hence the transformation matrix would have had yet again a different form. Depending on the convention chosen and the needs of every application, a particular form of the transformation and its matrix are derived.

There are several other problems with the perspective transformation. For instance, consider where the perspective transformation maps the point with *z* coordinate equal to zero. Since division by z is performed, that will be infinity, which will likely result in a division error. This is hardly a viable outcome.

Another problem is that calculations for points with negative *z* will produce negative results. The objects with such *z* coordinates will appear flipped over. Then again, objects with negative *z* coordinates are behind the viewing plane and effectively behind the viewer and should not be displayed in the first place.

The only way to deal with these problems is to guarantee that there are no points with invalid *z* coordinates. You can achieve this is by performing *3D clipping* of the original set of points. This will be discussed in Chapter 4, "Clipping."

The 3D clipping has to be performed immediately before the perspective transformation but after the affine transformation, which places the viewer into the origin of the space. Thus, representing all transformations by a single concatenated matrix is problematic because representing clipping in a conventional matrix form is hardly feasible. If it is known that none of the points will ever be behind the viewing plane, there is no need for clipping and in this instance all transformations can be represented as one concatenated matrix. In other cases, clipping cannot be avoided and the transformations are separated into two stages: before and after application of 3D clipping.

Fractional Arithmetic

Fractional numbers are necessary to implement the geometric transformations. For instance, scaling factors may be less than 1 and more than zero if the object is to be scaled down. The values of trigonometric functions *sin(x)* and *cos(x)* are also in the range from -1 to 1 and cannot be represented as integers. Thus, although the coordinates of points eventually become integers for the purposes of drawing in a raster display device (the screen consists of numbered discrete pixels, after all), intermediate calculations require fractional numbers.

It is worthwhile to review possible approaches for storing fractional numbers. There are multiple ways available and it helps to know several alternatives that exist. Of course, modern computers provide hardware support for at least one type of fractional number, notably *floating point* numbers. However, some graphics boards demand different representation, in particular some variation of *fixed point* format. Moreover, the latter type can be efficiently emulated using available operations for integers and hence may be used as a fast software alternative to floating point numbers under some circumstances.

It is beneficial to refresh how digital computers represent integer numbers. With any counting system, digits in a multi-digit number have different weight, so to speak. With decimal numbers, this weight is some power of ten. For instance, 102 is actually:

$$1 \cdot 10^2 + 0 \cdot 10^1 + 2 \cdot 10^0 = 100 + 0 + 2 = 102$$

It is difficult to built electronic circuitry that allows for representing ten different states for every digit. Thus, the simplest system with only two different states of each digit is chosen instead: the *binary system* (see Figure 2.21).

FIGURE 2.21
Representing integers.

1	0	0	1	1
$2^4 = 16$	$2^3 = 8$	$2^2 = 4$	$2^1 = 2$	$2^0 = 1$

With the binary system, the weight of digits or *bits* is an increasing power of two. Thus the number in Figure 2.21 should be interpreted in decimal base as:

$$1 \cdot 2^4 + 0 \cdot 2^3 + 0 \cdot 2^2 + 1 \cdot 2^1 + 1 \cdot 2^0 = 16 + 0 + 0 + 2 + 1 = 19$$

Whenever confusion might arise as to the base of a number, the base will be denoted in parentheses following the number—such as 1011(bin) for a binary number or 1010(dec) for a decimal.

It is also necessary to consider representation for negative numbers. While there are several methods, one has effectively prevailed today. This is the so-called *two's complement form*. It requires negating the weight of the leftmost digit (see Figure 2.22).

FIGURE 2.22
Representing negative integers.

1	1	1	1	1
$-2^4 = -16$	$2^3 = 8$	$2^2 = 4$	$2^1 = 2$	$2^0 = 1$

The number represented above is thus interpreted as:

$$1 \cdot (-2^4) + 1 \cdot 2^3 + 1 \cdot 2^2 + 1 \cdot 2^1 + 1 \cdot 2^0 = -16 + 8 + 4 + 2 + 1 = -1$$

The advantage of this approach is that it isn't necessary to change addition and subtraction algorithms that work for positive integers in order to accommodate two's complement integers. This is due to the natural wrapping of the integer numbers resulting from the way they are represented in computers. If 1 is added to the maximum number that can be represented, there is a carry from the most significant (leftmost) bit, which is ignored, and the result is exactly 0. In the signed representation, -1 is the maximum value that can be stored in the unsigned representation, and indeed -1 + 1 = 0. Although addition and subtraction algorithms don't have to be changed in order to accommodate two's complement negative numbers, multiplication and division algorithms do. That's why there are instructions for both signed and unsigned multiplication in most processors.

Since the leftmost digit in the two's complement representation carries negative weight and because that's the one with the highest power, the minimum negative number possible to represent in the preceding example will be 10000(bin) = -16(dec). All the other digits have positive weights, so the maximum possible positive number will be 01111(bin) = 15(dec).

Floating Point Arithmetic

A floating point number consists of several parts. Although particular formats may vary, there are two essential components: the *mantissa* and the *exponent*. Both are integers and can be positive or negative. If the mantissa is denoted as M and the exponent is denoted as E, the number that is represented is assumed to be $M \cdot 2^E$

The base of the exponent is most commonly binary but it doesn't have to be. For instance, old IBM mainframes used the base of 16. Since the exponent can be either positive or negative, 2^E can be either very small or very big. In the particular case, when the exponent is negative the following takes place:

$$M \cdot 2^{-E} = \frac{M}{2^E}$$

Since some number divides the mantissa, it reduces the weights associated with each bit, so to speak. Some of the weights may become fractional and, depending on the magnitude of the exponent, a different number of bits will thus have a fractional weight. A point in a fractional number separates those digits with integer weight from those with fractional weight. In this case, the position of the point depends on the value of the exponent, hence the name *floating point* format.

The key concept allowing for implementation of the arithmetic operations for floating point numbers is that the mantissa and the exponent can be adjusted in a coordinated manner and still describe the very same number.

Of course, the mantissa is just an integer, every digit of which has a weight of an increasing power of two. If all digits are shifted to the left by one position, every digit arrives at a location where the weight is twice as big. Thus, by shifting all digits to the left by one position, the resulting value is also twice as big as the original. A familiar example from everyday arithmetic is multiplication of a decimal number by ten. Obviously, it is enough to add an extra zero on the right to obtain the result. This operation does the very same thing—all original digits are shifted to the left by one position, increasing their corresponding weight by ten.

Thus, if the bits of the mantissa are shifted to the left by one, the mantissa's value becomes twice as big. This should be compensated for by dividing the whole expression by two in order to preserve the same value. Of course, since

$$\frac{2^E}{2} = 2^{E-1}$$

to compensate for the change, the exponent should be reduced by one. Using this procedure, the algorithm of adding two floating point numbers can be expressed as follows:

$$M_1 2^{E_1} + M_2 2^{E_2} = (M_1' + M_2)2^{E_2}$$

In other words, one of the mantissas is adjusted in such a way that the exponents become equal. After that, the mantissas are added and the common exponent is used for the result.

The multiplication operation is even easier—just multiply the mantissas and add the exponents:

$$M_1 2^{E_1} \cdot M_2 2^{E_2} = (M_1 \cdot M_2)2^{E_1+E_2}$$

Subtraction and division are reciprocal to addition and multiplication and are computed very similarly. Mantissas are subtracted during subtraction of floating point numbers. Mantissas are divided and exponents are subtracted for the division.

Although the idea is quite straightforward, there is an ample amount of subtleties such as ranges of numbers involved, possible overflow or underflow and their treatment, representation of critical situations such as infinitely small or infinitely big results, and so on. Whereas historically every computer manufacturer had a different format for floating point numbers, this has changed over the past two decades. Today, all hardware manufacturers adhere to the IEEE standard for floating point.

Most computers today have hardware support for floating point operations. In many cases, so much attention is paid to floating point performance that it exceeds integer performance. It is quite common, for instance, for floating point multiplication to be faster than integer multiplication, although that is not always the case. It should be noted that, algorithmically, integer multiplication is easier but due to hardware design it may work slower.

Fixed Point Arithmetic

A floating point number consists of the mantissa and the exponent. Both can change, which allows for the representation of a wide range of numbers. If the exponent is fixed as some negative number, the assumed fractional point for the mantissa is also fixed. With a fixed exponent, there is no need to store it anymore. Its value is simply assumed. Such a representation is known as *fixed point* format.

Suppose the exponent is equal to -2. The weight of the rightmost bit that used to be equal to 1 will now have to be divided by 2^2 becoming one quarter. The weights of other bits will change accordingly (see Figure 2.23).

FIGURE 2.23
Representing a fixed point number.

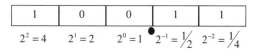

The number represented in Figure 2.23 should thus be considered as:

$$1 \cdot 2^2 + 0 \cdot 2^1 + 0 \cdot 2^0 + 1 \cdot 2^{-1} + 1 \cdot 2^{-2} = 4 + 0 + 0 + \frac{1}{2} + \frac{1}{4} = 4\frac{3}{4}$$

Let's find the range of numbers that can be represented in this particular format. Returning once again to the analogy with the decimal numbers, you can see that two digits to the right of the decimal point can cover the range from 0.00 to 0.99 in 0.01 steps. Numbers smaller than the minimal 0.01 precision step can't be represented without increasing the number of fractional digits. The same happens with the binary numbers. In the example in Figure 2.23, since there are two binary digits, the minimal number that can be represented is 1/4 (0.01(bin) = 1/4(dec)). And again, the numbers with higher precision can be represented only by increasing the number of binary digits after the binary point.

The format with only one integer digit and all remaining digits having fractional weight is quite convenient to store the values of trigonometric functions because the range of numbers such a format describes is close to [-1,1] (see Figure 2.24).

FIGURE 2.24
Fixed point number with a single integer field.

0	1	1	1	1

$-2^0 = -1 \quad 2^{-1} = \frac{1}{2} \quad 2^{-2} = \frac{1}{4} \quad 2^{-3} = \frac{1}{8} \quad 2^{-4} = \frac{1}{16}$

Since the weight of the leftmost digit in Figure 2.24 is negated to accommodate negative numbers, and it is also the digit with the greatest absolute weight, the smallest number that can be represented is 10000(bin) or -1(dec). Unfortunately, due to the asymmetry discussed previously there won't be any representation for positive 1, just its approximation: 01111(bin) = 1/2+1/4+1/8+1/16=15/16 (see Figure 2.24). For most graphics applications, when there are, for instance, 15 bits representing fractions, such an approximation is close enough and won't cause problems. Yet for some algorithms this may become an additional source of accumulated error, thus requiring the allocation of more fractional digits.

Normally there is no hardware support for fixed point arithmetic. However, corresponding integer operations can be used to achieve this result.

To add or subtract two fixed point numbers, integer addition and subtraction can be used. The weight of bits of the result in these operations is the same as corresponding weights in the arguments.

The situation is somewhat more complex with multiplication and division. Consider what is happening when two decimal numbers are multiplied. For example, when an integer is multiplied by a number with a decimal point and the result needs to be an integer (the fractional part could be neglected):

```
×      1.52
         11
       _____
+      1 52
      15 2
       _____
      16.72
```

As you can see, the actual result of the multiplication has as many digits after the decimal point as there were in both arguments. Since only the integer part is needed for the result, the digits following the point are discarded, effectively shifted to the right by two positions.

A similar approach is taken with the fixed point binary numbers. For instance, when multiplying an integer by a number having eight bits considered to be after the binary point, the result of the multiplication will also have eight bits after the point. If it is just the integer part that is required, the digits have to be shifted right by eight bits, destroying all fractional information. In general, the result of multiplication of two fixed point numbers is adjusted by shifting to have as many fractional digits as necessary. Consider the following example: Two binary numbers 00.10(bin) and 01.10(bin) having two binary digits each are multiplied.

```
×      00.10
       01.10
      _____
        0000
        0010
        0010
        0000
      _____
     000.1100
```

The result, 000.1100(bin), has four fractional digits. If the result is to have the same format as the arguments, it has to be shifted right by two digits. And indeed 1/2 times 3/2 equals 3/4, just what is computed in this case.

A similar technique is applied in the case of divisions. To divide two integers and obtain a fixed point result, the argument to be divided has to be shifted left (added fixed point fields), so that effectively a fixed point number is divided by an integer.

It is often helpful to implement a general-purpose fixed point arithmetic library. However, the fixed point algorithms depend on the selected precision, in particular exactly how the arguments and results must be adjusted by shifting. Since it is convenient to use different precision in different parts of graphics applications, it may become useful to choose several different formats of fixed point numbers, one for every specific place, and implement computations for some particular expressions directly.

It is important to also figure out whether it is possible to implement all the operations using just high level C, or whether it will be necessary to descend into the assembly level. In most assemblies, the result of multiplication has twice as many bits as each of the arguments, which is helpful since fixed point operations produce extra bits to be discarded by shifting. Besides, the result of multiplication will often be located in two registers. The operations can be organized in such a way that instead of adjusting the result by shifting, it can just be taken from the register carrying higher bits, effectively doing a zero-cost right shift by the bit length of the register. On the other hand, compromising code portability by coding in assembly can be considered a questionable practice in some situations. Obviously, depending on the particular application, the question can be resolved either way.

The fixed point arithmetic is clearly useful for the implementation of 3D transformations that require a lot of multiplications. Assume that coordinates of points are stored as integers. The result of a *sin(x)* or *cos(x)* function is clearly fractional and, therefore, so are the coefficients in the transformation matrices. Both of these can be represented using the same fixed point format.

In a typical 3D application that uses fixed point arithmetic, in order to construct the transformation matrices, fixed point numbers will be multiplied by other fixed point numbers. The result will have twice as many fractional digits as required and, thus, will have to be adjusted by right shifts (see Listing 2.4).

Assuming that the coordinates of points are represented as integers, in the routine implementation of the rotation transformation, integers will be multiplied by fixed point numbers. The result will also have fractional digits, which can be removed by right shifts if only the integer part of the result is needed (which is not unreasonable since the final destination of these coordinates is to index a discrete bitmap storing the image).

LISTING 2.4

Using Fixed Point Numbers for Building Rotation Coefficients (see /3DGPL3/ TRANS/ trans-bs.c *on the CD)*

T_P - denotes the number of fractional digits.

```
                               . . .
T_wx1=((singam*((sinbet*sinalp)>>T_P))>>T_P) + ((cosgam*cosalp)>>T_P);
T_wy1=((cosbet*sinalp)>>T_P);
T_wz1=((singam*cosalp)>>T_P) - ((cosgam*((sinbet*sinalp)>>T_P))>>T_P);
T_wx2=((singam*((sinbet*cosalp)>>T_P))>>T_P) - ((cosgam*sinalp)>>T_P);
                               . . .
```

Removing extra fractional digits.

It is often necessary to convert a floating point number into a fixed point number. This may be necessary, for instance, when the trigonometric functions are computed as floating point numbers but the transformations are done in fixed point. If a floating point number is simply assigned to an integer (used to store fixed point numbers), C will perform the necessary and meaningful conversion so that the whole part of the floating point number is transferred but the fractional part is discarded. Since it is necessary to transfer certain amounts of fractional information as well, you can attempt to move the floating point before the assignment. Adjusting the exponent moves the floating point. Since you cannot manipulate the mantissa or the exponent directly in C (or more precisely it could be done but not without some hacking and bit manipulation), it is nicer instead to exploit some underlying mathematics. To move a floating point in the mantissa by one position to the left, the exponent has to be increased by one. This can be done by multiplying the floating point number by the base of the exponent (*2*). Thus, to transfer N bits of fractional digits from a floating point number, the number has to be multiplied first by 2 to the power of N and the result should simply be assigned to the integer triggering all the necessary conversion.

There are several concerns related to the implementation of fixed point arithmetic. Care must be taken for the range of numbers the operations will work for. If 32-bit integers are used to store fixed point numbers and 16 of those bits are allocated as fractional digits and 1 bit relates to the sign, then only 15 bits can carry the integer part. After multiplication of the two fixed point numbers, all 32 bits will actually carry fractions since the result has as many fractional bits as in both arguments.

The integer part will simply disappear. When coding the operations in assembly, this problem can be avoided entirely since the result of multiplication there will physically have twice as many bits as in each of the arguments and no bits will be lost. However, when implementing fixed point arithmetic using only high-level language, this may become a serious problem.

The processors with fast floating point units available today do floating point multiplication faster than integer multiplication. However, this is not quite the case with addition. Integer addition on most processors is faster than floating point addition. It should again be underlined that integer arithmetic algorithms in general are less costly than floating point ones, but the latter are usually dedicated much more silicon by processor designers, hence the higher speed for multiplication. Some of this speed increase can be attributed to pipelining and it gives improved throughput only for sequences of floating point instructions. (Which, luckily, is the case with matrix operations.)

There are, thus, many different tradeoffs that make choosing the underlying arithmetic for algorithms difficult at times. If the algorithm is mostly incremental, fixed point is usually a good choice since addition will be the predominant operation. On the other hand, in the case where multiplication will be predominant, choosing the calculation scheme may depend on the targeted processor.

Hardware Assistance for Geometric Transformations

The geometric transformations constitute an important performance bottleneck for interactive 3D graphics applications. For every generated frame, many vertices describing the virtual scene have to be translated and rotated (perhaps several times each) and finally projected so that scene's image can be drawn.

It is not surprising that hardware manufacturers try to provide some hardware assistance so that the transformations can be done faster. The type of assistance ranges from simple vector instructions to full support of matrix operations.

For instance, the Sony PlayStation game platform has a dedicated unit named *Geometry Transfer Engine* (GTE), which performs multiplication of a scalar and a vector, multiplication of a vector and a matrix, and multiplication of two matrices. The unit uses fixed point representation of numbers.

These operations allow for performing all pertinent geometric transformations, especially with the help of a vector matrix multiplication. Concatenated matrices can be constructed using the matrix multiplication instruction.

The PlayStation, of course, is a dedicated game machine where it is admissible to have such special-purpose functionality implemented in hardware. Although similar auxiliary geometry units are appearing today on general-purpose video cards, it is still relatively rare. Instead, most general-purpose processors provide more generic instruction that can help speed up geometric transformations or other similar tasks. Multimedia Extensions (MMX), which were introduced by Intel for Pentium processors, do just that. Besides some changes to the processor's cache and data paths, these extensions also add several new instructions. Many of these instructions are known as *single instruction multiple data* (SIMD). They allow for performing several arithmetic operations in parallel. Thus, one instruction is issued to act on multiple arguments at the same time. These instructions are quite convenient for geometric transformations that have a significant amount of parallelism. After all, the same type of computation is done independently for each of the three coordinates.

The MMX instruction set contains 57 instructions, including the instructions of packed arithmetic. It is possible to do operations in parallel on eight 8-bit integer numbers, four 16-bit integer numbers, or two 32-bit integer numbers. The instructions of packed arithmetic perform parallel addition, subtraction, multiplication, and a combined multiply-add. The latter comes in handy for implementing the geometric transformations.

The following general matrix, where the m entries describe the linear portion of the transformation (rotation and scaling) and the t entries describe additional translation, can represent most geometric transformations.

$$
\begin{bmatrix} v_1 & v_2 & v_3 & 1 \end{bmatrix}
\begin{bmatrix}
m_{11} & m_{12} & m_{13} & 0 \\
m_{21} & m_{22} & m_{23} & 0 \\
m_{31} & m_{32} & m_{33} & 0 \\
t_1 & t_2 & t_3 & 1
\end{bmatrix}
$$

If this matrix multiplication is expanded, the following expressions have to be computed for each coordinate (see Figure 2.25).

FIGURE 2.25
*Parallelism
in matrix
multiplication.*

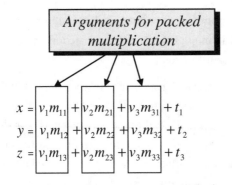

$$x = \boxed{v_1 m_{11}} + \boxed{v_2 m_{21}} + \boxed{v_3 m_{31}} + t_1$$
$$y = \boxed{v_1 m_{12}} + \boxed{v_2 m_{22}} + \boxed{v_3 m_{32}} + t_2$$
$$z = \boxed{v_1 m_{13}} + \boxed{v_2 m_{23}} + \boxed{v_3 m_{33}} + t_3$$

It is not hard to see that indicated multiplications are independent and can be done in parallel by a single packed multiplication instruction. Since all columns are to be added together, it is even more convenient to use multiply-add instruction so that each consecutive instruction performs the multiplication first and then adds its result to the current sum. Discounting the instructions to move and pack the arguments in the registers, entire vector matrix multiplication can be implemented in just three instructions.

It should be noted that MMX has several drawbacks. One is that packed instructions only do integer arithmetic, necessitating the use of fixed point numbers. This drawback is overcome, however, in *3Dnow* extensions from AMD, which extends the MMX instruction set with floating point packed instructions as well. The second disadvantage is the low combined bit size. Although it is possible to do arithmetic in parallel on four 16-bit values, these are not big enough. Only two 32-bit numbers can be acted on at the same time and, whereas the bit size is sufficient, the amount of parallelism of just two numbers at the same time is not good enough.

Approaches similar to MMX are used on a wide variety of hardware. For instance, the *Visual Instruction Set* of SPARC processors is also based on an SIMD strategy.

Generally, using the special provisions of processors permits speeding up the geometric transformations considerably. Using these features is quite straightforward and doesn't demand a lot of development effort. However, the strength of the features differs considerably across various platforms, making portable solutions quite difficult (if not impossible).

Summary

The geometric transformations in this chapter serve as the basis for describing location, orientation, and motion of virtual objects as well as their visibility to the viewer.

Rigid transformations such as translations and rotations keep the shapes and sizes of transformed objects unchanged. Shape deforming transformations such as scalings and shearings don't guarantee that. Geometric transformations and their computations can be represented with the help of matrices. The matrix approach allows for generalized expression of transformations as well as for representing several transformations in one, concatenated matrix.

The projection transformations compute an image of points in 3D space on a 2D plane. These could also be represented with the help of matrices. Computation of trigonometric functions and fractional arithmetic are important for the geometric transformations. There is often hardware support present for both, as well as some special provisions to speed up matrix operations.

CHAPTER 3

Rasterization

The mathematical techniques that you saw in Chapter 2, "Geometric Transformations," allowed for describing various positions and movements of virtual objects in space as well as their visibility to the viewer by means of projection transformations.

The projection transformations map the coordinates of key points of geometric primitives from 3D space into the screen 2D space. These primitives must now be drawn in their entirety based on the screen coordinates of their key points. Raster display devices represent an image as a square array of pixels. By changing a particular entry in this array, a corresponding screen pixel lights up. To draw a geometric primitive, many pixels that fall inside the area of the primitive must be lit in a coordinated manner. This process is called *rasterization*.

Some primitives, such as line segments and polygons, are easier to rasterize than others. In a lot of practical applications, a graphics module will support rendering of only these basic primitives. In cases where the description of some object demands more complex primitives, such as *cubic curves* or *bicubic patches* (which are discussed in Chapter 6, "Modeling"), rasterization can be achieved by approximating them with what is available. Curves are often approximated with line segments, and surface patches are approximated with polygons. Less commonly, there may be a routine rasterizing some more complex primitives directly, notably some curves.

It is true that modern graphics accelerators have some rasterization algorithms implemented in hardware. It is nevertheless important enough to examine the underlying algorithms in order to understand what hardware does and how to better interface with it.

This chapter considers rasterization of simple geometric primitives such as points, line segments, and polygons. Several techniques that allow you to enhance the appearance of rasterized primitives are also considered, notably shading and texture mapping.

Because a raster image is inherently discrete, algorithms drawing the primitives may introduce some visual degeneracies when the analytical shape of the primitive cannot be exactly represented by the discrete mosaic of pixels. Possible approaches to deal with these *aliasing* problems are discussed in the last section of the chapter.

> **Note**
>
> You will find the sample 3Dgpl programs `polygon.c` and `texture.c` on the accompanying CD useful for this chapter. Compile these for your platform using an appropriate makefile. Examine the implementation of the rasterization module located in the GRAPHICS subdirectory of 3Dgpl's source.
>
> See Appendix A, "3Dgpl Graphics Library" for more instructions about 3Dgpl and sample programs.

Rasterizing Points

On a somewhat simplistic level, rasterizing a point is very straightforward. It only involves setting a particular value describing the desired color into the specific entry of the bitmap memory. The difficulty, however, becomes apparent with the realization that the image bitmap is inherently discrete and nothing can be drawn in between pixels.

In other words, to plot a point whose real coordinates are between integer pixel coordinates, you have to decide how to resolve this ambiguity. Perhaps rounding to the nearest integer is a fairly logical and very common choice. However, the discrete nature of digital images is an inherent source of error and imperfection for raster graphics. This topic will be revisited in many contexts in this chapter. For the moment, however, round-off errors can be neglected assuming that the coordinates of points are already integers at this stage and the area of the point equals the area of the pixel. (When a point is referred to in this section, what is actually meant is some neighborhood of the point because in its mathematical sense, a point possesses, of course, neither area nor volume.)

The very first location of the bitmap most often describes the top, leftmost pixel. The locations that follow describe pixels in the first horizontal line, followed by locations for the second horizontal line of pixels, and so on. The typical arrangement of memory cells describing lines of pixels also determines a system of references, which is convenient to use in this case. The Y axis is directed from top to bottom and the X axis is directed from left to right (see Figure 3.1).

FIGURE 3.1
Image bitmap layout.

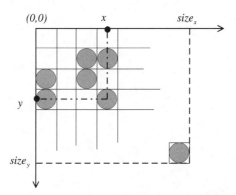

Assuming that each pixel is represented by one unit of memory (byte or word), and that the dimensions of the output bitmap are $size_x$ by $size_y$, the address of the pixel *(x,y)* in the image bitmap is computed as $y \cdot size_x + x$.

Setting a specific value into the memory location at the found offset from the beginning of the bitmap results in a point appearing at coordinates *(x,y)* on the screen.

In some practical settings, the distance in memory from the beginning of one row to the next one can be greater than the actual width of the image. This is due to the peculiarities of hardware and special software. If that is the case, it must be taken into account in the formula computing the pixel's address.

Rasterizing Line Segments

A line rasterization algorithm is quite important among the algorithms in your graphics toolbox. Besides rendering line segments, almost identical algorithms are used for other purposes such as determining edges of polygons before rasterization.

The goal of line rasterization is to find all pixels intersected by a given line, or more generally, those pixels that are close enough to the line's path. To specify a line segment, the Cartesian coordinates of its two endpoints, (X_{start}, Y_{start}) and (X_{end}, Y_{end}), are normally used (see Figure 3.2).

FIGURE 3.2
Finding points on a line.

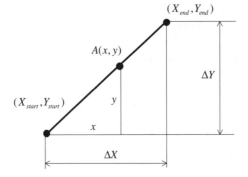

In Figure 3.2, which shows a line segment and an arbitrary point belonging to this line, you can see that there are two similar triangles. One is formed by the segments ΔX and ΔY and the other one is formed by the segments x and y. The latter represents the coordinates of some point A belonging to the line segment. Observing that these triangles are proportionate, you can see that if

$$\Delta X = X_{end} - X_{start}$$
$$\Delta Y = Y_{end} - Y_{start}$$

then

$$\frac{x}{y} = \frac{\Delta X}{\Delta Y}$$

and

$$y = \frac{x \cdot \Delta Y}{\Delta X}$$

Since the goal is to find all points along the line's path, the simplest strategy is just to take all integer values of x in the domain $[X_{start}, X_{end}]$ and compute their respective y according to the formula. There is a bit of a catch, however—there will be only as many as ΔX calculated points. But if the ΔY range was actually larger, the points obtained won't form a continuous path on the screen (see Figure 3.3). In the most degenerated case of vertical lines, ΔX will be equal to zero, making the preceding equation unresolvable in finite numbers at all. In those cases it is better instead to compute the x coordinate as a function of y. $x = \frac{y \cdot \Delta X}{\Delta Y}$

This will guarantee a continuous path and avoid the singular case (see Figure 3.3).

FIGURE 3.3

Calculating Y function of X versus X function of Y for some line.

Y function of X:

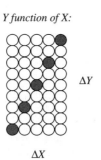

ΔY

ΔX

X function of Y:

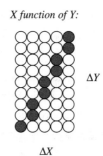

ΔY

ΔX

As far as performance, this method takes one multiplication and one division to compute a single point. In practice, this is rather expensive and leaves a lot to be desired.

A better technique is obtained by using *forward differences* to iteratively compute coordinates of multiple points. This technique is often used to rasterize various polynomial curves, and a line can also be thought of as the simplest curve with a constant slope. This approach uses the simple fact that the value of a function in some point $x+\delta$ is equal to the sum of its value in point x and the forward difference of the function on the interval δ. That is:

$$y(x + \delta) = y(x) + dy$$

Although in general dy is not a constant, in the particular case of the line it is. Using the formula for the line's coordinates, the forward difference can be found as

$$dy = y(x + \delta) - y(x) = \frac{\Delta Y(x + \delta)}{\Delta X} - \frac{\Delta Yx}{\Delta X} = \frac{\Delta Yx + \Delta Y\delta - \Delta Yx}{\Delta X} = \frac{\Delta Y}{\Delta X}\delta$$

The forward difference dy describes how much the function changes with respect to the change of the argument.

The derived expression implies that the value of $y(x+1)$, that is, the corresponding y coordinate for the next discrete x (assuming $\delta=1$), can be computed based on the value of y during the previous iteration:

$$y(x + 1) = y(x) + dy$$

where

$$dy = \frac{\Delta Y}{\Delta X}\delta$$

There is just one fractional (floating or fixed-point) addition involved per computed point, which is, of course, a considerable improvement compared with the original method. The technique of forward differencing is used on more complex curves as well, with the line just being the most trivial case. In a more complex situation (as seen in the following sections), the function's forward difference will not be constant. However, being a polynomial function itself, the forward difference can be found through forward differencing of its own rate of change.

It should be noted that this algorithm involves fractional numbers, either floating or fixed-point. It also potentially involves conversion or rounding of fractional numbers into integers—bitmaps are discrete, after all. It is at times preferable, for performance sake, to use only purely integer operations. Another iterative method for line rasterization doesn't involve either divisions or fractional numbers. Jack Bresenham, who was a researcher at IBM at the time, devised this algorithm.

The idea of this algorithm is to find a bigger range, either ΔX or ΔY, iterate the appropriate coordinate of this range, and have a variable signaling when it is time to advance the coordinate of the smaller range as well. To find conditions when this must occur, consider what is happening at some stage in line rasterization. Assume that ΔX is a longer range $(\Delta X > \Delta Y)$ and that in the given line segment $X_{start} < X_{end}$ and $Y_{start} < Y_{end}$ (see Figure 3.4).

FIGURE 3.4

Line passing through the pixel grid.

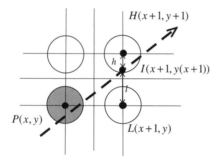

Figure 3.4 shows the situation where a pixel $P(x,y)$ (where P stands for previous) was just rendered at coordinates (x,y) and now the decision has to be made how to advance to the next pixel. Depending on the situation, the algorithm advances to pixel $L(x+1,y)$ (where L stands for lower) or to $H(x+1,y+1)$ (where H stands for higher). The points P,H,L represent the middles of the respective pixels. Since the actual line will pass somewhere in between the two points P and L, the algorithm should advance to the pixel that is closer to the line, that is, to the point whose center is closer to the intersection point $I(x+1,y(x))$. This can be measured by comparing the segments h and l resulting from the intersection.

Remembering the dependency used in the original line drawing method, you can see that

$$y(x+1) = \frac{\Delta Y \cdot (x+1)}{\Delta X}$$

and

$$h = y + 1 - y(x+1) \Rightarrow h = y + 1 - \frac{\Delta Y \cdot (x+1)}{\Delta X}$$

$$l = y(x+1) - y \Rightarrow l = \frac{\Delta Y \cdot (x+1)}{\Delta X} - y$$

To compare the segments l and h, the sign of l-h can first be examined:

$$l - h = 2\frac{\Delta Y \cdot (x+1)}{\Delta X} - 2y - 1$$

Thus, if l-$h>0$, that implies $l>h$, and the intersection point I is closer to the pixel H. This latter pixel should be plotted. Otherwise, if $l\leq h$, L should be plotted. To find a more usable expression, multiply both sides of the equation by ΔX:

$$\Delta X(l-h) = 2\Delta Y \cdot x + 2\Delta Y - 2\Delta X \cdot y - \Delta X$$

Since ΔX is assumed to be greater than zero, the signs of $(l$-$h)$ and $\Delta X(l$-$h)$ will be exactly the same. Denote $\Delta X(l$-$h)$ by d and find the value and sign of d at some iterations i and $i+1$:

$$d_i = 2\Delta Y \cdot x_{i-1} - 2\Delta X \cdot y_{i-1} + 2\Delta Y - \Delta X$$

$$d_{i+1} = 2\Delta Y \cdot x_i - 2\Delta X \cdot y_i + 2\Delta Y - \Delta X$$

It also helps to find the initial value of d. At the very first point, when $x=0$ and $y=0$, the following takes place:

$$d_1 = 2\Delta Y - \Delta X$$

Since the sign of d at iteration i determines which point (H or L) to move to at iteration $i+1$, find the value of d at $i+1$, assuming that its current value is known from the previous iteration:

$$d_{i+1} - d_i = 2\Delta Y \cdot x_i - 2\Delta X \cdot y_i - 2\Delta Y \cdot x_{i-1} + 2\Delta X \cdot y_{i-1} \Rightarrow$$
$$\Rightarrow d_{i+1} - d_i = 2\Delta Y(x_i - x_{i-1}) - 2\Delta X(y_i - y_{i-1})$$

If during the previous iteration the decision was made to plot the pixel at H, the following took place:

$$x_i - x_{i-1} = 1$$

and

$$y_i - y_{i-1} = 1$$

which means that

$$d_{i+1} - d_i = 2\Delta Y - 2\Delta X \Rightarrow d_{i+1} = d_i + 2\Delta Y - 2\Delta X$$

On the other hand, when the lower pixel, L, was plotted in the previous iteration, the following expressions hold:

$$x_i - x_{i-1} = 1$$

and

$$y_i - y_{i-1} = 0$$

This means that

$$d_{i+1} - d_i = 2\Delta Y \Rightarrow d_{i+1} = d_i + 2\Delta Y$$

This derivation may seem a bit complicated, but the implementation of the algorithm is certainly quite trivial. Before the iterative part of the algorithm, the initial value of d has to be computed, which is easy to do knowing the coordinates of the endpoints. Further, inside the loop, coordinates of the current pixel are computed. This computation depends on the sign of d. To update d for the next iteration, it is increased by either $2\Delta Y\text{-}2\Delta X$, or $2\Delta Y$. Since those two are constants for the duration of the loop, the values to update d can be calculated before actual work is started.

In the derivation above, it was assumed that $X_{start} < X_{end}$ and $Y_{start} < Y_{end}$

However, in real life this cannot be guaranteed. One way to take other cases into consideration is by changing increments to decrements when the preceding assumptions don't hold. It is equally possible to interchange the endpoints to satisfy at least one of the preceding conditions. Listing 3.1 presents a possible implementation for this line drawing algorithm.

LISTING 3.1

Line Rasterization

```
void G_line(int x,int y,int x2,int y2,HW_pixel color)
{
  int dx,dy,long_d,short_d;
  int d,add_dh,add_dl;
  int inc_xh,inc_yh,inc_xl,inc_yl;
  int i;

  dx=x2-x; dy=y2-y;                               /* ranges */

  if(dx<0){dx=-dx; inc_xh=-1; inc_xl=-1;}         /* making sure dx and dy >0 */
  else    {         inc_xh=1;  inc_xl=1; }        /* adjusting increments */
  if(dy<0){dy=-dy; inc_yh=-1; inc_yl=-1;}
  else    {         inc_yh=1;  inc_yl=1; }

  if(dx>dy){long_d=dx; short_d=dy; inc_yl=0;}/* long range, &making sure either*/
  else     {long_d=dy; short_d=dx; inc_xl=0;}/* x or y is changed in L case */

  d=2*short_d-long_d;                             /* initial value of d */
  add_dl=2*short_d;                               /* d adjustment for H case */
  add_dh=2*short_d-2*long_d;                      /* d adjustment for L case */

  for(i=0;i<=long_d;i++)
  {
    G_dot(x,y,color);

    if(d>=0){x+=inc_xh; y+=inc_yh; d+=add_dh;}/* previous point was H type */
    else    {x+=inc_xl; y+=inc_yl; d+=add_dl;}/* previous point was L type */
  }
}
```

Determining the ranges.

Initializing constants for the loop.

Rasterization loop. Depending on the kind of the previously rendered point different constant is used.

The loop of this algorithm doesn't involve divisions or fractional numbers at all.

As far as performance is concerned, the point of interest in the routine in Listing 3.1 is what's happening inside the loop, since for most line segments this part of the code will be executed multiple times. Along with some very inexpensive operations inside the line drawing loop, there is also a call to the G_dot function responsible for plotting a point. As discussed in the previous section, plotting a pixel requires computing its address in bitmap memory. This is done using the expression $y \cdot size_x + x$, which unfortunately involves multiplication. Avoiding the use of multiplication was one of the motivations behind the integer line drawing algorithm in the first place.

In order to avoid this potential performance problem, it is necessary to recall the representation of the image bitmap. To avoid the expensive computation, you can attempt to use the address of the previous pixel that was plotted to figure out the address of the next pixel (see Figure 3.5).

FIGURE 3.5
Neighboring pixels in the image bitmap.

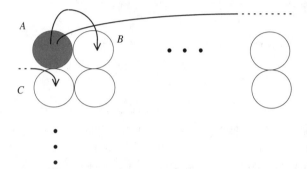

It is clear from examining Figure 3.5 that when advancing horizontally, along the *X* axis, the address of the pixel *B* will be equal to the address of *A* incremented by one. On the other hand, the pixels *A* and *C* are separated by exactly $size_X$ pixels—the width of the bitmap. Thus, in order to advance vertically, along the *Y* axis, the value of $size_X$ has to be added to the address of *A* to obtain the address of *C*. Using this strategy, it is possible to modify the line rasterization routine so that instead of coordinates *(x,y)*, it will directly compute addresses of pixels in the image bitmap. Listing 3.2 presents just the iterative part of such an implementation.

LISTING 3.2
Inner Loop of the Optimized Line Rasterization

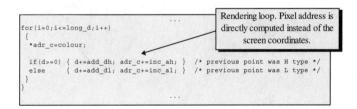

```
for(i=0;i<=long_d;i++)
{
    *adr_c=colour;

    if(d>=0) { d+=add_dh; adr_c+=inc_ah; }   /* previous point was H type */
    else     { d+=add_dl; adr_c+=inc_al; }   /* previous point was L type */
    }
}
```

Rendering loop. Pixel address is directly computed instead of the screen coordinates.

In Listing 3.2, you can see that the code inside the loop doesn't have any expensive operations left.

Incremental algorithms based on the same principle as the one presented above also exist for various curves, notably for circles. At times, especially in 2D applications, their use gives a fair performance gain. However, curves can also be approximated by numerous line segments, which is quite practical and doesn't require much in the way of development given that the line drawing routine is already implemented.

Rasterizing Polygons

A *polygon* is a planar geometric figure enclosed with edges formed by straight line segments. Of interest in computer graphics are non–self-intersecting or *simple polygons* whose edges are allowed to intersect only in a polygon's vertices.

The goal of rasterization is to assign the desired color to every pixel that falls inside this enclosed region. Most polygon rasterization methods use a variation of the *scan-line* approach. The idea behind this approach is to let a scan-line travel vertically along the polygon. At each different height, the scan-line will intersect the polygon by some line of pixels. These pixel lines are then drawn one at a time. The scan-lines have to be horizontal only because in the most common image bitmap, pixels forming horizontal lines occupy consecutive locations in memory, and as a result can be drawn somewhat faster than vertical lines.

Polygons are differentiated into *convex* and *concave*. By definition, a polygon is *convex* if the line connecting any two points inside the polygon never leaves the polygon's boundaries. This is not the case with concave polygons (see Figure 3.6).

FIGURE 3.6
Concave and convex polygons.

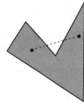

This differentiation has an implication for scan-line rasterization methodology. Only one continuous span of pixels is required for any horizontal scan-line when drawing a convex polygon. Clearly, multiple spans may be necessary to rasterize a concave polygon (see Figure 3.7).

FIGURE 3.7
Converting concave and convex polygons into pixel lines.

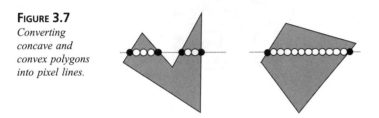

Figure 3.7 illustrates that rasterizing of concave polygons is inherently more complex. Thus, for the purposes of many applications it is suitable to limit allowable polygons to only convex ones whose rasterization and handling are generally much easier.

When such a relaxation is impossible, an attempt can be made to split a concave polygon into convex parts. For instance, any polygon can be triangulated; that is, it can be split into a set of triangles that cover the same area as the original polygon.

The following sections discuss rasterization of convex and concave polygons as well as an approach to performing triangulation that is used to simplify complex polygons into simple ones.

Rasterizing Convex Polygons

An algorithm rasterizing convex polygons must find and describe all horizontal pixel lines limited by the polygon's boundaries (see Figure 3.8). Any planar line segment can be represented by four parameters: two coordinates for each of the two endpoints. A horizontal line has an additional constraint and requires only three parameters: common heights and two horizontal coordinates, one for each endpoint.

Potentially, a polygon can have a pixel line at every possible height on the screen. Thus, an appropriate data structure for keeping these lines is an array whose length is equal to the vertical size of the screen where every entry stores two integers denoting the beginning and end of the appropriate pixel line.

FIGURE 3.8
Rasterized polygons.

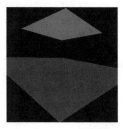

The information on the configuration of pixel lines is described, of course, by the polygon's edges. The algorithm can take one edge at a time, find all pixels belonging to this edge, and use this information to set the start and end values for appropriate pixel lines (see Figure 3.9).

FIGURE 3.9
Array to store polygon's pixel lines.

Start	End
1	5
2	8
2	7
3	7
4	6

When a point on some edge is found, it may not be immediately clear whether its x coordinate specifies the beginning or the end of the pixel line at its height y. An approach that is somewhat similar to sorting can be employed here. It is indeed a fact that the start value of the pixel line is less than or equal to the end value.

If the x coordinate of the found point is less than the existing value for the scan-line's start, the new point is, in fact, the actual start. Similarly, if the same x coordinate is greater than the existing value for the end point, this new point specifies the actual end.

By initially assigning the biggest possible value to the start values of all pixel lines and the smallest possible value to their ends, you ensure that the first point found at every height will be placed into both the start and the end locations. (After all, any value should be both smaller than the biggest possible value and bigger than the smallest possible value.) Figure 3.10 illustrates the process of finding the pixel lines from the polygon's edges.

FIGURE 3.10
Steps in finding a convex polygon's pixel lines.

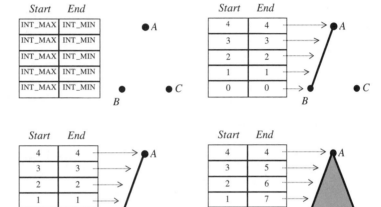

A convenient place to find the biggest and the smallest integer values is the standard header file `<limits.h>`. It is a good programming practice to use the `INT_MAX` and `INT_MIN` constants defined there. Besides extra clarity in the source code, it also guarantees platform independence (those values depend on the integer bit size, which, in turn, depends on the platform).

The process of finding points belonging to a polygon's edge, often referred to as *edge scanning*, is exactly the same as that in rasterization of a line segment. The only difference is that the purpose of found coordinates is not plotting a pixel but setting the pixel line boundaries. It should also be noted that for the purposes of finding the pixel line's boundaries, the horizontal edges can be completely ignored. Their neighbors, with which a horizontal edge shares its vertices, also carry the boundary information that such edges represent. Examine Figure 3.10. Edge *BC* was used to set the last pixel line, but should this edge be discarded, the last pixel line will still be correctly set after processing the edges *AC* and *AB*.

Once the configuration of every pixel line is found, the rasterization function has to set necessary locations in the image bitmap to the requested color value. This task is particularly simple because for the horizontal lines, the memory cells describing neighboring pixels occupy consecutive locations. Listing 3.3 presents a function that implements rasterization of convex polygons.

LISTING 3.3
Polygon Rasterization

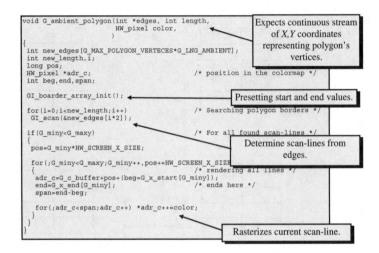

```
void G_ambient_polygon(int *edges, int length,
                       HW_pixel color,
                       )
{
 int new_edges[G_MAX_POLYGON_VERTECES*G_LNG_AMBIENT];
 int new_length,i;
 long pos;
 HW_pixel *adr_c;                         /* position in the colormap */
 int beg,end,span;

 GI_boarder_array_init();

 for(i=0;i<new_length;i++)                /* Searching polygon borders */
  GI_scan(&new_edges[i*2]);

 if(G_miny<G_maxy)                        /* For all found scan-lines */
 {
  pos=G_miny*HW_SCREEN_X_SIZE;

  for(;G_miny<G_maxy;G_miny++,pos+=HW_SCREEN_X_SIZE)
  {                                       /* rendering all lines */
   adr_c=G_c_buffer+pos+(beg=G_x_start[G_miny]);
   end=G_x_end[G_miny];                   /* ends here */
   span=end-beg;

   for(;adr_c<span;adr_c++) *adr_c++=color;
  }
 }
}
```

Expects continuous stream of *X,Y* coordinates representing polygon's vertices.

Presetting start and end values.

Determine scan-lines from edges.

Rasterizes current scan-line.

The algorithm that was considered enables drawing convex polygons on the screen. However, this algorithm does produce imperfections. Examine Figure 3.9 and you can see that the area occupied by the plotted pixels exceeds that of the actual polygon. Moreover, if there are several polygons that share the same edge, the pixels on the edge will be plotted twice, once for each polygon. A common practice to minimize both effects is not setting pixels that are on the extreme right of every pixel line and not drawing the last line.

This algorithm is a fairly practical one, yet it is not without performance shortcomings. It is necessary to initialize the array that stores the shape of all pixel lines before each polygon is drawn. This array has a considerable size and in the case of very small polygons, it may well happen that the task of initializing this array takes longer than drawing the pixels of the polygon itself.

An alternative approach, used quite commonly, is to avoid using such an array. Instead, you can first find the highest vertex of the polygon. The edges that intersect in this vertex necessarily belong to the opposite sides of the polygon and thus one describes beginnings of the pixel lines and the other one describes corresponding ends (see Figure 3.11).

Figure 3.11
Topmost vertex of a convex polygon.

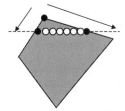

If the edges are traversed in a simultaneous way and the coordinates of points with the same *y* are found on both edges at the same time, there is no need for the array that was used in the previous algorithm and the performance can be potentially improved.

The only difficulty with this algorithm is that some care should be taken when a vertex is reached on one side and it is time to start traversing another edge. One potential solution is to subdivide the original polygon into even simpler shapes, such as trapezoids and triangles with horizontal bases. All the vertices except for the highest one and the lowest one are used to induce such a subdivision (see Figure 3.12).

Figure 3.12
Subdividing a polygon into trapezoids and triangles.

In these shapes, exactly one edge defines the left boundary and one edge defines the right boundary, making it easier to traverse both boundaries simultaneously to find coordinates of opposite points.

In all cases of polygon rasterization, the code drawing pixel lines remains to be the performance bottleneck. The ability to draw an arbitrary horizontal line of pixels efficiently is thus very important. When performance is of prime importance and an algorithmic shortcut is problematic, the last recourse still is hand-coding in assembly language. In practice, recoding a well-written C program into machine instructions might give an extra 10%–20% speed increase, which may be considered a fair gain. The loss of portability and clarity is a price to pay, however. It is also true that modern compilers do a pretty good job in optimization, to the degree that handwritten code may be less efficient. So recoding into assembly must definitely be done with care.

Rewriting everything into assembly is neither particularly appealing nor practical. Moreover, as you have already seen, the complexity of many algorithms is concentrated within relatively tight loops. Most of the potential performance gain from recoding into assembly is concentrated there. Thus, it is practical to employ assembly only in a few specific places.

That's perhaps one of the reasons why modern compilers have such a powerful feature as inline assembly. It allows mixing low-level machine code directly with the C instructions. Different C compilers have somewhat different provisions and syntax for inline assembly. GNU C, a compiler that is available for a variety of platforms (although mostly on UNIX machines) has an elaborate syntax designed for that purpose. See Listing 3.4.

LISTING 3.4
GNU C Inline Assembly

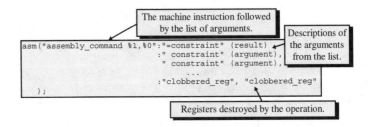

As you can see, an assembly instruction is specified with aliases that permit importing arguments from C variables. Aliases start with the percentage sign. A double percentage sign has the literal value of a single percentage sign. It is often the case that a register reference starts with this character in some assembly languages.

In many cases, a machine instruction spoils the contents of some registers in the course of its execution. To prevent C code from continuing to rely on values that might no longer exist, you should be careful to specify all the registers clobbered by the instruction. The compiler will make sure that no useful information is in these registers at the moment when the inline assembly code starts to execute.

For Intel 80x86 processors and GNU C compilers, the inline assembly code substituting the code to draw a pixel line can be implemented as illustrated in Listing 3.5.

LISTING 3.5
Intel 80x86 Assembly for the Pixel Line Filling Loop

```
asm("movl  %0,%%ecx" :: "g" (end):"%ecx");
asm("subl  %0,%%ecx" :: "g" (beg):"%ecx");       Names of
asm("movl  %0,%%edi" :: "g" (adr):"%edi");       variables from
asm("movl  %0,%%eax" :: "g" (colour):"%eax");    the C program.
asm("cld");
asm("rep");
asm("stosw %al,(%edi)");      The scan-line filling loop.
```

This code, which is particularly easy to introduce into a C program, gives a certain speed increase since it employs special processor instructions well suited for setting all elements of an array (rep prefix preceding the last instruction stosw).

Rasterizing Concave Polygons

As mentioned in the previous section, one approach for dealing with concave polygons is simply to disallow them from occurring. Such a strategy of dealing with a problem by ignoring it is in fact quite common in computer graphics.

In rare situations when it is necessary to rasterize an arbitrary polygon, thus potentially a concave one, several alternatives are available. One is to subdivide such a polygon into convex components—triangles, for instance—and the second alternative is to modify the rasterization algorithm to work correctly with concave polygons.

The fact that any polygon can be triangulated follows from an interesting geometric theorem by Meister. It states that any simple polygon with more than three vertices has at least two non-intersecting ears. An *ear* is determined by a vertex of a polygon such that its two neighbor vertices can be connected by a *diagonal*. For example, vertex *A* in Figure 3.13(a) determines an ear. However, vertex *C* in Figure 3.13(b) does not determine an ear because the connecting line of its two neighbors leaves the polygon's boundaries, and hence is not a diagonal.

FIGURE 3.13
Finding ears.

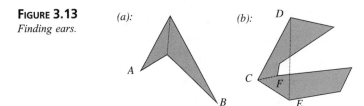

Clearly, the theorem is trivially true for a quadrilateral polygon (see Figure 3.13(a)). Only two possibilities exist, because there are two pairs of opposing vertices. One such pair absolutely must define two ears.

For polygons with more than four vertices, any vertex can either already determine an ear, or if it can't, it is always possible to find a diagonal connecting the given vertex to some other vertex and thus split the polygon into two sub-polygons with a smaller number of vertices. For example, vertex *C* in Figure 3.13(b) can be connected by a diagonal to vertex *F*. The vertex *F* is the closest to *C* in the direction orthogonal to the line through *C*'s neighbors: *D* and *E*. Assuming that both resulting sub-polygons have two non-intersecting ears each, even in the case when some ears were built using the newly introduced diagonal, there cannot be more than two such ears, one in each sub-polygon. This leaves the original polygon with at least two remaining ears.

The preceding presents compressed sketches of an *inductive prove*. In inductive proves, to show the hypothesis to be true, it is first demonstrated for the *base case* of some small size (quadrilateral in this case). Further, it is demonstrated that if the hypothesis is assumed true for problems of size less than *n*, it can also be shown to be true for problems of size *n+1*. As a consequence, it is concluded that the hypothesis must be true for all problems with *n* bigger than the size of the base case.

Meister's theorem immediately suggests the following triangulation algorithm:

- Select a vertex.

- Check if it determines an ear.

- If it does, cut off this triangle and reapply the algorithm on what remains of the polygon.

- If the selected vertex doesn't determine an ear, it is possible to use the suggested strategy to split the polygon into two sub-polygons and reapply the algorithm to both pieces.

Instead of using the recursion, another strategy is to cut the ears iteratively, one at a time. In other words, if a selected vertex doesn't determine an ear, just check another vertex. According to the preceding theorem, sooner or later an ear must be found.

It must be noted that testing whether a vertex determines an ear essentially reduces to testing whether some points are inside or outside a triangle. If all vertices of a polygon are outside of the triangle formed by some vertex and its neighbors, this vertex determines an ear. You will learn about polygon inclusion tests in Chapter 5.

Generally, it has been shown that the problem of triangulating a simple polygon requires linear time in the number of vertices. That is, the algorithm will perform the amount of basic operations proportional to the number of vertices. However, such a linear algorithm proposed not so long ago by prominent computational geometer B. Chazelle doesn't appear to be practical for actual implementation. In fact, it is so complex that very few people understand (and hence believe) its proof of correctness. Most of the time the developers opt for much simpler (although algorithmically more expensive) approaches similar in style to the ones suggested earlier.

Although attractive, the triangulation approach increases the number of polygons, and since rendering of each has a certain overhead, it may be cheaper to devise and use a more expensive concave polygon rasterization algorithm instead of calling many times cheaper convex rasterization.

As you have already seen, the main difficulty with rasterization of concave polygons is the fact that at each height there may be several spans of pixels to draw.

Clearly, knowing all the intersections at a given scan-line makes the remaining process quite easy. By sorting the intersection points according to their horizontal x coordinates, the sequence is obtained where all even entries will specify beginnings of spans followed by the spans' ends as odd entries.

As to the first portion of the algorithm, which must find the intersection points, the most immediate brute-force solution is to use line equations and check for intersection of the scan-line and every edge in the polygon (Chapter 5 discusses this topic). This, however, will involve many expensive computations and should be rejected in favor of a better approach. Instead, the property of locality can be exploited, which indicates that if a scan-line intersects an edge, there is a good chance that the next scan-line will also intersect the same edge. Looking at Figure 3.14, you can see that this property mostly holds true, and breaks down only in the few instances when a scan-line is passing through a vertex and thus no longer intersects the edge that ended at that vertex. Thus, an algorithm not unlike that for convex polygons can be used where a scan-line traverses the edges from top to bottom finding the appropriate pixel lines on-the-fly.

The algorithm to find the intersections of a scan-line with the edges can first pre-sort all edges (excluding useless horizontal ones) according to their least y coordinate. If some edges have the same least y, the value of x of the endpoint with greater y is used as an auxiliary sorting criterion. (An edge that starts the span will thus appear ahead of an edge that ends the span.) Further, an "active" edges list is maintained by adding to it the edges from the pre-sorted list. The edges will be added when their y coordinate will be equal to that of the current scan-line (see Figure 3.14).

FIGURE 3.14
Steps in finding a concave polygon's pixel lines.

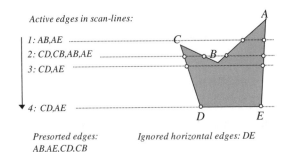

Active edges in scan-lines:

1: AB,AE
2: CD,CB,AB,AE
3: CD,AE
4: CD,AE

Presorted edges:
AB,AE,CD,CB

Ignored horizontal edges: DE

Figure 3.14 illustrates a concave polygon, with the list of pre-sorted edges. When the rasterization starts at the top of the polygon, the y coordinate of the scan-line will be equal to the y coordinate of the point A and thus, least y of edges AB and AE. These two edges are taken into the active edge list.

For each consecutive scan-line, the current x of all edges in the active list is computed using some iterative algorithm. It is also necessary to delete from this list all edges that have ended at the current scan-line. After that, verification is made to determine if y of some edges in the pre-sorted edge list became equal to y of the current scan-line, and if there are such, these are inserted into the active list, which is resorted each time there are insertions. The resorting should be quite cheap since the list is almost entirely sorted and requires only minor adjustments. At that point, current x coordinates for the edges in the active edge list are used to fill the spans of pixels and the iteration is repeated.

Figure 3.14 illustrates this algorithm on an example. When the rasterization starts, edges AB and AE are in the active edge list until the level of the point C is reached. At that stage, two more edges are inserted and after necessary sorting the list will become CD,CB,AB,AE. Further, at the level of the point B, two edges will get deleted with the active edge list becoming CD,AE.

By examining this algorithm, it should be noted that finding which edges to insert from the pre-sorted edge list is quite cheap. An index to the edge that should be inserted next can be maintained to help. Since the edges are sorted, it suffices to examine y of the currently indexed edge, and if its y is larger than that of the current scan-line, no other edges have to be examined. When some edge is inserted, the index is incremented and the examination is repeated until the current edge is not suitable for insertion anymore.

Although rasterization of concave polygons clearly seems more cumbersome than that of convex polygons and may force many developers to opt for convex only polygons, there are some other advantages to this algorithm, which will be seen in the examination of hidden surface removal techniques in Chapter 7.

Rendering Interpolatively (Gouraud) Shaded Polygons

Up to this point in this chapter you have learned only about polygons of constant color, or *flat* polygons. Flat polygons have been a choice for some time in many computer graphics applications due to the low cost of their rasterization. However, they present a fairly unrealistic portrait of the virtual world. After all, in the real world we don't often see polygonal patches of strictly constant coloring. Lighting introduces shading patterns on even monotonously colored surfaces. Surfaces themselves are not ideally smooth. Most have imperfections such as bumps or encrustation of different material. Ideally, this can be reproduced by a very big number of flat polygons, each having a different, yet constant, color. This approach will, of course, defeat the purpose of modeling with polygons, since the simplicity and small size of components involved in such a representation is crucial. An alternative approach is to introduce changes to polygon rasterization routines so that they become more sophisticated and produce more realistic images.

One technique is to consider lighting during rasterization. Another technique is to apply a material texture onto the polygon. Those two give a considerable visual improvement to the produced images. Lighting is considered at length in the next chapters, particularly how to compute illumination for different points in the virtual world. For the purposes of this section, it will be assumed that it is possible to compute values representing intensity of light in the vertices of the polygon. Since variation in illumination largely changes in some smooth way, the lighting for pixels within the polygon can be computed by interpolating the values in the vertices (see Figure 3.15). The fastest and perhaps simplest of the interpolating techniques comes from Henri Gouraud, one of the computer graphics pioneers who studied at the University of Utah.

FIGURE 3.15
Interpolatively (Gouraud) shaded polygons.

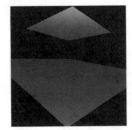

The idea behind this method is to integrate rasterization and computation of light intensity. It is done by keeping a color intensity value in every vertex of the polygon and linearly interpolating these values at the time of pixel line computation in order to find the color for each pixel inside the polygon (see Figure 3.16).

FIGURE 3.16
*Interpolating
color intensities.*

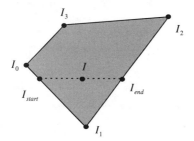

In other words, assuming that together with the screen space coordinates *(x,y)* every vertex also carries I, some sort of a color intensity value, it is easy to proceed with the original scan-line methodology, interpolating light intensity as it goes. The values on the left and right borders of a polygon can be obtained by interpolating the color intensity value along every edge. Afterwards, when rendering a horizontal pixel line, these can be further interpolated to find color for pixels in between (I in Figure 3.16).

An obvious implication of this algorithm for the edge scanning function that was used for flat polygon rasterization is that vertices now have more information associated with them. Moreover, depending on the lighting scheme used, a single color might be represented by several values (notably, the RGB scheme with three values—one for red, one for green, and one for blue). A possible design implication on the scanning function may be to opt for building a general-purpose scanner for N-dimensional edges. In fact, in this chapter you will soon encounter at least two other situations where it will be necessary to interpolate another kind of information, different from light intensities, across the polygon. Built generically, the scanning function will be capable of serving multiple purposes.

The function fragment presented in Listing 3.6 uses forward differences to compute values other than *x* and *y*, which are still calculated through Bresenham's iterations.

LISTING 3.6
Fragment of the Edge Scanning Routine

```
for(i=0;i<dimension;i++)                         ...          /* for all dimensions */
{
  cur_v[i]=((HW_32_bit)v1[i])<<G_fixed_dim[i];
  if(long_d>0)
    inc_v[i]=(((HW_32_bit)(v2[i]-v1[i]))<<G_P)/long_d;
}

for(i=0;i<=long_d;i++)                                        /* for all points in long range */
{
  if(x<G_x_start[y])                                         /* further then rightmost */
  {
    G_x_start[y]=x;                                          /* the begining of scan line */
    for(j=0;j<dimension;j++) G_start[j][y]=cur_v[j];
  }
  if(G_x_end[y]<x)
  {
    G_x_end[y]=x;                                            /* the end of scan line */
    for(j=0;j<dimension;j++) G_end[j][y]=cur_v[j];
  }

  if(d>=0){x+=inc_xh;y+=inc_yh;d+=add_dh;}  /* previous point was H type */
  else    {x+=inc_xl;y+=inc_yl;d+=add_dl;}  /* previous point was L type */
  for(j=0;j<dimension;j++)
    cur_v[j]+=inc_v[j];                                      /* for all other dimensions */
}
}
```

Compute fixed point *dy* for all extra dimensions.

Set the current values in the boundaries.

Proceed with regular iterative method for *x* and *y* coordinates.

Once pixel lines composing the given polygon are recovered, the rasterization function further interpolates the intensity value across each scan-line, using a simple case of forward differences. Similar to the scanning function, fractional numbers can be maintained in a fixed point form. The fragment of code in Listing 3.7 demonstrates the pixel line filling loop of a shaded polygon rasterization.

LISTING 3.7
Rendering Shaded Polygons

```
                                  ...
cur_i=G_I_INDX_START[G_miny];
inc_i=(G_I_INDX_END[G_miny]-cur_i)/span;

for(;beg<=end;beg++,adr_c++)
{
  {
    *adr_c=HW_colour(colour,cur_i>>G_P);  /* rendering single point */
  }
  cur_i+=inc_i;                                             /* incrementing colour */
}
                                  ...
```

Computing intensity increment .

There is one small catch, however, to interpolative shading. I mentioned that intensity can be handled pretty much as an extra dimension. In fact, a shaded polygon on the screen can be considered to have two space dimensions and one color dimension. But will all vertices of the polygon belong to the same plane in this 3D space? If they don't, it will be possible to arrive at a different shading value depending on which vertices the interpolation starts from.

In practice, when a shaded polygon that has this problem will rotate, there will be visible discontinuities in shading, which also change depending on the polygon's orientation. One solution is to limit polygons to just triangles. Three non-collinear points always belong to the same plane in any 3D space, thus linear interpolation will always give a smooth appearance to a triangle independent of its orientation.

Rendering Textured Polygons

Applying a texture to a polygon serves the purpose of improving visual realism of synthetic scenes. Ed Catmull first proposed this technique in his PhD thesis.

A texture associates some color value to two coordinates *(u,v)* of a polygon's area. One variation of textures is what's known as *procedural textures*, where some function (a procedure) computes a color for arbitrary *(u,v)* coordinates. Another, perhaps more common method is to store a texture as a bitmap. In this case, colors are explicitly stored for each *(u,v)* pair inside a two-dimensional array. A single element of this array is often called a *texel* (for texture element). Specifying the texture coordinates in each vertex of the polygon associates a texture to a polygon (see Figure 3.17).

FIGURE 3.17

A polygon and its texture.

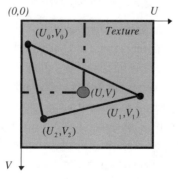

There are several methods to map a texture to a polygon's screen projection. The following sections consider three different yet related approaches.

Linear Texture Mapping

The interpolation technique used to compute color intensity for Gouraud shading can be easily extended to handle texture mapping. As was the case with color intensities, texture *(u,v)* coordinates could be stored in every vertex of the polygon, allowing for interpolating these two along edges during edge scanning, and then along horizontal lines, obtaining texture *(u,v)* for every pixel inside the polygon (see Figure 3.18).

FIGURE 3.18
Interpolating texture coordinates.

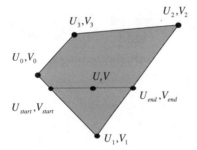

This approach, known as *linear* or *affine* texture mapping, however, does not quite work. Or, to be more precise, it stops working when the perspective projection is used to find the polygon's image on the screen. The reason is that the perspective transformation is not linear, and hence the change of texture coordinates across the polygon during texture mapping can't be computed properly by linear interpolation (see Figure 3.19).

You may ask why this method worked for interpolative shading—after all, it was implied that perspective may well be used. The answer is that it did not actually work, but the visual aspect of neglecting perspective effect for shading is quite permissible most of the time. Neglecting it for texture rendering, however, is not. It has to do with the density of visuals perceived by human eyes. A relatively small number of visual clues are introduced by shading, just a changing intensity across the polygon. There is a very large number of visual clues present on a textured polygon. Lack of realism is immediately evident in the latter case, while it may be completely unnoticed in the former.

Figure 3.19
*Linear texture
mapping; note
unnatural
warping.*

To recognize the effect of perspective distortion in linear texture mapping, just consider the following situation: A rectangular polygon is displayed on the screen so that one of its sides is much closer to the viewer than the opposite one, which is almost disappearing at infinity (see Figure 3.20). Evidently, texture coordinates will be interpolated along the edges *AD*, *AB*, and *DC*. However, the edge *BC* is extremely small in this example. So, no pixel line will ever be mapped close to what *BC* corresponds to in the texture map (see Figure 3.20).

Figure 3.20
*Linear texture
mapping for a
perspectively
projected
polygon.*

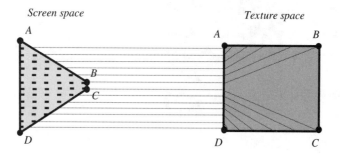

In this somewhat extreme case, the textured polygon on the screen will be missing a considerable portion of the actual texture, with other parts unnaturally joined and distorted (see Figure 3.19).

However, in less dramatic cases, texture rendered in this way may look quite nice, being perfect when the effect of perspective transformation is negligible: all points are at roughly the same distance from the viewer, or very far away from the viewing plane. In Figure 3.19, note that the texture of the background polygon doesn't appear unrealistic, whereas the texture of the foreground polygon, where the effect of perspective transformation is larger, is unnaturally warped.

There is an advantage to implementing linear texture mapping: It is less expensive than non-linear mapping, which considers the perspective effect. For many applications, it may be desirable to implement both methods. It is not hard to do a simple analysis on the location of the polygon, and if the situation is suitable, proceed with linear mapping and do the non-linear one only in critical situations. Such a critical situation occurs when a polygon is too close to the projection plane and thus is significantly distorted by the perspective transformation.

Perspective Texture Mapping

Perspective texture mapping, as its name suggests, attempts to compensate for the non-linear perspective projection (see Figure 3.21). The first, immediate solution is to simply subdivide the polygon prior to the perspective projection so that more vertices with precisely known mappings between screen and texture are present, and the linear mapping is limited to small polygons on which the distortions are less severe.

FIGURE 3.21
Perspective texture mapping.

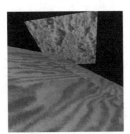

This solution, however, increases the number of polygons and thus may not be very attractive. To find a different approach, where subdivisions are not required, it is important to examine what is happening with the polygon and its texture during the transformation stages (see Figure 3.22).

As discussed in Chapter 2, the perspective projection can be considered a two-step process. During the first step, some affine transformation is applied to move the viewer into the space origin. While the viewer moves to the origin, the polygon for which texturing is to be done also moves to some new position. Later on, a simplified projection onto a plane parallel to the *XY* plane is performed. This determines three spaces (see Figure 3.22): the texture space, the view space (the one before the perspective projection where the viewer is located in the beginning of the coordinates), and, finally, the contents of the screen (the screen or image space). The first space is local to the polygon. Position and orientation of the polygon and position and orientation of the viewer in the world determine the affine transformation necessary to transform the polygon into the view space. (Chapter 5 covers this topic in the necessary detail.) The screen space contains the perspective image of the polygon that depends on the focus distance of the perspective transformation.

FIGURE 3.22

Stages in trans-
formations of a
textured polygon.

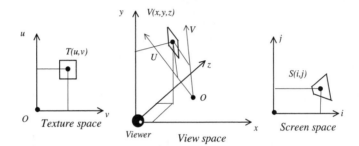

As you learned in Chapter 2, an affine 3D transformation is necessary to move the viewer into space origin. Such a transformation can be represented by a four-by-four matrix. Thus, the transformation of a point $T(u,v)$ into the view space point $V(x,y,z)$ can be expressed as $(\,u \quad v \quad 0 \quad 1\,)[T] = (\,x \quad y \quad z \quad 1\,)$ where *[T]* is a four-by-four matrix. It could be assumed that there are two vectors U and V in the view space that are the mappings of the unit length vectors *(1,0)* and *(0,1)* from the texture space. These vectors describe how the main axes of the texture became oriented as the result of the affine transformation. Let's also suppose that the mapping of the texture space origin into the view space is also known as the point O. Knowing these makes it easy to express mappings of three points from the texture space representing the origin and unit vectors along main axes as

$$(0 \quad 0 \quad 0 \quad 1)[T] = (\,O_x \quad O_y \quad O_z \quad 1\,)$$

$$(1 \quad 0 \quad 0 \quad 1)[T] = (\,O_x + V_x \quad O_y + V_y \quad O_z + V_z \quad 1\,)$$

$$(0 \quad 1 \quad 0 \quad 1)[T] = (\,O_x + U_x \quad O_y + U_y \quad O_z + U_z \quad 1\,)$$

Knowing these mappings, and remembering that texture is only two-dimensional, it is not hard to recover the transformation matrix *[T]* as

$$
(\begin{array}{cccc} u & v & 0 & 1 \end{array})
\begin{bmatrix}
U_x & U_y & U_z & 0 \\
V_x & V_y & V_z & 0 \\
0 & 0 & 0 & 0 \\
O_x & O_y & O_z & 1
\end{bmatrix}
= (\begin{array}{cccc} x & y & z & 1 \end{array})
$$

Knowing the transformation, individual formulas mapping texture coordinates *T(u,v)* into view coordinates *V(x,y,z)* can be expressed as

$$
\begin{aligned}
x &= O_x + v \cdot V_x + u \cdot U_x \\
y &= O_y + v \cdot V_y + u \cdot U_y \\
z &= O_z + v \cdot V_z + u \cdot U_z
\end{aligned}
$$

Further, a point from the view space *V(x,y,z)* is perspectively transformed into the screen space appearing at *S(i,j)*:

$$
i = focus \cdot x/z
$$

$$
j = focus \cdot y/z
$$

In order to perform the mapping, what is required is a procedure to compute the texture coordinates *(u,v)* as a function of the screen coordinates *(i,j)*. In other words, it is necessary to find out which color to fetch from the texture for certain pixels on the screen. To do that, first it is necessary to express view space coordinates as a function of screen coordinates:

$$
x = i \cdot z/focus
$$

$$
y = j \cdot z/focus
$$

Further, the meaning of x, y and z can be expressed in terms of the texture space coordinates:

$$
O_x + v \cdot V_x + u \cdot U_x = i(O_z + v \cdot V_z + u \cdot U_z)/focus
$$

$$
O_y + v \cdot V_y + u \cdot U_y = j(O_z + v \cdot V_z + u \cdot U_z)/focus
$$

By trying to express *u,v* through *i,j* the following expression is obtained:

$$v(V_x - i \cdot V_z/focus) + u(U_x - i \cdot U_z/focus) = i \cdot O_z/focus - O_x$$

$$v(V_y - j \cdot V_z/focus) + u(U_y - j \cdot U_z/focus) = j \cdot O_z/focus - O_y$$

By solving these equations in *u* and *v* the following reverse mapping formulas are derived:

$$u = \frac{i(V_z \cdot O_y - V_y \cdot O_z)/focus + j(V_x \cdot O_z - V_z \cdot O_x)/focus + (V_y \cdot O_x - V_x \cdot O_y)}{i(V_y \cdot U_z - V_z \cdot U_y)/focus + j(V_z \cdot U_x - V_x \cdot U_z)/focus + (V_x \cdot U_y - V_y \cdot U_x)}$$

$$v = \frac{i(U_y \cdot O_z - U_z \cdot O_y)/focus + j(U_z \cdot O_x - U_x \cdot O_z)/focus + (U_x \cdot O_y - U_y \cdot O_x)}{i(V_y \cdot U_z - V_z \cdot U_y)/focus + j(V_z \cdot U_x - V_x \cdot U_z)/focus + (V_x \cdot U_y - V_y \cdot U_x)}$$

These two formulas allow for computing texture coordinates for any screen pixel using the two vectors describing texture orientation and a point describing the mapping of the origin of the texture space into the view space. These three additional parameters must be obtained before the formulas can be employed. Thus, each polygon possessing a texture can be initially associated with two vectors describing the texture orientation and a point describing the origin of the texture space. At the same time the transformations on the polygon's vertices are performed, it is also necessary to apply the very same transformations to the three parameters. The only exception is that there is no need to apply translation transformation to vectors because they are unaffected by such. As a result, the necessary view screen parameters enabling the texture mapping computations are found. Although this method is relatively easy to implement, the additional data for each polygon may be too troublesome to maintain. Moreover, for the purposes of linear texture mapping, texture coordinates in every vertex are necessary. To be able to render the polygon using either of the methods, the amount of extra information becomes even larger. In Chapter 5, this problem is revisited and a strategy is found to use texture coordinates in the vertices to recover the information required for perspective texture mapping.

By examining the formulas, you can see that some of the subexpressions are constant for the entire polygon and some are constant for every scan-line. Thus, proper arrangement of the computation can give a substantial performance gain. However, even with this consideration it will be necessary to use several expensive divisions for every pixel.

Perhaps the easiest way to optimize the performance of this computation is through horizontal line subdivision. Real texture mapping is computed only every N pixels, and then these are linearly interpolated to find texture mapping coordinates for pixels in between (see Figure 3.23).

FIGURE 3.23
Scan-line subdivision and linear approximation.

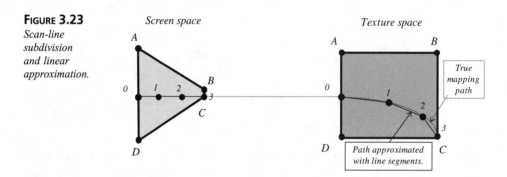

As you can see from Figure 3.23, the real texture mapping *(u,v)* is computed as a function of the screen coordinates *(i,j)* only at a couple of points along the pixel line. Other points along the line obtain their *(u,v)* from linear interpolation on the texture coordinates of the neighboring points where the precise mapping is known. Although the exact result is not achieved and the true mapping path is only approximated, the performance can still be increased dramatically. It should be noted that the computation of the exact mapping in the next point and interpolation on the current segment are independent. On some CPUs it is possible to assign these two jobs two different units and perform the computations in parallel. For instance, on an Intel CPU the integer unit and the floating point unit may operate in parallel. With these modifications, the subdivision method will be as fast as linear texture mapping.

Texture Mapping Using Quadric Curves

Another possible approach to perspective texture mapping is to approximate the mapping path with some polynomial curve. As Figure 3.23 illustrates, sufficiently good approximation with line segments (which can be considered as first degree polynomial curves) requires a lot of subdivisions. By employing a higher degree polynomial curve, better approximation can be expected and hence fewer or no subdivisions are required. Quadrics (polynomials of degree two) are good candidates since the true mapping path is relatively smooth. Thus, texture coordinates *(u,v)* along some pixel line could be found by evaluating parametric quadrics:

$$u = a_2 x^2 + a_1 x + a_0$$
$$v = b_2 x^2 + b_1 x + b_0$$

where *x* is a parameter describing location along the pixel line (see Figure 3.24).

FIGURE 3.24
*Quadric approxi-
mation.*

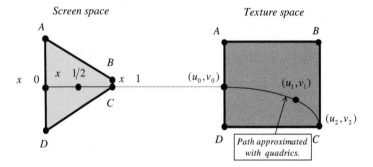

Clearly, finding six coefficients in the preceding expressions requires six different equations with known left sides. This can be obtained if there are three points where the texture mapping is known precisely (see Figure 3.24). Such points can be found by employing the technique of reversed mapping discussed previously. Suppose that the mapping is known for points in the beginning, the middle, and the end of the current pixel line. Also suppose that the parameter *x* varies in the range *[0,1]* along the scan-line, so that *x=0* in the beginning, *x=1/2* in the middle, and *x=1* in the end. Based on these assumptions, six equations can be constructed.

for $x = 0$:

$$u_0 = a_0$$

$$v_0 = b_0$$

for $x = \frac{1}{2}$:

$$u_1 = \frac{a_2}{4} + \frac{a_1}{2} + a_0$$

$$v_1 = \frac{b_2}{4} + \frac{b_1}{2} + b_0$$

for $x = 1$:

$$u_2 = a_2 + a_1 + a_0$$

$$v_2 = b_2 + b_1 + b_0$$

By solving these equations simultaneously, expressions for the coefficients can be obtained:

$a_0 = u_0$

$a_1 = -3u_0 + 4u_1 - u_2$

$a_2 = 2u_0 - 4u_1 + 2u_2$

$b_0 = v_0$

$b_1 = -3v_0 + 4v_1 - v_2$

$b_2 = 2v_0 - 4v_1 + 2v_2$

With the coefficients computed, it is possible to find texture mappings for any pixel along the pixel line by evaluating the two quadrics. Of course, the straightforward evaluation does involve several multiplications and is quite expensive. Fortunately, since the pixels along the scan-line are processed iteratively one after another, the technique of forward differencing can be used. This technique was first considered in the section "Rasterizing Line Segments" earlier in the chapter.

As you have seen, the value of a function in some point can be computed knowing the value in the previous point and the forward difference, which, in the case of the u texture coordinate, will mean that $u(x+1) = u(x) + du$

The first forward difference can be found as $du = u(x+1) - u(x) =$

$$(a_2(x+1)^2 + a_1(x+1) + a_0) - (a_2x^2 + a_1x + a_0) = a_2(2x+1) + a_1$$

Since the resulting expression is not a constant but a polynomial function, it can be efficiently evaluated using the same technique of forward differences:

$$ddu = du(x+1) - du(x) = (a_2(2(x+1)+1) + a_1) - (a_2(2x+1) + a_1) = 2a_2$$

The same reasoning applies, of course, for *v(x)*, *dv*, and *ddv*. Having these, the current function value can be found by adding the first differences to the function values known during the previous iteration. At the same time, the correct values for the first differences for the next iteration are updated by adding the second differences to the current values of the first differences:

$$u(x+1) = u(x) + du(x)$$

$$du(x+1) = du(x) + ddu$$

It is also possible to use higher degree polynomials (such as qubics, degree three) for approximation of the texture mapping path of a pixel line. The method of coefficient derivation and consecutive evaluation will remain exactly the same, but it will require more points, more equations, and more levels of forward differencing. Polynomials of degrees higher than three are practically never used since the improvement they give isn't significantly better and additional overhead becomes appreciable.

Anti-Aliasing

As noted before, there is a source of imperfections inherent to some of the relaxations that were implicitly or explicitly introduced in raster graphics. For instance, when drawing polygons, a pixel even partially covered by the analytical area of the polygon was often plotted. This produced the familiar "staircase" effect of jagged lines and edges that often results when straightforward rasterization algorithms are used. In another instance—namely, when picking a color value from the texture—only one texture entry was considered to figure out the color of the pixel. The problem is that at a greater distance from the viewer, due to the perspective foreshortening, not a single texel but some area from the texture will project into a single pixel on the screen. A popular example of artifacts of this type is a checkerboard moving away from the viewer. At some point, the projections of the squares become smaller than pixels on the screen. Naturally, if both black and white squares project to the same pixel, this pixel should appear as some shade of gray. Unfortunately, the simpler texture mapper will not consider areas, so either black or white pixels will be drawn depending on the rounding. This can cause the image to look quite unnatural, and in the case of textures with regularities, such as a checkerboard, it will produce artifacts such as Moiré patterns.

Both of these examples demonstrate *aliasing* problems caused by the discrete nature of raster graphics. There exists a wide spectrum of *anti-aliasing* techniques that attempt to alleviate these problems. Such techniques range from very simple to extremely sophisticated and complex. They can be roughly separated into two categories. The algorithms from the first category are integrated with the drawing routines. The algorithms from the second category perform post processing on the rendered images, improving their quality.

Area Sampling

To fight aliasing problems, a texture mapper can consider the actual area of a pixel and find which area in the texture should be mapped into it. It can further average colors to arrive at a smoother image. Such a technique is rather expensive, however. A simpler approach with a similar result is to always consider four (or at least some fixed number) of neighboring texture entries and average their colors to figure out how to light current screen pixels.

This is known as *bilinear sampling*, which is linear averaging in two directions. Because more of a texture was considered for every screen pixel, the result of bilinear sampling is generally better than the product of a straightforward mapping where only one texel is considered. The latter is also known as *point sampling*.

Another popular technique is known as *mip mapping*. The essential idea is to precompute the texture at different levels of detail, and then to use smaller textures for polygons further away from the viewer. Since it guarantees less area difference between texture entries and pixels, there is less room for aliasing problems. With relatively small associated overhead, the resulting images exhibit considerable improvement.

Mip mapping and bilinear sampling can be combined to form *trilinear sampling*. There you average across two neighboring levels of detail of the texture taking several pixels in each.

Current graphics accelerators that implement texture mapping practically always provide bilinear or even trilinear sampling.

Filtering

The techniques of the second category perform filtering on the rendered image so that the resulting image is smoother. The original image can be *supersampled*, meaning rendered at higher resolution. The filtering procedure will take a group of pixels from the original image and compute the weighted sum of their intensities. The result is placed into the filtered image bitmap, which is later displayed to the viewer. Figure 3.25 illustrates the filtering process. In this example, the filter is a three-by-three matrix with the assigned weights used to compute the intensity of the resulting pixel, which is then placed into the filtered bitmap.

The filters are often produced from a variety of analytical functions, of which the simplest and the most common are *Box*, *Triangle,* and *Gaussian.* These functions associate weights to the points of the area spanning across several pixels we want to filter (see Figure 3.26).

Instead of using an analytical filter, another approach is to sample some random points within a certain neighborhood. This approach is called *stochastic sampling* and the results obtained often look better because this method tends to leave visual noise rather than regular patterns in the filtered image. The human visual system appears to be capable of ignoring visual noise, yet it exaggerates regular patterns.

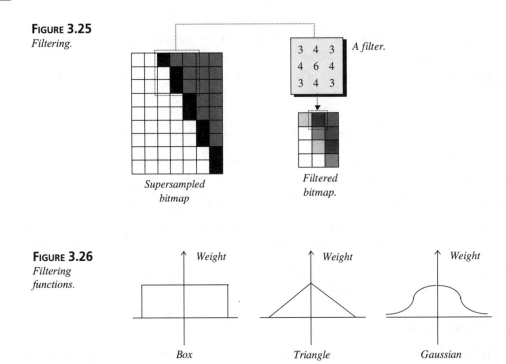

FIGURE 3.25
Filtering.

A filter.

Supersampled bitmap

Filtered bitmap.

FIGURE 3.26
Filtering functions.

Box   Triangle   Gaussian

As a result of filtering, sharp edges of the polygons and other artifacts that were introduced by unsophisticated rasterization algorithms are smoothed. Although it is generally impossible to completely nullify the problems caused by *undersampling* (computing color in too few points), the general appearance of the images can be considerably improved by using filtering. The limitation of this technique is in its usage of supersampling. The image has to be computed at higher resolution, which can be limited by both available memory and processing time.

Besides spatial aliasing, interactive computer graphics applications that display objects in motion may encounter the problem of *temporal aliasing*. A familiar example of temporal aliasing, often seen in movies, is rotating wheels reversing the direction of their rotation due to a higher revolution rate of the wheel with respect to the sampling rate of the camera.

One way to combat this problem in a computer graphics application is through the introduction of *motion blur*. This is similar to the filtering strategy used to alleviate problems of spatial aliasing. In this case, the intensity of the pixel in the current image bitmap is determined by finding the weighted sum of corresponding pixels in several consecutive frames that capture the object at slightly different moments in time. Of course, besides its use to reduce problems of temporal aliasing, the effect of motion blur (especially of exaggerated motion blur) is often used in its own right to produce special effects in graphics applications (games in particular).

It is important to consider another issue in this context—how many frames per second a graphics program should generate to present an appearance of smooth motion. Human eyes are fast enough for only about 25–30 frames per second. It is even less if the scene is dark enough. Many graphics programs, however (flight simulators and video games in particular), strive to produce as many as 60 frames per second. It may seem like overkill but it really isn't. What happens is that human eyes blur several consecutive frames that switch too fast. Thus, even though not all frames are seen, they still contribute toward smoother motion. By introducing motion blur in the application itself it is possible to reduce the amount of frames generated and yet to preserve a similar impression of smooth motion.

Use of these techniques is very much dependent on the application's objectives and available resources. High-end rendering applications may use very sophisticated techniques to improve visual realism, whereas lower-end applications, or those having performance constraints, may have to sacrifice realism for speed. It should also be noted that many of the current graphics accelerators provide filtering in hardware (this is also often referred to as FSAA—Full Screen Anti-Aliasing).

Summary

Rasterization routines are used to picture geometric primitives in a raster display device. It is expensive to rasterize complex geometric objects, so these are usually drawn as a collection of simpler primitives, such as line segments or polygons, which are easy to rasterize. In order to enhance the appearance of polygons, and depending on available resources, shading and texture mapping can be added to improve visual realism.

Texture mapping can be done in several ways. Linear texture mapping simply interpolates texture coordinates originally given in the vertices. This method will not produce a correct image if perspective transformation was used—a more complex, perspectively-correct texture mapping has to be done in that case.

The discrete nature of raster graphics often gives rise to various aliasing problems. Anti-aliasing techniques that are either introduced into drawing algorithms or used as a post-processing step attempt to alleviate these problems.

CHAPTER 4

Clipping

In the previous chapters, it was assumed that the primitives to be drawn were completely within the screen boundaries. Of course, this cannot be guaranteed in the general case. In real life, geometric transformations may produce primitives that are either completely outside the screen boundaries or just partially inside them. In both cases, the computation of addresses for some pixels may be outside of the bitmap's allocated storage space. Attempting to set or read such a location will inevitably crash the program. Since this is hardly a viable alternative, you must restrict the coordinates of primitives to the boundaries of the screen.

You also saw that, in the case of perspective transformation, there is another constraint on the coordinates. It is impossible to transform a point with $z = 0$ into the screen space. Besides, portions of the object that have negative z are effectively behind the viewer and, thus, aren't visible. In order to avoid problems such as division by zero or parts of the object being flipped over by the perspective transformation, you must ensure that only valid points ever get transformed into the perspective screen space. The process to locate a primitive's part or parts that satisfy some spatial constraints is called *clipping*.

Of the preceding two examples, in the first case it is necessary to perform 2D or *screen boundaries clipping,* and in the second case it is necessary to perform 3D or *volume clipping*. This chapter looks at both techniques.

It should be noted that most graphics accelerators perform screen boundaries clipping in hardware. The functionality implemented there as a rule doesn't include volume clipping, for which most graphics applications must provide a software solution.

> ### Note
>
> For the following sections, examine the implementation of the clipping module located in the `/3DGPL3/CLIPPER` subdirectory on the enclosed CD.
>
> Refer to Appendix A, "3Dgpl Graphics Library," for more instructions about the 3Dgpl library.

2D Clipping Strategies

The clipping algorithm receives as an input a description of a certain primitive, as well as a specification for another primitive (an area in 2D or a volume in 3D) against which the clipping has to be performed. Similar to rasterization, it is often hard to find a clipping strategy for arbitrary shapes and clipping volumes, primarily due to the cost constraints. There are three different approaches to 2D clipping. The first approach is to clip before the rasterization phase. This usually works for simple primitives such as polygons that are restricted by a simple clipping area, such as a rectangle. In some situations, especially for complex primitives, it may be suitable to clip during the rasterization stage. On obtaining the screen coordinates of a pixel, you first check whether it is within the proper bounds, and then proceed with plotting the pixel only when this is the case. When the geometry of the clipping area is complex, the chosen strategy may be to rasterize the primitive into some bigger rectangular bitmap and then select from this bitmap only those pixels that are inside the complex clipping area (see Figure 4.1). This is often achieved by having another buffer where all pixels that should be displayed are masked. The second buffer is referred to as a *stencil buffer* and the technique is known as *stenciling*.

FIGURE 4.1
Types of clipping.

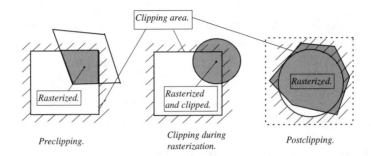

Preclipping.

Clipping during rasterization.

Postclipping.

As usual, cost considerations govern the decision about which clipping strategy to employ. The first strategy, preclipping, works well when it is inexpensive to analytically find and describe a portion of the primitive within the clipping area. When preclipping is relatively expensive to do (for instance, to find and analytically describe an intersection of a circle and a rectangle), the second strategy, clipping during the rasterization, can be used. When it is expensive both to preclip and to validate the location of a pixel with respect to the clipping area in the runtime, the third strategy, postclipping, can be considered. For example, this could be done when the clipping area is a circle or an ellipse or, perhaps, some complex shape representing a cockpit window in a flying computer game.

Because most of the time computer graphics deals with the rectangular clipping area (the computer screen), and because other algorithms often favor simple geometric primitives, this section concentrates primarily on the first strategy—more particularly, clipping points, line segments, and polygons against a rectangular clipping area.

For polygons and lines, the cheapest strategy is to clip prior to rasterization. Other strategies are much more expensive.

Clipping Points

The rectangular clipping area, which is of special interest in computer graphics, is described by four infinite lines that limit the least and the greatest horizontal coordinates and the least and the greatest vertical coordinates of the screen. Clipping a point to this area is achieved by checking its coordinates against these four constraints.

Although this is a fairly cheap operation as it is, the performance can be improved a bit further when the least limiting lines of the area pass through the beginning of the coordinates (both are zeros). Negative numbers reinterpreted into the unsigned representation appear as very big positive numbers (refer to the section "Fractional Arithmetic" in Chapter 2, "Geometric Transformations"). Thus, it suffices to compare against only upper limits to make the correct decision.

Clipping Line Segments

To ensure that a line draws inside the screen, you must check to see whether every pixel is within the boundaries. However, by employing the strategy to clip simultaneously with the rasterization, the complexity of the line rasterization routine's inner loop is increased. Moreover, the optimized line drawing may well be working with addresses of points within the image bitmap rather than with the screen coordinates.

The preclipping method analyzes the location of the primitive with respect to the constraints and finds the part of the primitive that satisfies them. A line segment requires that you find an intersection or intersections between the segment and the borders of the clipping area. Often, it is not immediately clear where such intersections occur (see Figure 4.2). In one case, the intersection may be with the horizontal boundary and in another case it may be with the vertical boundary.

Figure 4.2
Line segments intersecting a rectangular clipping area.

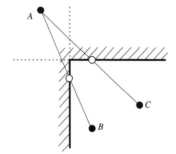

A common strategy is to employ one of the varieties of divide-and-conquer clipping algorithms that were first described by Cohen and Sutherland in the early seventies. By clipping against some boundary, possibly locating an intersection, and proceeding to other boundaries with the subproblem, it is guaranteed that the line segment that satisfies all the conditions will eventually be found. Consider Figure 4.3. The line segment AB is clipped first by the boundary B_1.

The intersection point I_1 is found and, further, the algorithm proceeds to clip the segment I_1B by the boundary B_2 that represents a subproblem of the original. Such a strategy is very general and can be employed for clipping a line against any polygonal area, not necessarily a rectangle.

FIGURE 4.3
*A line segment
intersecting
rectangular
clipping area.*

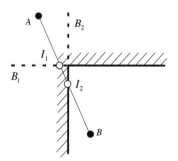

Because it may be necessary to find multiple intersection points, some of which may be useless, it becomes very important to avoid doing the calculations whenever possible. Sometimes, entire lines can be trivially rejected or accepted. For instance, when the horizontal coordinates of both endpoints of a line segment are less than the least acceptable screen coordinate, such a segment can be safely rejected. The same reasoning applies for the other boundary and the horizontal coordinates as well.

One approach to trivial acceptance or rejection, which speeds up the chain of comparisons, is based on what are called *region outcodes*. A bit pattern is assigned to regions of the plane in such a way that each bit signals the presence of the primitive in a certain region outside of the clipping rectangle (see Figure 4.4).

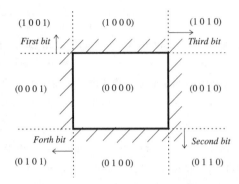

FIGURE 4.4
Region outcodes.

In a typical example of this technique, illustrated in Figure 4.4, the first bit of the outcode depicts the region above the clipping rectangle. If you assign the outcodes to the two endpoints of the segment, it becomes possible to use bitwise operations ("and" and "or") to check the endpoints' combined location in the plane. If some bits are set for both endpoints it signals that the entire line segment is in that region and, thus, outside of the clipping area. This fact can be verified for all bits using the bitwise "and" operation. If the result is non-zero, the segment can be safely rejected. On the other hand, if any bit is set for either endpoint, the segment should be taken through the clipping process. Only if there are no set bits can the segment be trivially accepted. Application of the bitwise "or" operator can verify this fact. The outcodes also help to determine which clipping edges are crossed by the line, and thus the cases where the intersections should be computed.

Whenever a segment cannot be trivially accepted or rejected, it must be taken through the clipping process. As noted, this process involves finding intersections. For the vertical and horizontal clipping edges, finding an intersection with the line segment is particularly easy (see Figure 4.5).

As the example in Figure 4.5 illustrates, the solution involves analyzing the relations of two similar triangles. Since the intersection point will belong to the clipping edge for which coordinate x_i is known, finding the corresponding y_i coordinate is all that remains. It can be computed as

$$\frac{y_2 - y_i}{x_2 - x_i} = \frac{\Delta y}{\Delta x} \Rightarrow y_i = y_2 - \frac{\Delta y(x_2 - x_i)}{\Delta x}$$

Similar expressions are also used for the vertical edges where it is necessary to locate x_i of the intersection point knowing its y_i.

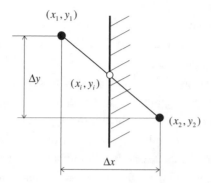

FIGURE 4.5
*Clipping a
segment against
a vertical edge.*

The cost of clipping a line segment is not particularly high. It only involves a multiplication and a division for each intersection point. However, as seen in Chapter 3, "Rasterization," in some cases lines or edges may have multiple values defined in every vertex. For instance, shaded polygons possess light intensity values in addition to spatial coordinates, and textured polygons also possess the texture coordinates. Hence, as a result of the clipping process, the correct values for all the coordinates, spatial or non-spatial, must be found. This can be achieved, of course, by invoking the found formula multiple times, once for each coordinate or parameter. However, by doing this, the cost is increased to the degree that it may be worthwhile to consider an alternative solution.

The methods that don't involve divisions or multiplications are often attractive for graphics applications due to their low cost. In the case of clipping, you can use the *binary search* technique. This technique involves only inexpensive integer operations (see Figure 4.6).

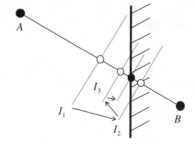

FIGURE 4.6
*Binary search
clipping.*

The binary search algorithm is often used to find roots of equations. It iteratively reduces the size of the problem until the solution is found. Applied to the clipping problem, this algorithm finds the midpoint of the line segment and compares its location to the clipping edge. Of the two line segments that are obtained at that stage, one can be discarded and the next iteration can be started for the remaining, smaller than the original, segment. For example, the line segment AB in Figure 4.6 is split into two segments. One segment spans from the endpoint A to the midpoint I_1 and another from I_1 to the endpoint B. By comparing the x coordinate of the midpoint with the x coordinate of the clipping edge, you can conclude that the edge is located to the right of the midpoint and thus intersects segment I_1B.

The remaining segment AI_1 is discarded. The iterations of the algorithm are repeated until the x coordinates of the midpoint and the edge are equal or close enough.

Although there may be several iterations involved, during each iteration the size of the new subproblem is only half of the original, thus the algorithm should terminate quite promptly. Only very cheap operations are needed for the computation of the midpoint:

$$x_{mid} = \frac{x_1 + x_2}{2}$$
$$y_{mid} = \frac{y_1 + y_2}{2}$$

As you can see, only additions and divisions by two are needed. The latter operation, as was already discussed, can be performed with the help of the shifting instruction.

Listing 4.1 is an implementation of the routine that clips against the least vertical boundary using the binary search technique. Clipping against other boundaries is done in a similar manner, and combining all four produces the effect of clipping against the rectangular screen area.

LISTING 4.1

*Binary Search
Clipping (see*
`/3DGPL3/`
`CLIPPER/`
`clipp-2d.c`
on the CD)

```
int C_line_min_x_clipping(int **vertex1,int **vertex2,int dimension)
{
 int i;
 int whereto;
 int *l,*r,*m,*t;
 static int g_store0[C_MAX_DIMENSIONS];      /* static vertex storage */
 static int g_store1[C_MAX_DIMENSIONS];
 static int g_store2[C_MAX_DIMENSIONS];
 int **vmn,**vmx;

 if((*vertex1)[0]<(*vertex2)[0])
 { swap=0; vmn=vertex1; vmx=vertex2; }        /* so that *vmn[0] < *vmx[0] */
 else
 { swap=1; vmn=vertex2; vmx=vertex1; }

 if(*vmx)[0]<C_x_clipping_min) return(0);
 else
 {
  if((*vmn)[0]<=C_x_clipping_min)             /* clipping */
  {
   HW_copy_int(*vmn,m=g_store0,dimension);    /* copying old vertices */
   HW_copy_int(*vmx,r=g_store1,dimension);
   l=g_store2;

   whereto=1;
   while(m[0]!=C_x_clipping_min)
   {
    if(whereto==1)  { t=l; l=m; m=t; }
    else            { t=r; r=m; m=t; }
    for(i=0;i<dimension;i++) m[i]=(l[i]+r[i])>>1;
    whereto=m[0]<C_x_clipping_min;
   }
   *vmn=m;                                    /* that is why m[] is static */
  }
 }
 return(1);                                   /* partially or not clipped */
}
```

Pointers to arrays passed, and returned back in the same variables.

Intersection point will be placed into this static storage.

Trivial rejection test.

Termination condition.

One of the subsegments is getting discarded by swapping vertex pointers.

Note that the routine in Listing 4.1 is designed to handle multiple dimensions in every vertex so that it can be used not only for the clipping of line segments, but also for the clipping of edges in shaded or textured polygons. Calls to the clipping functions must be placed into the line segment rasterization routine, which will then be able to assume that the primitive is entirely within the screen boundaries.

Although only simple cases of horizontal and vertical clipping edges were considered, a very similar method can be used for any kind of polygonal clipping area. This, however, involves finding an intersection of two arbitrarily oriented line segments. The next chapter discusses how to mathematically describe geometric primitives and how to use the primitive's equations in the computation of intersections.

Clipping Polygons

Similar to the line segment clipping discussed in the previous section, polygon clipping involves searching intersections between the edges of the polygon and the edges of the clipping area. The difficulty compared with the method used for lines is that a polygon can change its shape quite substantially as a result of clipping. As Figure 4.7 illustrates, the number of edges and vertices may change.

FIGURE 4.7
Different cases of polygon clipping.

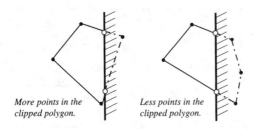

More points in the clipped polygon.   Less points in the clipped polygon.

Similar to the case of lines, polygonal clipping can be done using a divide-and-conquer strategy. A popular algorithm to do that was devised by Sutherland and Hodgman in the early seventies. This algorithm is very general and permits clipping of a polygon against any other polygonal clipping area. In the case of the rectangular screen, the clipping routine is invoked for each clipping edge, at the end producing the polygon that meets all the imposed criteria (see Figure 4.8).

FIGURE 4.8
Iterating clipping edges.

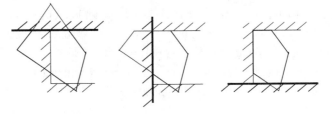

The previous section considered the technique that allows you to find an intersection of a line segment with a clipping edge. A polygon consists of multiple edges and thus the algorithm considered for line segments will be of use.

A polygon is commonly represented as a sequence of vertices. Each consecutive pair of vertices describes an edge. Whenever one of the edges intersects the clipping line, an intersection point is found and necessarily becomes a vertex of the clipped polygon (see Figure 4.9).

FIGURE 4.9

Iterating a polygon's edges against a single clipping edge.

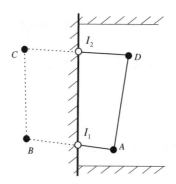

As Figure 4.9 illustrates, the polygon *ABCD* becomes AI_1I_2D after clipping. In order to deduce this fact, the edges are considered in the order of their appearance in the polygon's description. When the edge *AB* crosses the clipping line, the intersection point is added into the description of the resulting polygon. Further, following the order of the polygon definition, some edge must cross the clipping line back. In this case, it happened at the intersection point I_2.

The segment of the clipping line between the intersection points limits the clipping area and thus defines an edge I_1I_2 of the clipped polygon. It should also be noted that the edges that are trivially accepted remain in the new polygon, whereas the edges that are trivially rejected are discarded.

It must also be recognized that each vertex belongs to two edges and the polygon description is a sequence of vertices where each vertex forms an edge with its successor and its predecessor in the list. Thus, when analyzing an edge, the fact that the first vertex in each pair may have already been considered by the previous iteration should be taken into account. Following are all the possible situations that may occur:

- When an edge is trivially accepted, only its second vertex must be copied into the resulting list. It is assumed that the first one has been considered already.

- When an edge is rejected, none of its vertices can be copied.

- When the second vertex in the pair is outside of the clipping area, the intersection point must be found and placed into the result.

- When the first vertex in the pair is outside the area, it is necessary to find the intersection point and copy it into the result together with the second vertex in the pair since the second one has not been considered yet.

The completely clipped polygon is further passed to the rasterization routine, which is likely to draw the polygon as a set of horizontal pixel lines. In view of this fact, horizontal edges of the clipped polygon don't carry any additional information for the rasterization routine. Since any horizontal edge shares its endpoints with two other edges, its only pixel line can be found from the neighboring edges. Thus, assuming that the left and right boundaries delimiting the pixel lines are found by scanning the edges, you can avoid passing horizontal edges to the scanning routine without loss of consistency (see Figure 4.10).

FIGURE 4.10

A scan-line coinciding with the horizontal edge.

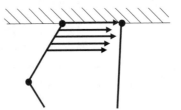

The following routine implements simultaneous clipping of a polygon against two vertical clipping edges. It is interesting to observe that the algorithm used to decide which vertices to copy into the result doesn't require modifications after this change. Further, when you have a vertically clipped polygon, its edges are passed one at a time to the edge scanning function that finds the parameters of the pixel lines. The scanning function must first clip the edge horizontally. Such a two-step approach also guarantees that the horizontal lines of the polygon will never be explicitly created, which slightly improves the overall performance (see Listing 4.2).

LISTING 4.2

Clipping a Polygon (see /3DGPL3/ CLIPPER/ clipp-2d.c on the CD)

```
int C_polygon_x_clipping(int *from, int *to,
                          int dimension, int length
                        )
{
 register int i;
 int *v1,*v2,new_lng=0;
 int *first_vrtx=to;                       /* beginning of the source */

 for(i=0;i<length;i++)                      /* for all edges */
 {
  v1=(int*)from; from+=dimension; v2=(int*)from;

  if(C_line_x_clipping(&v1,&v2,dimension))
  {
   if(C_2D_clipping)
   {
    HW_copy_int(v1,to,dimension); to+=dimension;
    HW_copy_int(v2,to,dimension); to+=dimension;
    new_lng+=2;
    }                                       /* first or both clipped */
   else
   {
    HW_copy_int(v2,to,dimension); to+=dimension;
    new_lng++;                              /* second point clipped */
    }
   }
  }
 HW_copy_int(first_vrtx,to,dimension);

 return(new_lng);
}
```

A polygon is represented as a continuous stream of vertices.

Clips an edge against both vertical boundaries.

First or second or both vertices clipped. Must be set by line clipping routine.

Note that the function presented in Listing 4.2 calls an edge clipping function that must clip against two vertical boundaries and report which of the vertices were clipped, so that the polygon clipping routine can copy the right vertices into the resulting polygon description.

It must be mentioned that the suggested algorithm can also be used to clip concave polygons as well as convex ones. However, in many cases clipping may split a concave polygon into multiple pieces. For example, a polygon *ABCDE* in Figure 4.11 is clipped into two pieces:

$$AI_1I_2$$

and

$$DI_3I_4$$

It is not hard to see that the described algorithm will in this case produce a single polygon unifying the two pieces: $AI_1I_4DI_3I_2$ (see Figure 4.11).

Strictly speaking, this produced polygon isn't simple since edges I_1I_4 and I_3I_2 coincide at some length. Such polygons, however, are often called *weakly-simple* since many computational geometry algorithms don't have to be changed to accommodate them. Rasterization algorithms aren't exceptions and would be able to correctly draw weakly-simple polygons with only minor changes. You must ensure that the line is not drawn where the edges coincide at some length.

FIGURE 4.11

A scan-line coinciding with the vertical edge.

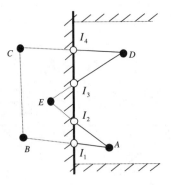

3D Clipping Strategies

As discussed in Chapter 2, the perspective projection is applicable only to a subset of all points in space. Because the perspective transformation employs the inverse of the distance from the viewer, it produces an infinite result for the points with $z=0$. It also negates the coordinates of the points that are behind the viewer, potentially flipping over parts of a primitive. The goal of 3D or volume clipping is to ensure that only valid points are getting transformed.

Thus, the perspective transformation restricts the world space to the points in front of the viewer. The previous section discussed the methods for clipping primitives against vertical and horizontal edges. In just a slightly more general form, the same algorithms are applicable for the purposes of the view plane clipping. The only difference is that three instead of two spatial dimensions must be taken into account.

Clipping against a plane slightly in front of the viewer prior to the perspective transformation discards the points that would have otherwise caused division by zero. Points that are only slightly in front of the plane will satisfy the imposed restriction, yet they may be mapped into the screen space with big absolute values of the coordinates. In fact, it is not unlikely that some of the transformed coordinates could be so big that they overflow the bit size of the variables that store them (see Figure 4.12).

FIGURE 4.12

Effects of the overflow.

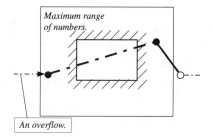

Values stored in signed representation are especially vulnerable to overflow problems. Because negative numbers are represented as very big positive numbers, numerically big coordinates of a projected point may suddenly change sign and appear in a different region of the plane. If this happens to only a few of the vertices describing some primitive, the consistency of the projection will be lost and, in the most dramatic situations, this primitive may suddenly occupy a considerable area of the screen space. For instance, a line with one of its endpoints overflowed may span across the screen from left to right or from top to bottom.

A simple fix is to attempt to move the clipping plane further ahead of the viewing plane. It doesn't solve the fundamental problem, however; it only shifts the inevitable to a greater distance. This may be sufficient in situations with a limited size of the world space. However, the majority of the applications must consider a more fundamental solution.

Observing that the ultimate goal of rendering algorithms is to present a drawing on the screen, you can separate the points in space by their ability to be projected on the screen. All points that are projected inside the screen are said to belong to the *view volume*. The points that project to the outside of the screen are also outside of the view volume in space. The problem with overflow happens for the points that are not possibly able to appear inside the screen. If some constraint is introduced limiting the space to the view volume, the overflow problem can be completely avoided.

Consider both parallel and perspective projections and their view volumes. In both cases, points that are projected to the screen boundaries separate the points that are inside the volume from the rest. In the case of the parallel projection, the projecting lines are mutually parallel and usually orthogonal to the projection plane. The lines that pass through the boundaries of the screen thus define a prism-like view volume limited in the front by the projection plane that may coincide with the screen plane. In the case of the perspective projection, the projecting lines intersect in the viewer's eye. The projecting lines that pass through the screen boundaries form a pyramid-like view volume in space, which is also limited by an additional clipping plane in the front, slightly ahead of the viewer (see Figure 4.13).

FIGURE 4.13
View volumes of perspective and parallel projections.

 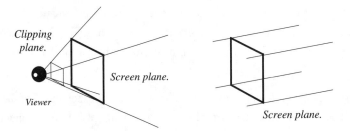

For the applications using parallel projection, 2D screen boundaries clipping restricts the coordinates to the prism-like view volume. Applications that use the perspective projection and do restrict, through some method, the coordinates to the pyramid-like view volume, don't require screen boundaries clipping since the volume clipping step ensures that all primitives are projected to the inside of the screen.

Besides being necessary to ensure the correct functioning of the perspective transformation and rasterization algorithms, volume clipping also limits the number of primitives by discarding those that cannot appear in the image. Of course, the earlier it can be decided that a primitive cannot appear in the image, the less the amount of processing that has to be dedicated to it. In the case of perspective transformation, due to the inverse of the distance that is used, the primitives that are far from the viewer appear very small on the screen. In these cases, it is unreasonable to spend processing time to draw them. The visual effect of such objects is quite negligible. Therefore, a back-clipping plane is often added to the view volume, which allows disposing of objects far away.

Clipping against the perspective view volume has an additional complication. It is necessary to clip against planes, some of which are directed almost arbitrarily in space. In all previous cases it was possible to exploit simple geometry of the clipping edges and planes. In this case, however, a fairly general situation takes place. Only two planes of the six limiting the volume have simple orientations. They are the front and the back clipping planes. The other four are located quite inconveniently.

The next chapter discusses how to mathematically describe geometric primitives such as planes and how to find intersections in the general case. The techniques examined are also applicable to the clipping problem. The generality of solutions is very often paid for in the loss of performance, however. This particular case is not an exception. Although it is relatively straightforward to analytically solve the intersection problems, it may often be too expensive to undertake. A more efficient alternative may be necessary.

Because the difficulty of volume clipping is due to the presence of arbitrarily oriented clipping planes, the first solution is to attempt to fix this situation. A much more convenient view volume results when the angle of the field of view is 90 degrees. In that case, the planes forming the perspective viewing pyramid have very simple equations: $Y=Z$, $-Y=Z$, $X=Z$, $-X=Z$ (see Figure 4.14). It is much easier to clip against such planes.

FIGURE 4.14
Viewing volumes of perspective projection with a 90 degree angle.

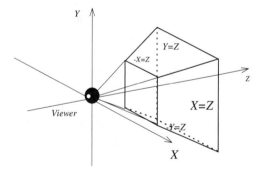

However, it is often the case that the chosen field of view angle is less than 90 degrees. In those cases, the original space can be properly scaled to arrive at the view volume with the sought angle. The clipping can be performed against the view volume of a simple geometry, and once this is done the space is scaled back into the original configuration.

As an alternative to this multistep process, you could clip in the simple volume, yet further employ the perspective transformation with a smaller field of view angle. As a result of that, some important qualities of 3D clipping are lost. The projected points may be located outside of the screen and, thus, 2D screen boundaries clipping must also be performed to ensure that this is not happening.

It is unreasonable, of course, to do two expensive clipping procedures. Thus, another approach could be used. Volume clipping could be done against the front and perhaps back clipping planes and only trivial rejection/acceptance tests performed against the remaining planes. Further, the primitives would be going through a complete 2D clipping process in the screen space.

During the first pass, future problems caused by divisions by zero are avoided thanks to clipping against the front clipping plane. It also helps to statistically avoid possible overflow problems since the great majority of the points that caused the overflows are removed through the trivial rejection tests. This problem can only occur if there are primitives that span long distances in the world space both inside the view volume and on the boundary of the maximum numerical value for the coordinates. Most of the time you can safely assume that this won't be the case.

The trivial rejections against the view volume with a 90 degree angle is very much aided by volume's simple geometry. Consider Figure 4.13. Since the clipping planes are described by the equation $Y=Z$, $-Y=Z$, $X=Z$, $-X=Z$, it is easy to observe that the space outside of the volume can be described as $Y>Z$, $-Y>Z$, $X>Z$, $-X>Z$. If all the points of some primitive satisfy the same inequality, the primitive is trivially rejected.

Individual primitives in the world space are often combined into some complex objects. Such objects may consist of many hundreds of primitives. The vertices of these primitives are very often closely located in space. If some vertex is trivially rejected, other vertices are probably going to be rejected as well. This property of locality can be exploited so that initially the trivial rejection tests are done for entire objects as opposed to individual primitives. For these tests you need some exact property of the object to consistently tell if it can be rejected. For instance, the center of the object is not suitable because when the center is outside the volume, some part of the object may well still be inside. A better approach is to enclose the object with a bounding volume of some simple geometry. If the bounding volume doesn't intersect with the view volume, the rejection can be safely done. The bounding volumes that are commonly used are a *bounding box* or a *bounding sphere* (see Figure 4.15).

FIGURE 4.15
*Bounding box
and sphere for an
object of complex
geometry.*

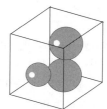

The bounding box represents minimal and maximal spatial coordinates of the object, whereas the most remote point from the object's center determines the radius of the bounding sphere.

Using the parameters of the bounding box, you can check for possible rejections from the view volume. For instance, when the minimal x coordinate is greater than the maximal z coordinate of the box, the object is outside of $X=Z$ plane and can be rejected. Although the bounding boxes were considered for the trivial rejection of complex objects, they may also help in rejecting individual primitives, such as polygons that may have many vertices, making a sequence of individual computations somewhat cumbersome.

Listing 4.3 is a routine implementing trivial rejection of some primitive or object specified through the parameters of its bounding box.

LISTING 4.3
*Bounding Box-
Based Approxi-
mate Clipping
(see* /3DGPL3/
CLIPPER/
clipp-3d.c
on the CD)

```
int C_volume_clipping(int *min, int *max)          Parameters of the
{                                                  bounding box.
 if((max[2]<min[0])||(max[2]<min[1])||(max[2]<-max[0])||
    (max[2]<-max[1])||(max[2]<=C_Z_CLIPPING_MIN))
  {
   return(0);                         /* outside */    Trivial rejection.
  }
 else
  {
   if(min[2]<C_Z_CLIPPING_MIN) return(-1);  /* partly behind the plane */
   else return(1);
  }                                          Further clipping is required.
}
```

Bounding spheres can be handled in a similar manner. However, you will have to compute the distance from the clipping plane to the center of the sphere. If this distance is bigger than the sphere's radius, the object can be rejected. The mathematics necessary to compute the distance from a point to a plane are examined in the next chapter.

Summary

Clipping algorithms are necessary to ensure consistency of other algorithms, such as rasterization or perspective transformation. They are also used to trivially discard the objects that could not contribute to the generation of the image. It is often expensive to consider general cases of clipping against any polygonal area in 2D or any polyhedron volume in 3D. Somewhat simplified solutions are commonly used instead. For instance, it is common to consider clipping against rectangles since this is the shape of the display device. Clipping against an arbitrary shape is often done with the help of stenciling, where an image is drawn in a big rectangular buffer and then some pixels, which belong to the insides of a complex clipping shape, are moved on screen. In the case of volume clipping, it is possible to either simplify the geometry of the clipping volume or use approximate accept/reject tests followed by full clipping against the screen boundaries.

CHAPTER 5

Viewing

All the techniques that process geometric descriptions of the virtual scene so that scene's projection on the screen can be computed are referred to as *viewing processes*. In all discussions up to this point, a certain viewing technology was assumed without actually being defined. It was assumed that viewing was done through projection of geometric primitives—polygons, for instance—onto the viewer's screen space. This approach, however, is not unique. There are two mainstream viewing methods, often referred to as the *world-to-screen method* and the *screen-to-world method*. Projection of primitives is world-to-screen. The second method, screen-to-world, is also called *ray-casting* or *ray-tracing*. The idea of ray-casting is quite different from world-to-screen viewing: For every pixel on the screen, you cast a ray into the representation of the virtual world until it intersects with some surface. The color of the surface in the intersection point is what is supposed to be seen at that pixel on the screen.

Both methods attempt to mimic how the viewing process appears to happen in nature. In nature, light sources emit scores of particles. Whenever these particles are reflected by some object, their wavelength composition (their color) changes. The viewer captures some of the particles and thus, through analyzing their color, can reconstruct the images of objects from which the light particles were last reflected. Although it is possible to express this process as an algorithm, its efficiency in terms of utilization of computer resources is quite low.

Only a tiny portion of all emitted rays ever reaches the viewer. The rest are dissipated in space without contributing to the generation of the image, so their simulation would only waste the processor's time.

The virtual viewing methods that are commonly used in the field of computer graphics differ in their approach to limiting the complexity of the natural viewing. World-to-screen methods attempt to limit viewing to a set of objects in the scene and handle visibility of primitives as a whole rather than through the individual rays that contributed to it. Screen-to-world methods limit the amount of rays. By tracing back from the screen, this method considers only those rays that were emitted by some light source and actually reached the viewer. This chapter discusses the relative advantages and disadvantages of both types of viewing. You will see why world-to-screen methods are currently more attractive than screen-to-world methods for interactive graphics applications, despite their relative complexity in implementation.

World-to-Screen Methods

World-to-screen methods create an image of the virtual world by projecting primitives from the world onto the viewer's screen space (see Figure 5.1). When considering the transformations and processes that form this viewing method, it is also necessary to examine the general ideas behind the representation of the 3D world and the viewer's camera.

FIGURE 5.1
World-to-screen projection.

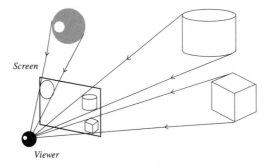

Screen

Viewer

The 3D scene is described in terms of geometric primitives, such as polygons. Individual objects in the scene may be composed of some number of primitives. Since it is feasible that the objects are capable of moving in the virtual world, it is convenient to describe their primitives using some local coordinate system rather than the world coordinates. It is often said that this local coordinate system is given in the *object space*.

Objects assume a certain orientation and position in the world space. If you know the location and the orientation, it is easy to obtain an object's coordinates in the world space by applying some affine coordinate transformation. You have already seen these transformations in Chapter 2, "Geometric Transformations." Further, once the coordinates are in the world space, it is necessary to perform the projection transformation that maps the coordinates to the viewer's screen space so that you can start the rasterization process and display the image. As discussed in Chapter 2, the projection transformation can be thought of as a two-step process. During the first step, the world space transforms in such a way that the viewer will assume the position in the beginning of the coordinates, viewing along the Z axis. From such transformed world space, which is often called the *view space*, it is easy to apply the actual projection transformation and obtain the coordinates in the screen (see Figure 5.2).

FIGURE 5.2
Transformations of an object.

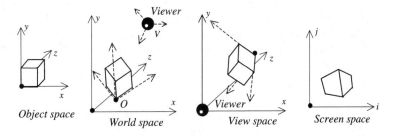

Thus, in order to display a primitive of some object, an affine transformation of its vertices is performed. This transformation depends on the object's position and orientation in the world. Further, depending on the viewer's position and orientation, another affine transformation must be applied to produce the coordinates in the view space. Finally, a projection transformation (parallel or perspective) is applied so that the screen space coordinates can be computed.

Assuming that the position of the object in the world is described by the point O and the orientation is given through the rotation angles α, β, γ (yaw, pitch, roll), to obtain world coordinates, you will have to first apply the rotation transformations using the given angles and then apply the translation transformation using the coordinates of the point O.

$$\begin{bmatrix} x_{world} & y_{world} & z_{world} & 1 \end{bmatrix} = \begin{bmatrix} x_{object} & y_{object} & z_{object} & 1 \end{bmatrix} \begin{bmatrix} R_{\alpha}^{world} \end{bmatrix} \begin{bmatrix} R_{\beta}^{world} \end{bmatrix} \begin{bmatrix} R_{\gamma}^{world} \end{bmatrix} \begin{bmatrix} T^{world} \end{bmatrix}$$

Concatenation of the four transformation matrices produces the sought affine transformation. Another affine transformation, dependent on the viewer, is performed in order to transform the coordinates from world space into view space.

Tip

There is one common mistake that those who first implement movements of models usually make. It seems reasonable to change all coordinates of the model to represent its position in a new point. When computing the next position, the coordinates of the previous position are used as arguments for the transformations. This doesn't work well since small numerical errors present in every transformation accumulate and the shape of the model will eventually change. For instance, when you rotate a model using coordinates in the previous position to compute the coordinates of the next one, it is very likely that the model will eventually collapse into a point. The correct way is to compute the coordinates for the current position from the original model's coordinates. This way, errors don't accumulate.

It should be noted that the representation of the orientation using the three angles (also called *Euler angles*) has some problems. Since these angles are given with respect to moving axes, there are some rotations where the effect of the loss of one degree of freedom (called *gimbal lock*) can be observed. When that happens, two of the angles suddenly start describing the same rotation. This usually is a complication for applications in which a user can interactively specify the orientation for some object. The Euler angles are also not very good for interpolation between two specified orientations. For instance, an animation application may have two positions of some object with specified orientations and it may need to find the intermediate orientations in between the given two. If the Euler angles are interpolated to obtain such intermediate orientations, the resulting motion may be visually unsatisfactory. The mechanism of *quaternions* should be used if this presents a problem. Despite these problems, however, representing the orientation using Euler angles is widely used thanks to its simplicity and the ease with which rotation transformation can be described.

Although a point and the rotation angles is, perhaps, quite a convenient way to specify an object in the world, many different ways are used to specify the viewer's camera. The following section discusses various ways to describe the camera and the methods to retrieve proper affine transformation in each case.

Parameters of the Viewing System

There are multiple ways to specify the viewing camera. To uniquely describe it, it is necessary to have at least six different parameters that correspond to the number of degrees of freedom for a rigid body in 3D space. Additional variables to parameterize projection transformations may also be needed. One approach is to specify the coordinates of the point V where the viewer is located, and the rotation angles α, β, γ of the camera's orientation. To obtain the view space coordinates, the translation transformation that brings the viewer into the origin of the world space must be performed first, followed by the rotations in an order more convenient for world space (γ, β, α) :

$$\begin{bmatrix} x_{view} & y_{view} & z_{view} & 1 \end{bmatrix} = \begin{bmatrix} x_{world} & y_{world} & z_{world} & 1 \end{bmatrix} \begin{bmatrix} T^{view} \end{bmatrix} \begin{bmatrix} R_\gamma^{view} \end{bmatrix} \begin{bmatrix} R_\beta^{view} \end{bmatrix} \begin{bmatrix} R_\alpha^{view} \end{bmatrix}$$

Concatenated together, the four transformation matrices produce the necessary affine transformation. In turn, the combined matrix obtained at this stage can be concatenated with the matrix describing the transformation from the object into the world space:

$$\begin{bmatrix} x_{view} & y_{view} & z_{view} & 1 \end{bmatrix} =$$

$$\begin{bmatrix} x_{object} & y_{object} & z_{object} & 1 \end{bmatrix} \begin{bmatrix} R_\alpha^{world} \end{bmatrix} \begin{bmatrix} R_\beta^{world} \end{bmatrix} \begin{bmatrix} R_\gamma^{world} \end{bmatrix} \begin{bmatrix} T^{world} \end{bmatrix} \begin{bmatrix} T^{view} \end{bmatrix} \begin{bmatrix} R_\gamma^{view} \end{bmatrix} \begin{bmatrix} R_\beta^{view} \end{bmatrix} \begin{bmatrix} R_\alpha^{view} \end{bmatrix}$$

Alternatively, the orientation of the camera can be specified through three unit vectors $\overline{n}, \overline{s}, \overline{t}$ describing the direction of viewing and the orientation of the rectangle of the screen in the world space (see Figure 5.3).

FIGURE 5.3
Specifying the camera.

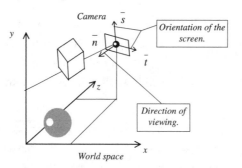

It must be noted that despite the fact that three vectors contain nine scalar parameters, these parameters are not independent. There are also six additional equations that govern their dependencies (three equations describing the fact that vectors are unit length, and three equations saying that the vectors are mutually orthogonal). As a result, there are only three independent parameters for specifying the camera's orientation, which, combined with the three independent coordinates used to specify the position of the viewer, gives the six degrees of freedom of a rigid body in 3D space.

The first step in finding the transformation is the same for both methods of camera representation: You must apply the translation transformation that will bring the viewer into the beginning of the coordinates of the world space.

As for the second step, in this case, there are no rotation angles that enable easy construction of the rotation matrix. Thus, the transformation matrix should be deduced by different means. It must be noted that the rotation is a linear transformation and thus can be represented using a three-by-three matrix. Consider trying to find it in this form, understanding that it is necessary to increase the dimension when multiplying by the other transformation matrices. Analyzing the available information, you can see that the vector of the viewing direction in the world space $\bar{n} = (\begin{array}{ccc} n_x & n_y & n_z \end{array})$, must map into $(\begin{array}{ccc} 0 & 0 & 1 \end{array})$ in the view space (recall that in this space the camera is directed along the Z axis). The other two vectors describing the screen orientation $\bar{t} = (\begin{array}{ccc} t_x & t_y & t_z \end{array})$ and $\bar{s} = (\begin{array}{ccc} s_x & s_y & s_z \end{array})$ are mapped into $(\begin{array}{ccc} 0 & 1 & 0 \end{array})$ and $(\begin{array}{ccc} 1 & 0 & 0 \end{array})$ respectively.

Using these facts, it is not difficult to establish a system of equations

$$\bar{t} = (\,t_x \quad t_y \quad t_z\,)[X] = (\,1 \quad 0 \quad 0\,)$$

$$\bar{s} = (\,s_x \quad s_y \quad s_z\,)[X] = (\,0 \quad 1 \quad 0\,)$$

$$\bar{n} = (\,n_x \quad n_y \quad n_z\,)[X] = (\,0 \quad 0 \quad 1\,)$$

where *[X]* is the unknown transformation matrix.

Combined, these equations can be written in a matrix form as

$$\begin{bmatrix} t_x & t_y & t_z \\ s_x & s_y & s_z \\ n_x & n_y & n_z \end{bmatrix} \begin{bmatrix} x_{1,1} & x_{1,2} & x_{1,3} \\ x_{2,1} & x_{2,2} & x_{2,3} \\ x_{3,1} & x_{3,2} & x_{3,3} \end{bmatrix} = \begin{bmatrix} 1 & 0 & 0 \\ 0 & 1 & 0 \\ 0 & 0 & 1 \end{bmatrix}$$

By solving this equation in all *x*, you obtain the sought transformation matrix that transforms any point from the translated world space into the view space.

Perhaps the most popular technique for solving the matrix equations of low dimension of the type *[A][X]=[B]* is the *Gaussian elimination* algorithm. In this algorithm, the equation is transformed in such a way that the coefficient matrix *[A]* attains the upper triangular form:

$$\begin{bmatrix} a_1'1 & a_2'1 & a_3'1 \\ 0 & a_2'2 & a_3'2 \\ 0 & 0 & a_3'3 \end{bmatrix}$$

This is done through exploiting a property that allows for subtracting different rows times a constant without losing the consistency of the equation. Consider a simple matrix equation:

$$\begin{bmatrix} a_1^1 & a_2^1 \\ a_1^2 & a_2^2 \end{bmatrix} \begin{bmatrix} x \\ y \end{bmatrix} = \begin{bmatrix} b_1 \\ b_2 \end{bmatrix} \Rightarrow \begin{cases} a_1^1 x + a_2^1 y = b_1 \\ a_1^2 x + a_2^2 y = b_2 \end{cases}$$

CHAPTER 5

By subtracting the first row times constant t from the second row, an equivalent system of equations is obtained:

$$\begin{cases} a_1^1 x + a_2^1 y = b_1 \\ (a_1^2 - t a_1^1)x + (a_2^2 - t a_2^1)y = b_2 - t b_1 \end{cases} \Rightarrow \begin{bmatrix} a_1^1 & a_2^1 \\ a_1^2 - t a_1^1 & a_2^2 - t a_2^1 \end{bmatrix} \begin{bmatrix} x \\ y \end{bmatrix} = \begin{bmatrix} b_1 \\ b_2 - t b_1 \end{bmatrix}$$

Using this property, it is possible to continuously subtract one row from another in such a way that the coefficients are eliminated in the lower triangle of the matrix *[A]*. Once the matrix is in the upper triangular form, the resulting matrix equation can be trivially resolved for *[X]*. Because the last row of the coefficient matrix has a single coefficient, it translates into linear equations of the type $a_n^n x_{n,n} = b_n^n$ from which it is easy to deduce all x in the last row. With this done, there is enough information to resolve for the row preceding the last one. This process is repeated until all x are resolved. The following routine implements the Gaussian elimination algorithm (see Listing 5.1).

LISTING 5.1

Solving a System of Linear Equations Using Gaussian Elimination

```
void T_linear_solve(float a[T_MAX_MATRIX_SIZE][T_MAX_MATRIX_SIZE],
                    float b[T_MAX_MATRIX_SIZE][T_MAX_MATRIX_SIZE],
                    float x[T_MAX_MATRIX_SIZE][T_MAX_MATRIX_SIZE],
                    int n, int m
                   )
{
  float max,tmp,pivot,sum;

  int i,j,k,num;

  for(max=0,num=0,i=0;i<n-1;i++)
  {
    for(j=i;j<n;j++)
    {
      if(a[j][i]>=0) pivot=a[j][i]; else pivot=-a[j][i];
      if(pivot>max) { max=pivot; num=j; }
    }

    if(max!=0)
    {
      if(num!=i)
      {
        for(j=0;j<n;j++) { tmp=a[i][j]; a[i][j]=a[num][j]; a[num][j]=tmp; }
        for(j=0;j<m;j++) { tmp=b[i][j]; b[i][j]=b[num][j]; b[num][j]=tmp; }
      }

      for(j=i+1;j<n;j++)                    /* for all coefs below */
      {
        for(k=i+1;k<n;k++) a[j][k]=a[j][k]-a[i][k]*a[j][i]/a[i][i];
        for(k=0;k<m;k++)   b[j][k]=b[j][k]-b[i][k]*a[j][i]/a[i][i];
      }
    }
  }

  for(i=n-1;i>=0;i--)                       /* reversed direction */
  {
    for(k=0;k<m;k++)
    {
      for(sum=0,j=i+1;j<n;j++) sum=sum+a[i][j]*x[j][k];
      x[i][k]=(b[i][k]-sum)/a[i][i];
    }
  }
}
```

Selecting a row with the maximum lead coefficient to prevent division by 0 and reduce numerical errors.

Interchanging rows to further use found maximum lead coefficient.

Subtracting rows to obtain the matrix in the upper triangular form.

Resolving for the unknown matrix.

Consider the following tiny example of using Gaussian elimination:

$$\begin{bmatrix} 1 & 2 \\ 2 & 6 \end{bmatrix}\begin{bmatrix} x_1 \\ x_2 \end{bmatrix} = \begin{bmatrix} 1 \\ 4 \end{bmatrix}$$

By subtracting the first row times 2 from the second row, the matrix assumes the upper triangular form:

$$\begin{bmatrix} 1 & 2 \\ 0 & 2 \end{bmatrix}\begin{bmatrix} x_1 \\ x_2 \end{bmatrix} = \begin{bmatrix} 1 \\ 2 \end{bmatrix}$$

From that point it is easy to find that $x_2 = 2/2 = 1$, and knowing this fact, the first row that can be represented as $x_1 + 2x_2 = 1$ can now be resolved to obtain $x_1 = 1 - 2 = -1$.

There are a number of problems that may appear while solving matrix equations. Some of them arise from numerical rounding errors. Rounding, however, is usually not a big problem for the low dimension matrices that are important in geometric transformations. Another set of problems may appear because of inconsistencies in the equation itself. This might happen if you initially selected parallel vectors when formulating the matrix equation. Parallel vectors translate into linearly dependent rows (one row is equal to a constant multiple of another row) and this leads to difficulties in finding a unique solution. Due to the linear dependency, trying to create a zero in a particular position creates zeros in the entire row. Having the whole row turned into zeros translates into the equation *0X=0,* which has an infinite number of solutions.

Using the Gaussian elimination method, the formulated equation can now be solved to produce the rotation matrix that can be concatenated to the right of the translation matrix to produce the sought affine transformation.

This approach of formulating a matrix equation and retrieving the transformation matrix is very general and can be applied to cameras whose direction of view is not necessarily orthogonal to the projection plane. In the particular situation when it is, a much simpler solution is available.

If it is known that all vectors describing the camera are unit length, the following statements are true (the reason for this will be seen later when the scalar product is considered):

$$\begin{bmatrix} t_x & t_y & t_z \end{bmatrix} \begin{bmatrix} t_x \\ t_y \\ t_z \end{bmatrix} = 1$$

$$\begin{bmatrix} s_x & s_y & s_z \end{bmatrix} \begin{bmatrix} s_x \\ s_y \\ s_z \end{bmatrix} = 1$$

$$\begin{bmatrix} t_x & t_y & t_z \end{bmatrix} \begin{bmatrix} t_x \\ t_y \\ t_z \end{bmatrix} = 1$$

It is also known that all vectors are mutually orthogonal, and thus also

$$\begin{bmatrix} t_x & t_y & t_z \end{bmatrix} \begin{bmatrix} s_x \\ s_y \\ s_z \end{bmatrix} = 0$$

$$\begin{bmatrix} t_x & t_y & t_z \end{bmatrix} \begin{bmatrix} n_x \\ n_y \\ n_z \end{bmatrix} = 0$$

$$\begin{bmatrix} s_x & s_y & s_z \end{bmatrix} \begin{bmatrix} n_x \\ n_y \\ n_z \end{bmatrix} = 0$$

Considering the matrix multiplication rule, it is not hard to see that the preceding statements describe individual cases of row column multiplication in the equation that was built. Noting the value that must be produced, the matrix can be reconstructed as follows:

$$\begin{bmatrix} t_x & t_y & t_z \\ s_x & s_y & s_z \\ n_x & n_y & n_z \end{bmatrix} \begin{bmatrix} t_x & s_x & n_x \\ t_y & s_y & n_y \\ t_z & s_z & n_z \end{bmatrix} = \begin{bmatrix} 1 & 0 & 0 \\ 0 & 1 & 0 \\ 0 & 0 & 1 \end{bmatrix}$$

As you can see, the coefficients of the vectors that describe the orientation of the viewer should only be placed into a matrix column by column to describe the necessary transformation.

When the coordinates in the view space are known, the projection transformation is applied. This transformation could be also represented in the matrix form and concatenated with the other transformation matrices. This is only possible, however, if the clipping process was not required. Some projections need additional parameters. For instance, the perspective transformation requires the focus distance. Such parameters are also a legitimate part of the viewer's camera description.

Choosing which of the two camera representation methods to use depends on the particular application. For moving viewers, the first method is often more intuitive because it allows easily expressing the change in the orientation through increasing or decreasing the rotation angles. The second method is helpful when the precise viewing direction should be selected. If you know the coordinates of the point to look at and the coordinates of the viewer's position, the vector specifying the viewing direction can be immediately found.

Polygonal Pipeline

A polygon is a fundamental primitive for object representation used in the world-to-screen viewing method. This primitive is the easiest to manipulate, especially during the rasterization stage. It is often the case that other primitives are tessellated (subdivided) into polygons at one stage or another. In the previous section you saw how a single point is transformed from the object space into the screen space. The process for taking a polygon from the world space into the screen space is often called the *polygonal pipeline*. Although there are complications caused by the presence of multiple polygons (some polygons may be obscured by others), we'll concentrate for the moment on a single polygon passing all the stages until it appears on the screen.

You have already seen that in addition to the transformations, a primitive must pass the clipping stages. You must ensure that there are no vertices outside of the viewing volume, and if the 3D clipping was approximate, it is also necessary to guarantee to the rasterization routine that the primitive is within the boundaries of the screen. In order to do the latter, 2D clipping algorithms are employed.

Chapter 4, "Clipping," discussed how to perform the volume clipping immediately before the perspective transformation—that is, in the view space. Since another reason for volume clipping is to reduce the scene complexity, it is potentially advantageous to do clipping earlier, in the world space. You will have to transform the viewing volume from the view space back into the world space to apply clipping there, thus possibly rejecting many primitives even before they are transformed into the view space. In many situations, however, this is not practical. For one thing, clipping will have to be done against planes arbitrarily oriented in space, which is fairly expensive to do. Moreover, if a single concatenated matrix is performing the transformations directly from the object space into the view space, there is no gain to be made by clipping in the world space because world coordinates are never computed explicitly. For example, in applications picturing interior scenes, there may be a lot of objects described in terms of world space. These objects could be static elements of the interior such as walls or floors. Moving objects, however, will be specified in their own object space. In such applications, clipping earlier may bring a potential gain because some vertices would not have to be transformed at all.

Depending on the type of polygon, extra work may be required. Chapter 3, "Rasterization," considered flat polygons, interpolatively shaded polygons, linearly textured polygons, and finally, perspectively textured polygons. There is no extra work to do for the first three types, except that a different number of coordinates per vertex has to be pushed through the pipeline. It is just (x,y,z) coordinates for the flat polygons, $(x,y,z,red,green,blue)$ for interpolatively shaded ones, (x,y,z,u,v) for linearly textured, or $(x,y,z,red,green,blue,u,v)$ for the combination of the latter two.

For the purposes of the transformations, you just have to worry about spatial coordinates. Clipping, on the other hand, has to be applied to all of the values defined in a vertex. Because all of the values mentioned above represent parameters that change linearly across the polygon, treating intensity or texture coordinates as space coordinates in the clipping algorithms is valid. This property was already exploited for performing polygon scan-conversion. There, the intensity and the texture coordinates were linearly interpolated along the edges to obtain the values on the left and right boundaries of the polygon, and then linearly interpolated again along the scan-lines.

An extra complication comes with perspectively textured polygons. In order to do proper perspective texture mapping, you need a projection of two orthogonal unit vectors from the texture space into the view space since they are used in the reverse mapping equations. Chapter 3 considered this algorithm. Because perspectively textured polygons are crucial for creating realistic looking virtual worlds, the following section considers this problem in deeper detail.

Textured Polygons

As discussed in Chapter 3, the algorithm performing the perspective texture mapping requires the information about the orientation of the polygon's plane in the view space. This information is represented by the mappings of two orthogonal unit vectors from the texture space into the view space and the mapping of the texture space origin.

Recovering texture mapping vectors is a very simple task if you are dealing with rectangles. The big advantage is in the property of the edges being orthogonal (see Figure 5.4).

FIGURE 5.4

Texture mapping vectors for a rectangle.

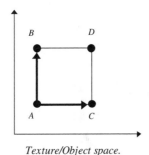

Texture/Object space.

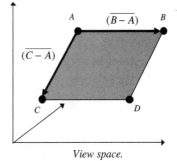

View space.

As Figure 5.4 illustrates, it is easy to recover the scaled version of texture mapping vectors as $\overline{(B-A)}$ and $\overline{(C-A)}$ from the view space coordinates of vertices. Similarly, the coordinates of the point A in the view space may serve as the mapping of the texture space origin. The same strategy can be applied for triangles that have two orthogonal edges.

However, if there are no orthogonal edges in a polygon, the problem becomes somewhat more complicated. One solution is to store two vectors that describe texture orientation and a point that describes the texture space origin with every polygon. You will apply transformation to them during the transition from the object into the view space. Then you will obtain the proper mappings. This method, however, assumes storing redundant information for every polygon. The same information can be deduced by examining the coordinates of the vertices in the view space.

Recall that for the linearly textured polygons, the texture coordinates were kept in every vertex that allowed rendering polygons of any shape. The texture coordinates were treated just as space coordinates for the purposes of clipping so that there were correct texture coordinates in all vertices at the rasterization stage, whether or not the vertices were created during clipping. Although the situation is different with the perspectively textured polygons, a similar strategy can be employed. Texture coordinates stored in every vertex may help to obtain the texture mapping vectors.

Consider again why rectangles were so simple in this respect. Corners of a rectangle correspond exactly to the corners of the texture. That may not be the case for an arbitrary polygon (see Figure 5.5).

FIGURE 5.5

A polygon and its texture.

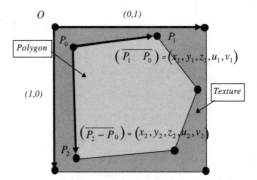

Yet in the vertices of an arbitrary polygon in the view space, there are both the spatial coordinates and the texture coordinates that each vertex has originated from. Thus, it is possible to establish a correspondence between some vectors in the texture space and the view space by building these vectors from the coordinates of the vertices (see Figure 5.5).

$$(u_1 \quad v_1 \quad 0)[T] = (x_1 \quad y_1 \quad z_1)$$

$$(u_2 \quad v_2 \quad 0)[T] = (x_2 \quad y_2 \quad z_2)$$

What you require, on the other hand, and what is easy to obtain in the case of rectangles without complex calculations, are the mappings of the orthogonal texture space vectors $(1 \quad 0 \quad 0)$ and $(0 \quad 1 \quad 0)$. Obviously, combining these two equations results in a matrix equation. By solving the matrix equation, it is possible to retrieve the transformation matrix *[T]* that performs the transformation from the texture into the view space.

$$\begin{bmatrix} u_1 & v_1 & 0 \\ u_2 & v_2 & 0 \end{bmatrix} \begin{bmatrix} t_{1,1} & t_{1,2} & t_{1,3} \\ t_{2,1} & t_{2,2} & t_{2,3} \\ t_{3,1} & t_{3,2} & t_{3,3} \end{bmatrix} = \begin{bmatrix} x_1 & y_1 & z_1 \\ x_2 & y_2 & z_2 \end{bmatrix}$$

Noting that the texture is two dimensional, the preceding equation is trivially transformed into

$$\begin{bmatrix} u_1 & v_1 \\ u_2 & v_2 \end{bmatrix} \begin{bmatrix} t_{1,1} & t_{1,2} & t_{1,3} \\ t_{2,1} & t_{2,2} & t_{2,3} \end{bmatrix} = \begin{bmatrix} x_1 & y_1 & z_1 \\ x_2 & y_2 & z_2 \end{bmatrix}$$

This matrix equation can be resolved by using, for example, the Gaussian elimination algorithm that was examined in the previous section. When the equation is resolved, the transformation matrix *[T]* is obtained that transforms any point from the texture space into the world space. Since you need the mappings of the unit vectors for the purposes of texture mapping, this can be computed as follows:

$$(1 \quad 0) \begin{bmatrix} t_{1,1} & t_{1,2} & t_{1,3} \\ t_{2,1} & t_{2,2} & t_{2,3} \end{bmatrix} = (t_{1,1} \quad t_{1,2} \quad t_{1,3})$$

$$(0 \quad 1) \begin{bmatrix} t_{1,1} & t_{1,2} & t_{1,3} \\ t_{2,1} & t_{2,2} & t_{2,3} \end{bmatrix} = (t_{2,1} \quad t_{2,2} \quad t_{2,3})$$

In addition to these two, it is also necessary to have the mapping of the texture space origin, the point O, into the view space. Although it is not explicitly present, you can use the mapping in any vertex of the polygon $P = (P_x, P_y, P_z, u_P, v_P)$ and change the direct mapping equations that were derived in Chapter 3 accordingly to reflect the fact that an arbitrary point is used rather than the origin:

$$
\begin{aligned}
x &= P_x + (v - v_P) \cdot V_x + (u - u_P) \cdot U_x \\
y &= P_y + (v - v_P) \cdot V_y + (u - u_P) \cdot U_y \\
z &= P_z + (v - v_P) \cdot V_z + (u - u_P) \cdot U_z
\end{aligned}
$$

Thus, the reverse mapping equations will assume a slightly different form:

$$
u = \frac{i(V_z \cdot P_y - V_y \cdot P_z)/focus + j(V_x \cdot P_z - V_z \cdot P_x)/focus + (V_y \cdot P_x - V_x \cdot P_y)}{i(V_y \cdot U_z - V_z \cdot U_y)/focus + j(V_z \cdot U_x - V_x \cdot U_z)/focus + (V_x \cdot U_y - V_y \cdot U_x)} + u_P
$$

$$
v = \frac{i(U_y \cdot P_z - U_z \cdot P_y)/focus + j(U_z \cdot P_x - U_x \cdot P_z)/focus + (U_x \cdot P_y - U_y \cdot P_x)}{i(V_y \cdot U_z - V_z \cdot U_y)/focus + j(V_z \cdot U_x - V_x \cdot U_z)/focus + (V_x \cdot U_y - V_y \cdot U_x)} + v_P
$$

The method of relying upon texture coordinates defined in every vertex allows for treating linearly and perspectively textured polygons in a uniform manner as far as the data representation is concerned. Although the final purpose of texture coordinates stored in each vertex is different, their presence permits rendering the same polygon using both techniques. This is attractive because linear texture mapping is inherently less expensive and the perspective texture mapping can then only be used in the situations where the perspective distortion cannot be neglected.

Screen-to-World Methods

Screen-to-world methods find images of the virtual world by tracing back the rays from the viewer's eye into the space.

A common strategy is to generate a ray passing through every pixel on the screen and to compute the intersections with all the primitives in the world that result. Of all the intersection points, the one with the least distance to the viewer is of interest because this will be the visible point at the selected screen pixel (see Figure 5.6).

FIGURE 5.6

Screen-to-world projection (ray-casting).

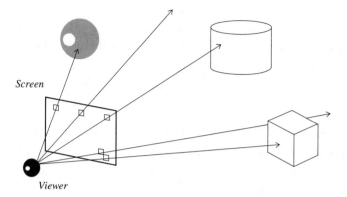

Although this solves the visibility problem, it doesn't completely help in determining the color that should be assigned to the pixel on the screen. (Lighting and color are discussed in Chapter 8, "Lighting.") For the moment, assume that it is possible to deduce the color by examining attributes of the surface intersected by the ray.

It must also be noted that you can obtain the coordinates of individual objects in the world space from their object space coordinates by applying coordinate transformations in exactly the same way as in the world-to-screen method. For this viewing method, however, it is not necessary to explicitly transform the coordinates into the view space and then into the screen space. Since the viewing is achieved through intersection calculations, these can just as easily be performed in the world space. The calculations will be the same in either space (see Figure 5.7).

FIGURE 5.7

Definition of camera for screen-to-world projection (ray-casting).

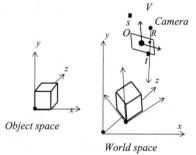

Figure 5.7 illustrates that if the camera is specified through the point O describing the position of the screen center in the world, orthogonal vectors $\bar{s}(S_x, S_y, S_z), \bar{t}(T_x, T_y, T_z)$ describing screen orientation, and the point V specifying the position of the viewer, it is easy to find the world coordinate (R_x, R_y, R_z) of any screen pixel $R(s,t)$ as

$$R_x = O_x + sS_x + tT_x; \qquad R_y = O_y + sS_y + tT_y; \qquad R_z = O_z + sS_z + tT_z.$$

These expressions are obtained in the very same way as was done in a similar situation with the perspective texture mapping in Chapter 2. Further, when you have the world coordinates for a point R, it is possible to define a ray that is passing through this point as having originated in the point V.

Although other ways of defining the camera are possible, in all cases it is easy to avoid extra coordinate transformations by constructing the necessary rays in the world space. Therefore, the major problem that remains is how to find intersections between rays and geometric primitives. You need to consider first the mathematical form of representing basic primitives—lines, planes, polygons, spheres, and cylinders—and then how to compute the coordinates of the intersection points.

Line Equation

A line can be specified in a number of ways. For instance, it can be specified using a point Q through which the line passes, and a vector $\overline{C}$ co-directed with the line. The goal is to tie these in an expression with an arbitrary point X belonging to the line (see Figure 5.8). Such an expression will thus describe all valid X.

FIGURE 5.8
A line and its co-directed vector.

It is not hard to see that any other way of representing a line can be brought to this case. For instance, if there are two points Q_1 and Q_2 belonging to the line, a vector co-directed with this line can be found as $\overline{(Q_2 - Q_1)}$. Either of the two points can be taken in addition to the vector to serve as the point Q.

Using a variable point X and the given point Q, it is easy to construct another vector co-directed with the line $\overline{(X - Q)}$. The two vectors $\overline{C}$ and $\overline{(X - Q)}$ are parallel and thus linearly dependent. Both have the same direction and only differ in length. In other words, one vector is a scalar multiple of the other. This fact gives us the sought line equation:

$$\overline{(X - Q)} = t\overline{C}$$

In this equation, parameter t is some real scalar value, and the equation can be further rewritten into what's known as the *parametric form*:

$$X = Q + t\overline{C}$$

Thus, by varying the parameter t, you arrive at a different point belonging to the line. It should be noted that X, Q, and $\overline{C}$ have three coordinates each and the preceding equation has, in fact, the following meaning:

$$\begin{bmatrix} x \\ y \\ z \end{bmatrix} = \begin{bmatrix} Q_x \\ Q_y \\ Q_z \end{bmatrix} + t \begin{bmatrix} C_x \\ C_y \\ C_z \end{bmatrix}$$

This form gives rise to several different representations written in components as opposed to vector form. For instance, if two vectors are equal, it follows that their respective components should be equal too. Thus, it is easy to obtain three equations. From each of these equations, the parameter t can be found.

$$\begin{bmatrix} x \\ y \\ z \end{bmatrix} = \begin{bmatrix} Q_x \\ Q_y \\ Q_z \end{bmatrix} + t \begin{bmatrix} C_x \\ C_y \\ C_z \end{bmatrix} = \begin{bmatrix} Q_x + tC_x \\ Q_y + tC_y \\ Q_z + tC_z \end{bmatrix} \Rightarrow \begin{cases} x = Q_x + tC_x \\ y = Q_y + tC_y \\ z = Q_z + tC_z \end{cases} \Rightarrow \begin{cases} t = (x - Q_x)/C_x \\ t = (y - Q_y)/C_y \\ t = (z - Q_z)/C_z \end{cases}$$

Equating all the different ways the parameter t can be found gives another common form of expressing lines:

$$\frac{(x - Q_x)}{C_x} = \frac{(y - Q_y)}{C_y} = \frac{(z - Q_z)}{C_z}$$

For the purposes of screen-to-world viewing, the parametric form is the most convenient. When looking for intersections of a line with several geometric objects, it is convenient to compare distances between the intersections by analyzing the parameters t. At the same time, the ray equation can be obtained by computing the corresponding line equation with the origin of the ray taken as the point Q, and combining it with an extra condition limiting the parameter t to positive numbers only.

Plane Equation

Before a formula for a plane equation can be derived, it is important to consider an important concept of multiplying vectors. Two different kinds of products are defined for the vector space: a *cross product* (also known as a *vector product*) and a *scalar product* (also known as a *dot product*). As their names suggest, multiplication of two vectors produces a vector in the first case, and a scalar value in the second case.

By definition, a vector product denoted as $\overline{A} \times \overline{B}$ is a vector satisfying these three properties:

$$\|\overline{A} \times \overline{B}\| = \|\overline{A}\| \|\overline{B}\| \sin(A, B)$$

Length of the vector product of two vectors is the product of their lengths and the sin of the angle between the vectors (Note the *norm* notation $\|\bar{a}\|$ specifying length for vector $\bar{a}$).

$\overline{A} \times \overline{B}$ is orthogonal to both $\overline{A}$ and $\overline{B}$.

$\overline{A}, \overline{B}$ and $\overline{A} \times \overline{B}$ form right triple of vectors. When looking from the end of $\overline{A} \times \overline{B}$ the rotation to get from $\overline{A}$ to $\overline{B}$ is counterclockwise (see Figure 5.9).

FIGURE 5.9
Right triple of vectors.

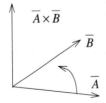

Of the three properties, property number two is of particular interest: the vector product of two vectors is orthogonal to the two given vectors. For a plane, the normal vector (the one orthogonal to the plane) can be computed as the vector product of any two vectors that lie in it. Property number three specifies in which of the two possible directions the vector product will point, and the first property indicates the resulting length.

Let's derive a formula to compute the vector product given two vectors.

Any vector can be represented as a linear combination of the *basis*. The usual basis of the 3D vector space is formed by a right triple of three mutually orthogonal unit length vectors:

$$\bar{i} = \begin{bmatrix} 1 \\ 0 \\ 0 \end{bmatrix}, \bar{j} = \begin{bmatrix} 0 \\ 1 \\ 0 \end{bmatrix}, \bar{k} = \begin{bmatrix} 0 \\ 0 \\ 1 \end{bmatrix}$$

What this means is that a vector A can be expressed as

$$\bar{A} = \begin{bmatrix} x \\ y \\ z \end{bmatrix} = \begin{bmatrix} x \\ 0 \\ 0 \end{bmatrix} + \begin{bmatrix} 0 \\ y \\ 0 \end{bmatrix} + \begin{bmatrix} 0 \\ 0 \\ z \end{bmatrix} = x \begin{bmatrix} 1 \\ 0 \\ 0 \end{bmatrix} + y \begin{bmatrix} 0 \\ 1 \\ 0 \end{bmatrix} + z \begin{bmatrix} 0 \\ 0 \\ 1 \end{bmatrix} = x\bar{i} + y\bar{j} + z\bar{k}$$

which is clearly true based on the definition of vector addition and multiplication by a scalar.

From the definition of the vector product, it is easy to see that the product of any two basis vectors is the remaining third vector or its negative. For instance, the product of $\bar{i}$ and $\bar{j}$ must be orthogonal to them both. Since the length of the product is

$$\|\bar{i} \times \bar{j}\| = \|\bar{i}\| \|\bar{j}\| \sin(i, j)$$

and both $\bar{i}$ and $\bar{j}$ are unit vectors crossed at the right angle, the length of the product must be equal to 1 as well.

This automatically leaves either $\bar{k}$ or $-\bar{k}$. Considering property number three and the fact that the rotation from $\bar{i}$ to $\bar{j}$ observed from the end of $\bar{k}$ is indeed counterclockwise in the usual basis, it is easy to conclude that $\bar{k} = \bar{i} \times \bar{j}$.

Similarly, $\bar{j} \times \bar{k} = \bar{i}, \bar{k} \times \bar{i} = \bar{j}$. To find an expression to compute the vector product, it is necessary to represent two arbitrary vectors as the linear combinations of the basis and perform some algebraic manipulation with the resulting expressions:

$$\overline{A} \times \overline{B} = (A_x \bar{i} + A_y \bar{j} + A_z \bar{k}) \times (B_x \bar{i} + B_y \bar{j} + B_z \bar{k}) =$$

$$A_x B_x \bar{i} \times \bar{i} + A_y B_x \bar{j} \times \bar{i} + A_z B_x \bar{k} \times \bar{i} +$$
$$A_x B_y \bar{i} \times \bar{j} + A_y B_y \bar{j} \times \bar{j} + A_z B_y \bar{k} \times \bar{j} +$$
$$A_x B_z \bar{i} \times \bar{k} + A_y B_z \bar{j} \times \bar{k} + A_z B_z \bar{k} \times \bar{k}$$

Further, with the help of the definition of the vector product, it is not hard to see that $\bar{i} \times \bar{i} = \bar{0}, \bar{j} \times \bar{j} = \bar{0}, \bar{k} \times \bar{k} = \bar{0}$ due to the fact that the vector forms a 0 degree angle with itself and $sin(0)=0$. Substituting known products into the expression, the formula to compute the vector product is obtained:

$$\overline{A} \times \overline{B} = (A_y B_z - A_z B_y)\bar{i} + (A_z B_x - A_x B_z)\bar{j} + (A_x B_y - A_y B_x)\bar{k}$$

It is customary to represent this formula with the help of the definition of the *matrix determinant* because this formula represents precisely how you compute the determinant for a particular matrix containing the vectors' coordinates:

$$\overline{A} \times \overline{B} = \bar{i}(A_y B_z - A_z B_y) + \bar{j}(A_z B_x - A_x B_z) + \bar{k}(A_x B_y - A_y B_x) =$$

$$= \bar{i}\det\begin{bmatrix} A_y & A_z \\ B_y & B_z \end{bmatrix} + \bar{j}\det\begin{bmatrix} A_x & A_z \\ B_x & B_z \end{bmatrix} + \bar{k}\det\begin{bmatrix} A_x & A_y \\ B_x & B_y \end{bmatrix} = \det\begin{bmatrix} \bar{i} & \bar{j} & \bar{k} \\ A_x & A_y & A_z \\ B_x & B_y & B_z \end{bmatrix}$$

Unlike the vector product, the scalar product of two vectors is a scalar number. By definition, this number is a product of the vectors' length and the *cos* of the angle formed by the two vectors:

$$\overline{A} \cdot \overline{B} = \|\overline{A}\|\|\overline{B}\|\cos(A, B)$$

Just as for the vector product, consider the scalar product of the basis vectors. This time, it is even simpler. Since *cos(90)=0*, it is obvious that $\bar{i} \cdot \bar{j} = 0, \bar{j} \cdot \bar{k} = 0, \bar{k} \cdot \bar{i} = 0$. Representing two arbitrary vectors as the linear combinations of the basis vectors, you can see that

$$\overline{A} \cdot \overline{B} = (A_x\bar{i} + A_y\bar{j} + A_z\bar{k}) \cdot (B_x\bar{i} + B_y\bar{j} + B_z\bar{k}) =$$

$$A_xB_x\bar{i} \cdot \bar{i} + A_yB_x\bar{j} \cdot \bar{i} + A_zB_x\bar{k} \cdot \bar{i}+$$
$$A_xB_y\bar{i} \cdot \bar{j} + A_yB_y\bar{j} \cdot \bar{j} + A_zB_y\bar{k} \cdot \bar{j}+$$
$$A_xB_z\bar{i} \cdot \bar{k} + A_yB_z\bar{j} \cdot \bar{k} + A_zB_z\bar{k} \cdot \bar{k}$$

By definition $\bar{i} \cdot \bar{i} = \|\bar{i}\|\|\bar{i}\| \cos(0) = 1$. Taking this fact into consideration, the formula for computation of the scalar product can be expressed simply as

$$\overline{A} \cdot \overline{B} = A_xB_x + A_yB_y + A_zB_z$$

You can see that this is exactly how a row and a column vector are multiplied.

$$[A_x \quad A_y \quad A_z] \begin{vmatrix} B_x \\ B_y \\ B_z \end{vmatrix} = A_xB_x + A_yB_y + A_zB_z$$

There is an important property of the scalar product. This product of two orthogonal vectors is *0* since *cos(90)=0*.

With the help of the two products, it is now possible to find an equation describing a plane.

If there is a point *P* located in the plane, any vector in this plane can be represented as $(X - P)$ where *X* is a variable point in the same plane. If there is also a vector $\overline{N}$, normal to the plane, the plane equation can be expressed as an equality of the scalar product of the two vectors to zero (see Figure 5.10):

$$(\overline{X - P}) \cdot \overline{N} = 0$$

Only those *X* that lie in the plane will make the preceding equation evaluate to *0*.

FIGURE **5.10**

A plane.

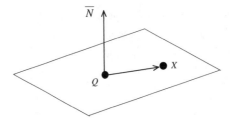

In the context of computer graphics, it is often necessary to find an equation of the plane for a given polygon. In that case, there may not be a normal vector available; however, with the help of the vector product it could be easily found. It is only necessary to have two vectors in the plane, which are found as differences of a polygon's vertices.

Intersection of a Line and a Plane

The equation of a geometric surface holds for any point in space that belongs to that surface. Thus, simultaneously resolving the system of equations consisting of formulas describing several geometric primitives can lead to finding the points that belong to all the primitives in the system—their intersection.

Suppose there is a line represented in the parametric form $X = Q + t\overline{C}$ and a plane represented as $(\overline{X - P}) \cdot \overline{N} = 0$. This system can be resolved in the following way:

$$\begin{cases} X = Q + t\overline{C} \\ (\overline{X - P}) \cdot \overline{N} = 0 \end{cases} \Rightarrow (Q + t\overline{C} - P) \cdot \overline{N} = 0 \Rightarrow$$

$$\Rightarrow t\overline{C} \cdot \overline{N} = (\overline{P - Q}) \cdot \overline{N} \Rightarrow t = \frac{(\overline{P - Q}) \cdot \overline{N}}{\overline{C} \cdot \overline{N}}$$

By resolving the two equations together, an expression for the parameter t was found corresponding to the point on the line that also belongs to the plane. The coordinates of the intersection point can be further deduced by substituting found t into the line equation.

Note that if the line is parallel to the plane, the co-directed vector of the line and plane's normal will be perpendicular. The scalar product of two perpendicular vectors is equal to 0. Because in the preceding equation you divide by this scalar product, in this particular case the operation won't make much sense because mathematically t will resolve to infinity. This is to indicate that the intersection doesn't occur.

Intersection of a Line and a Polygon

The computation of the intersection of a line and a plane is quite important. However, the 3D scene is normally populated by polygons that are only patches of their respective planes. Thus, although by using the formula from the previous section it is possible to find the intersection with the plane, it may be of little use if it doesn't lie within the polygon's borders.

Once the intersection with the polygon's plane is found, all further computations are essentially planar, proceeding in the polygon's plane.

Even for a purely planar case, determining whether a point is within the boundaries of an arbitrary polygon is somewhat troublesome. A common approach is to use what is sometimes called the *plumb-line* or *odd intersection* rule. This rule is an immediate consequence of a fundamental geometric theorem known as *Jordan's curve* theorem, which simply states that any simple polygon subdivides a plane into two regions: the interior of the polygon and its exterior.

Thus, if a horizontal line passing through a given point is drawn, it may intersect the polygon at several edges. If there is an odd number of intersections on either side of the point, it must be within the polygon. If there is an even number of intersections on either side, it must be on the outside. Note that since 0 is considered to be even, the case when the line doesn't intersect any edge falls into the second category as well (see Figure 5.11).

Since this method works entirely in the plane, it is necessary to have the coordinates of all the points with respect to this plane. What's available instead are 3D coordinates. It is possible, of course, to deduce this information by applying the techniques used in previous sections for camera transformations.

FIGURE 5.11
Odd intersections rule.

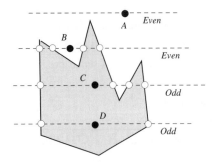

In this particular case, it is easy to build a normal to the plane and select two orthogonal vectors in the plane. The goal is to find the transformation that maps the three selected vectors into the usual basis. Further applying it to the point in the world space produces the coordinates, two of which can be used as the coordinates in the plane. It is somewhat expensive to employ this strategy.

When looking for a cheaper solution, it becomes clear that it is possible to use projections of all points onto one of the reference planes of the coordinate system for the intersection calculations. If the point is within the polygon in a given plane, it is within the polygon in any projection of that plane. Reference planes are attractive because the projections onto them are the easiest to find. Finding them only involves discarding one of the three 3D coordinates in every point. For instance, for a point *(x,y,z)*, its projection onto the *XY* plane is just *(x,y)* (see Figure 5.12).

FIGURE 5.12
Projections of a polygon onto the reference planes.

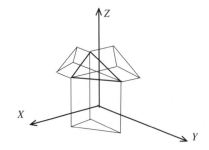

A small problem with this approach is that it is not impossible that a given plane maps into a line in some projections. When this happens, all further computations are severely impeded. Thus, before you select which projection to use, you must analyze the positioning of the plane in space and select the biggest of the three projections. The information for this decision is implicitly contained in the normal to the plane. If you find which of the three components of the normal has the greatest absolute value, you should select the projection onto the plane that is orthogonal to that coordinate's axis.

The method based on the odd intersection rule involves looking for intersection of the line with every edge of the polygon. It is relatively expensive to do.

Another technique is available that is very much reminiscent of clipping. This technique, however, sacrifices generality by limiting the consideration to only convex polygons.

A convex polygon is a set of connected line segments. A line passing through each edge, due to the property of convex polygons, leaves all other vertices on one side. All the points in space to one side of a line define what's called a *half-plane*. The area of the polygon is, thus, the intersection of the half-planes formed by every edge (see Figure 5.13).

Figure 5.13
Polygon as an intersection of half-planes.

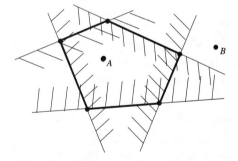

If it is possible to decide whether a point is in the proper half-plane, it is also possible to conclude whether it belongs to the inside of a polygon by examining all the half-planes formed by the edges.

It should be noted that this algorithm, similar to the one considered previously, also involves analyzing every edge. However, the individual step is somewhat cheaper, since it is relatively inexpensive to find whether or not a point belongs to a half-plane (as you will see later in this section).

This algorithm can be easily improved and made logarithmic in the number of vertices considered by employing the technique of binary search. Consider the polygon in Figure 5.14. By using the fan-like subdivision shown there, you can first use the binary search to find which of the slices the point is in. It is necessary to then test, just as in the previous algorithm, whether the point is in the proper half-plane defined by the edge limiting the slice (see Figure 5.14).

FIGURE 5.14

Using binary search on a fan-like subdivision.

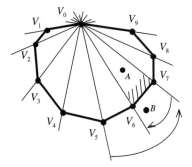

As Figure 5.14 shows, you first find the median (the middle entry) of the list of the polygon's vertices, so that if you connect the first vertex of the list V_0 with the median vertex V_5, half of the vertices will be on one side of this line and half will be on the other side. By checking where the point is with respect to this line, it is possible to reject half of the input and repeat the iteration again till only a single slice remains. It is important to note that in many cases you deal with polygons having only a few vertices. The advantage of the algorithm involving subdivision, however, becomes significant only when there is a relatively large number of vertices in the polygons. In light of this, the algorithm checking all half-planes is often favored because it is simpler than the other one.

A somewhat similar subdivision strategy can be used for inclusion tests on concave polygons. Figure 5.15 demonstrates a possible slab-like subdivision. With such a subdivision, assuming use of a proper pre-computed data structure, you can pre-sort edges within each slab. Further, it is possible to use a binary search to first locate the slab necessary for the inclusion test and then perform another binary search within the slab to find whether a given point is within a part of a polygon or its exterior.

FIGURE 5.15
*Using binary
search on slab
subdivision.*

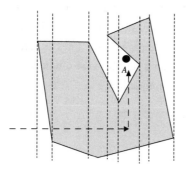

In all of these techniques, however, it is necessary to have a way to test whether or not a point is in a certain half-plane. To do that, it is possible to use the equation of a line in the plane. Such an equation was already derived for the 3D case, and the current planar task is even simpler.

It is customary and convenient to express an equation of a line in the plane as $Ax + By + C = 0$ where A,B,C are some constants. There are two equivalent methodologies you can use in order to derive this formula. One derivation of a line equation based on the co-directed vector has already been considered:

$$(\overline{X - Q}) = t\overline{C}$$

For the planar case, this translates into

$$\begin{bmatrix} x - Q_x \\ y - Q_y \end{bmatrix} = t \begin{bmatrix} C_x \\ C_y \end{bmatrix} \Rightarrow \begin{cases} x - Q_x = tC_x \\ y - Q_y = tC_y \end{cases} \Rightarrow$$

$$(x - Q_x)/C_x = (y - Q_y)/C_y \Rightarrow C_y(x - Q_x) - C_x(y - Q_y) = 0 \Rightarrow$$

$$C_y x - C_x y + C_y Q_x - C_x Q_y = 0$$

This formula must be used when you need to find the line equations given two points since, in such a case, the co-directed vector is computed as simply the difference of these two points.

An equivalent derivation method is based on the vector orthogonal to the line. A similar approach was used to find the plane equation. It was not useful for the case of a line in 3D because it doesn't uniquely describe the situation. Many lines are orthogonal to a vector in 3D. It is meaningful, however, for the planar case because a unique line is specified. Thus, it is similar to the derivation of the plane equation:

$$(\overline{X - P}) \cdot \overline{N} = 0$$

or brought into a conventional form

$$(x - P_x)N_x + (y - P_y)N_y = 0 \Rightarrow$$

$$N_x x + N_y y - P_y N_y - P_x N_x = 0$$

This line equation has a nice property that helps to determine the relationship between an arbitrary point and a half-plane. Since, fundamentally, the equation is expressing some scalar product, it should be easy to see that

$$(\overline{X - P}) \cdot \overline{N} = \|(\overline{X - P})\| \|\overline{N}\| \cos((X - P), N)$$

If the angle between the two vectors is less than 90 degrees, *cos(x)* is positive, and since the lengths are always positive that makes the whole expression positive. However, if the angle is greater than 90 degrees, *cos(x)* is negative, making the whole expression negative. At exactly 90 degrees, the expression evaluates to 0. This has the following geometric interpretation: The line equation evaluates to zero for any point on the line (90 degrees). It evaluates to a positive number for the points that are in the half-plane pointed to by the normal vector. That is because the angle between the normal and the vector pointing to the point is less than 90 degrees in this case. For the rest, the equation evaluates to a negative number because the angle between the normal and the vector toward the point is greater than 90 degrees (see Figure 5.16).

FIGURE 5.16

Sign of the scalar product.

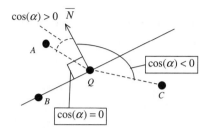

Thus, whenever one of the algorithms performing polygon inclusion computation requires testing whether a point is in a certain half-plane, you can first compute the necessary line equation using the first derivation. Since the derivations are equivalent, you can further exploit the property found in the second case to deduce which side of the line the point is on by evaluating the line equation for that point.

Thus, for the algorithm that uses the fact that a polygon is an intersection of the half-planes formed by its edges, in the case when all line equations evaluate with the positive sign for a given point, it is possible to conclude that this point is indeed inside the polygon.

Intersection of a Line and a Sphere

By definition, a sphere is a surface formed by points, all of which are equidistant from a single point—the center of the sphere (see Figure 5.17).

FIGURE 5.17

Intersection of a line and a sphere.

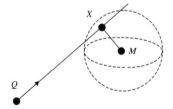

Simple use of this fact allows deriving the sphere's formula as $\left\| (\overline{X - M}) \right\| = r$.

In this formula, X is any point on the sphere, M is the center of the sphere. and r is its radius. This equation uses the length of the vector $(\overline{X - M})$. The length of any vector can be derived from the definition of the scalar product. By definition, the scalar product of the vector multiplied by itself is

$$\overline{A} \cdot \overline{A} = \|\overline{A}\| \|\overline{A}\| \cos(0) = \|\overline{A}\|^2$$

from which the length of the vector can be found as $\|\overline{A}\| = \sqrt{\overline{A} \cdot \overline{A}}$. Hence, the sphere equation can be expressed more conveniently as

$$\sqrt{(\overline{X - M})(\overline{X - M})} = r$$

or

$$(\overline{X - M})(\overline{X - M}) = r^2$$

In order to find intersections of a sphere and a line, you must simultaneously solve the two equations representing both primitives:

$$\begin{cases} X = Q + t\overline{C} \\ (\overline{X - M})(\overline{X - M}) = r^2 \end{cases} \Rightarrow$$

$$(Q + t\overline{C} - M)(Q + t\overline{C} - M) = r^2 \Rightarrow$$

$$(\overline{Q - M})(\overline{Q - M}) + 2t\overline{C}(\overline{Q - M}) + t^2 \overline{C} \cdot \overline{C} - r^2 = 0$$

When resolving this quadric equation in t, you can find a single root that represents the case where the sphere is touched by a line in a single point. Alternatively, you can find two roots in the case where the line pierces the sphere, or there might be no real roots in the case when the intersection doesn't exist.

Intersection of a Line and a Cylinder

A cylinder is a surface whose points have the same shortest distance to some line—the axis of the cylinder (see Figure 5.18).

FIGURE 5.18

*Intersection of
a line and a
cylinder.*

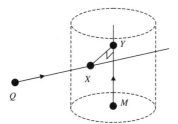

Suppose that the cylinder's axis is described by the following equation:

$Y = M + k\overline{N}$ where M is some point on the line and $\overline{N}$ is a vector parallel to this line. By varying the parameter k, all point Y belonging to this line are enumerated.

By definition of the cylinder, any point on it has a fixed distance r to the line. The shortest distance from a point to a line is a perpendicular. These two facts expressed as equations give the formula for the cylinder. From the first fact it could be derived that the length of $\overline{X-Y}$ is thus equal to r, which can be expressed as $(\overline{X-Y})(\overline{X-Y}) = r^2$ or $(X - M - k\overline{N})(X - M - k\overline{N}) = r^2$ at the same time it is known that $\overline{X-Y}$ is perpendicular to the cylinder axis. With the use of the fact that the scalar product of two orthogonal vectors is equal to zero, it can be expressed as $(\overline{X-Y})\overline{N} = 0$ or $(X - M - k\overline{N})\overline{N} = 0$.

In order to find the intersection point, the equations describing the cylinder and a line must be solved simultaneously.

$$\begin{cases} X = Q + t\overline{C} \\ (X - M - k\overline{N})(X - M - k\overline{N}) = r^2 \\ (X - M - k\overline{N})\overline{N} = 0 \end{cases}$$

Solving these equations is a small exercise in algebra, not unlike the one that took place in the case of the line-sphere intersection. There is also a quadric equation in parameter t that is obtained, which could thus have two, one, or zero solutions. It corresponds with the situations with two, one, or zero intersection points.

Finding the Proper Intersection

Of all the intersection points of the current ray that are found, of interest is the one with the minimal distance to the viewer. This is because light particles reflected from the surface in that point will travel into the eye unimpeded.

In the previous sections, the intersections of lines and primitives were solved in the parameter of the line equation t. The parameter t can be considered as a distance along the line from the point Q to the variable point X measured with the vector $\overline{C}$ as a unit. It is easy to show this fact by exploring the line equation expressed as an equality of two vectors:

$$(\overline{X - Q}) = t\overline{C}$$

If the vectors are equal, their lengths are equal too, thus

$$\left\|(\overline{X - Q})\right\| = t\|\overline{C}\| \Rightarrow t = \frac{\left\|(\overline{X - Q})\right\|}{\|\overline{C}\|}$$

According to the ray-casting algorithm, you project a ray for each pixel on the screen. If you use the coordinates of the viewer and the current pixel for the definition of the ray, the parameter t can be used as a measure of the distance from the viewer (see Figure 5.19).

FIGURE 5.19
Finding the proper intersection.

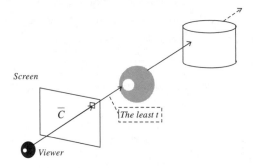

This property could be exploited further to compare parameters t obtained from different intersection points. The least t must define the intersection that is the closest to the viewer. Performing this computation for every pixel allows for solving the visibility for the entire image. It should also be noted that texture mapping is easily accommodated into this method, since in order to do it you basically need to know the coordinates of the intersection point in the object space where the texture is defined. Such coordinates are quite easy to obtain knowing the world coordinates of the intersection points and figuring out the reverse transformation taking you from the world space into the object space.

As noted earlier, additional work must be done to ensure proper lighting. Because this topic is both extensive and extremely important, it is covered in detail in Chapter 8.

Optimizing Ray-Casting

The ray-casting method is extremely attractive due to its simplicity. You are spared the unpleasant tasks of rasterization, clipping, and hidden surface removal (which is discussed at length in Chapter 7, "Hidden Surface Removal"). Moreover, lighting and generation of shadows can be almost trivially achieved by extending the ray-casting methodology.

The biggest problem, however, is in the fairly high cost of the individual step of casting a ray. Potentially, you must find an intersection of each ray with every surface in the world. Since there might be thousands of surfaces, it incurs an enormous cost. Straightforward implementation will hardly be able to achieve the real-time frame rates, at least not with modern hardware.

Thus, ray-casting is mostly used for non–real-time applications, yet it produces stunning images, at times indistinguishable from photographs. Only some relaxations may allow for real-time performance by the ray-tracer. The applications that achieve that do exist, for instance, in the field of computer games. One such example is, of course, Wolfenstein 3D by id Software, the predecessor of DOOM and Quake, where instead of casting a ray for each pixel, one ray was cast for a column of pixels. The penalty for the real-time performance was a simplified geometry of the world that only allowed the polygons parallel or orthogonal to the imaginary ground and reduced the number of degrees of freedom (no roll or pitch). Such relaxations are suitable for an indoor renderer but not feasible for a flight simulator. Still, it signals that you must not completely discount ray-casting as a method to use in interactive 3D applications (games in particular). Moreover, since computations for rays are mutually independent, there exists an opportunity to parallelize the problem and achieve a measurable speed increase in applications running on multiprocessors. Perhaps not so far in the future it will be feasible to have a simple processor for every pixel of the screen. For such a computer, world-to-screen graphics will rapidly become obsolete.

It is not difficult to see that the main cost of ray-casting comes from computing intersections of a ray with every surface in the scene. You may attempt to make the individual calculation cheaper, and may also try to avoid computing the intersection when it is easy to deduce that it doesn't exist.

One possible approach is to precompute projections of the polygons to the selected reference planes and the equations of their edges in that projection. This will lower the cost of otherwise expensive computations.

The biggest performance gain comes, however, from avoiding unnecessary intersection computation. It is often very easy to deduce that an intersection of a ray and a certain primitive can't possibly exist. Chapter 3 discussed the binding volumes approach. Using that technique, you can enclose a complex object of many primitives in a volume of a simple geometry. If the intersection with the volume doesn't exist, there is no need to analyze the enclosed primitives any further. Spheres and boxes are the most commonly used binding volumes.

Another approach, which employs a similar strategy, is that of space subdivision. If the space is separated into cells, you can compute the intersections for only those primitives whose cell is intersected by the ray (see Figure 5.20).

FIGURE 5.20
Space subdivision.

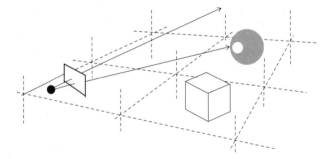

The simplest partition strategy is to separate the space into uniform cells. This also allows for employing integer-based algorithms to find out which cells are intersected by the current ray. Such algorithms were already discussed in the description of rasterization techniques. Other partitioning strategies involving trees will be discussed in conjunction with modeling and hidden surface removal. These are perhaps even more suitable due to their more economical control of space.

Summary

There are two fundamental methods of viewing a 3D scene: the world-to-screen method and the screen-to-world method.

The world-to-screen method projects primitives composing a geometric model onto the screen and then rasterizes the projections of the primitives.

The screen-to-world method handles the visibility on a per-pixel basis. For every pixel on the screen, a ray is cast into the representation of the virtual world. The closest intersection point determines what should be visible on the screen at the position of that pixel.

The screen-to-world method is conceptually simpler, only requiring many intersection calculations between rays and primitives of the virtual world. However, it is computationally intensive and very rarely used for applications generating images in real-time.

Although the world-to-screen method involves a lot of complex processes, such as geometric transformations, clipping, projection, rasterization, shading, texture mapping, and hidden surface removal (to be discussed in Chapter 7), it is nevertheless easier to produce images in real-time with its help.

CHAPTER 6

Modeling

All the previous chapters discussed the basics of 3D computer graphics. Using the algorithms and techniques that were talked about, it is possible to view images of an individual primitive from various angles and distances. However, actual objects that you want to display in the virtual world are often complex and consist of many hundreds or even thousands of primitives. It is important to consider modeling techniques that allow the representation of complex virtual objects in 3D applications.

There are a number of factors to consider when choosing a data structure to represent a 3D model. For instance, it is important to consider convenience of creation and manipulation, precision, storage efficiency, and applicability of rendering algorithms, as well as other criteria. Since the complete set of criteria is often unattainable, you are often forced to trade one factor for another. It is also often the case that a particular class of objects allows for certain relaxations that induce a distinct choice of a data structure. At other times, there may not be a clear favorite.

For instance, consider a modeling scheme that was implicitly used in the previous chapter. For the purposes of ray-casting, spheres and cylinders were represented as mathematical equations. This method of modeling suits the ray-casting algorithm very well because its basic operation, the calculation of an intersection, is achieved through resolving the primitive and ray equations together. However, an application that employs the world-to-screen rendering technique does not gain from such a representation because a sphere is hard to rasterize directly. Thus, for that application, modeling a sphere as a set of polygons may be more appropriate. Although this may be a logical choice, it is still an inadequate one as far as other criteria are concerned. The storage efficiency of approximating a sphere with a set of polygons is definitely inferior to the analytical description, and the higher the precision of such an approximation, the more polygons there must be. Moreover, natural properties of a sphere, such as its radius, are trivial to change in the first model, whereas changing them requires a fair amount of manipulations for the second one.

This chapter discusses several different techniques used by interactive applications, from the simplest wireframes to more complex models, which represent a solid body as a set of plane polygons or patches of curved surfaces. Although convenient in rendering, these techniques are often inadequate for representation of models created through automated sampling of the real-life objects. Voxel models, which address this problem, are covered in the last section of this chapter.

Wireframe Models

Wireframe models represent objects as a set of key vertices connected by key edges. Very few, if any, real-life objects can be represented in this manner. Yet, despite their unrealistic appearance, the wireframes play an important role in many graphics applications. These models are, perhaps, the cheapest to draw using world-to-screen rendering techniques because their rendering doesn't involve rasterization of complex primitives or hidden surface removal. When you need only an approximate overview of a complex scene (for instance, while creating and editing models) it is often easy to turn the scene's description into a wireframe and present it to the viewer (see Figure 6.1).

FIGURE 6.1
Wireframe models.

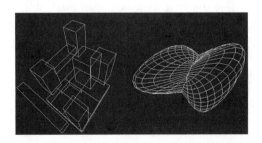

This representation is not very advantageous for use with screen-to-world (ray-casting) techniques, since the complexity of that algorithm will remain almost the same compared with more complex representations of objects. You still need to cast a ray for each screen pixel. It is also true that the computation of an intersection of a ray and a model's edge presents a challenge on both a conceptual level and the level of numerical precision.

If you employ the world-to-screen viewing method, the edges of a wireframe model must pass the coordinate transformation, clipping, projection, and rasterization stages. The edges are convenient to describe by specifying two endpoints. Since several edges may share some endpoints, and the first process in the pipeline involves only coordinate transformations, it is reasonable to employ a data structure that reflects the sharing. The vertices can be placed separately from the edges, which are described as two references to the proper vertices rather than storing actual coordinates (see Figure 6.2).

This approach is also beneficial from the editing perspective. If the coordinates of some vertex change, you don't have to examine every edge to make the adjustments.

FIGURE 6.2

A data structure for wireframe models.

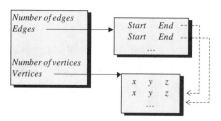

The viewing process for this model involves the coordinate transformations performed on the vertex set. Subsequently, edges must pass the clipping stage where some of the endpoints may be discarded and an edge may be limited by a newly created vertex. Thus, starting from the clipping stage, you must have an edge description that explicitly contains the coordinates. The clipping and the last two stages—the projection and the rasterization—are performed for each edge, eventually producing an image of the complete model on the screen.

Polygonal Models

The wireframe models present an inherently unrealistic appearance, because most of the objects in real life are solid. A logical modeling scheme for solid bodies is to describe the surfaces that enclose their volume. Because many of the objects from real life have planar surfaces that can be represented using polygons, and because there exists an efficient technique to rasterize polygons (as seen in Chapter 3, "Rasterization"), you can model objects as sets of polygonal patches (see Figure 6.3).

FIGURE 6.3
A polygonal model.

Both screen-to-world and world-to-screen rendering techniques are applicable to the models represented in this manner. Chapter 5, "Viewing," discussed ways to implement both rendering methods with respect to individual polygons. In the case of ray-casting, the most important operations were geometric transformations and computing intersections between rays and the polygons of the model. In the world-to-screen method, you must perform the coordinate transformations on the vertex set and further take all the polygons through the rendering pipeline consisting of the clipping, the projection transformation, and the rasterization. This is not unlike the process used for wireframe models.

Because the polygons are likely to share vertices and since fairly expensive coordinate transformations involve only the vertex set, a data structure reflecting the sharing is often chosen (see Figure 6.4).

In runtime, this data structure may be reorganized or augmented to help a particular stage of visualization. For instance, a ray caster may want to compute the bounding box of the object and the equations of the polygons' planes.

Figure 6.4

A vertex-based data structure.

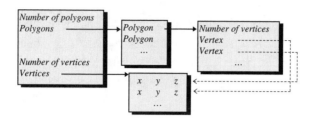

For the purposes of world-to-screen viewing, you perform the coordinate transformations on the vertex set, and further take each polygon through the rendering pipeline. Since the polygon description can potentially change at the clipping stage (new vertices can be created and old vertices can be deleted), it is no longer possible to use shared vertices. Thus, before each polygon enters the clipping stage, its full description containing the actual coordinates is built.

Considering again the objects, which this method attempts to represent, you can see that many of the edges can be shared by two polygons. In fact, if the model is completely closed, every edge should belong to two polygons. When you clip the polygons, you are effectively clipping the edges twice, once for each of the polygonal patches that are joined at that edge. To avoid doing extra work, it is possible to represent the polygons in relation to their edges rather than the vertices (see Figure 6.5).

Figure 6.5

An edge-based data structure.

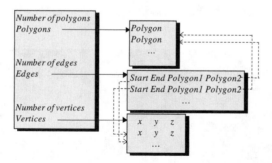

Such a representation has, of course, many implications on the rendering pipeline and usually means using scan-line–based hidden surface removal, which is discussed in Chapter 7. In that method, rendering of all polygons is done simultaneously rather than one at a time. There is no apparent gain for the ray-caster in such a representation.

Specialized graphics hardware often prefers particular arrangements of polygons. The models that are built from *triangle strips* and *triangle fans* (see Figure 6.6) can be drawn particularly fast. Some hardware also provides support for strips of quadrilaterals. Chapter 9, "Application Design," examines what makes these arrangements so convenient for hardware.

FIGURE 6.6
*Triangle fans(a)
and strips(b).*

(a):

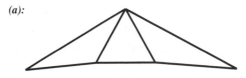

(b):

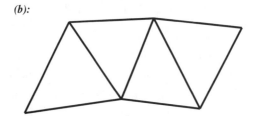

Many objects can be represented as strips and fans of triangles. Consider the sphere in Figure 6.7, which is modeled in this fashion.

FIGURE 6.7
*A sphere built
from triangle fans
and strips.*

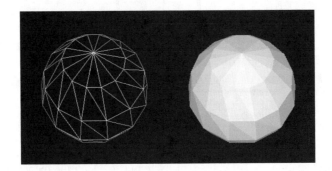

Billboards

Modeling with the help of geometric primitives is quite expensive, both to create a proper geometric model and to visualize it in the runtime. A cheap alternative that was heavily used in computer games until recently is to substitute geometric models of objects with prefabricated images to be textured on rectangular polygons.

A billboard is a textured rectangle, which captures the image of a modeled object from a certain direction. There could be several different textures available as viewed from different directions. The proper texture is selected depending on the orientation of the model and the viewing direction of the camera (see Figure 6.8).

Figure 6.8
Displaying a billboard.

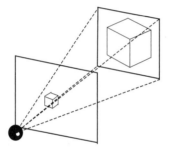

The billboard is always parallel to the viewing plane in the view space. This is done to maximize the projection of the image and to prevent the viewer from seeing the entire billboard as a single edge.

The goal of this modeling scheme is to substitute objects of complex geometry with images. Objects that are represented in this way may not necessarily be rectangular. Since a billboard is a rectangle with a textured image, an approach called *color keying* is used. A special color is chosen in the texture image to represent transparency. During the rasterization, if a texture element with that color is encountered, the pixel is not drawn. This approach permits having an image of some object with complex geometry drawn in the middle of the texture, surrounded by transparent texture elements that will not be drawn. When displayed, it will create the appearance of complex geometry rather than a rectangle with an image.

You can use billboards in both world-to-screen and screen-to-world graphics. Since this type of model is represented using polygons, they are processed exactly as such. The only difference is the possible use of color keying and the selection of a proper texture depending on the orientations of the model and the camera.

Cubic Curves and Bicubic Patches

As you saw in the previous section, there are several problems that result from representing solid bodies as polygonal meshes. Precision in such a representation is the biggest problem. Many real-life objects, which you may want to model, have curved surfaces. This includes anything from an aircraft fuselage to a human face. To realistically represent the curved surfaces using polygonal patches, which are only planar, you must use increasing numbers of polygons (see Figures 6.9 and 6.10).

FIGURE 6.9
Increasing precision of approximation of curves with lines.

A bigger set of polygons, besides being expensive to store and process, is also a very inconvenient representation for the modeling stage. Discrete points of the polygonal mesh don't provide a natural handle for the properties of the surface. Changing a single property of the surface, such as curvature, requires changing the positions of many points in some coordinated manner. To increase precision, offset difficulties in modeling, and reduce the number of involved polygons, simple curved patches are often used. These represent locality of some more complex curved surface. This section discusses the apparatus that is necessary to store and manipulate simple curved surfaces.

FIGURE 6.10
Modeling a sphere with 18, 50, 98, and 162 polygons, respectively.

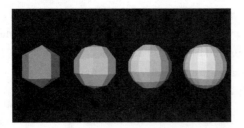

To a large degree, this approach to modeling is just an extension of approximating curves with plane polygonal patches. Planar patches can, in fact, be considered as curved surfaces of degree one, since when a plane equation is represented in parametric polynomial form, the highest degree of the parameter will be exactly one. By choosing an approximating polynomial of higher degree you can expect to achieve much higher quality with the same number of primitives.

Thus, the most popular approximating objects are polynomial curves, specifically *cubic curves* (polynomials of degree three):

$$f(t) = at^3 + bt^2 + ct + d$$

Polynomials of degrees lower than three, notably *quadrics* (polynomials of degree two describing parabolas), often don't have enough flexibility because they define a curve with just one flexing point. On the other hand, polynomials of degrees higher than three, although giving more flexibility than cubics, are more expensive to evaluate. They also are often less stable, meaning that a relatively small change to a parameter controlling the properties of the polynomial causes a considerable change in the curve itself.

2D Curves

Let's consider first the planar parametric curves, which will further serve as a base for consideration of three-dimensional curves and curved surface patches.

Parametric cubics representing a curve in a plane have the following form:

$$x(t) = A_x t^3 + B_x t^2 + C_x t + D_x$$
$$y(t) = A_y t^3 + B_y t^2 + C_y t + D_y$$

This form is referred to as *parametric* because instead of giving the relationship of y and x directly ($y=f(x)$ or $f(x,y)=0$), both x and y are expressed as a function of a third variable: the parameter t. By evaluating both formulas for a certain t, you obtain x from one equation and y from the other. Together (x,y) defines the coordinates of a point on the curve. By evaluating formulas in some range of t, you can obtain all points on a portion of the curve. It is often convenient to combine both formulas using vector notation:

$$\begin{pmatrix} x(t) \\ y(t) \end{pmatrix} = \begin{pmatrix} A_x \\ A_y \end{pmatrix} t^3 + \begin{pmatrix} B_x \\ B_y \end{pmatrix} t^2 + \begin{pmatrix} C_x \\ C_y \end{pmatrix} t + \begin{pmatrix} D_x \\ D_y \end{pmatrix}$$

or

$$\begin{pmatrix} x(t) \\ y(t) \end{pmatrix} = At^3 + Bt^2 + Ct + D$$

This form is not very convenient because it is hard to relate the coefficients $A_x, A_y, B_x, B_y, C_x, C_y, D_x, D_y$ to any specific curve.

Different forms of cubics have been derived to give a better handle to the properties of the curves. The forms differ in the kinds of controls that are used in order to specify a curve's properties, and as a consequence, the way to derive the coefficients given the controls.

Hermite forms are based on four controls: two points P_1, P_2 specifying the beginning and the end of the curve, and two vectors V_1, V_2 specifying the direction of the curve in these endpoints (see Figure 6.11).

FIGURE 6.11
Hermite controls for cubic curves.

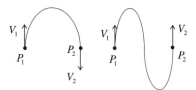

As Figure 6.11 shows, these controls are quite convenient to use in order to specify the exact shape of the curve. They are also convenient for derivation of coefficients used in the cubic equation. Let's consider a possible derivation technique.

The goal of the formulas is to compute all points on the curve between the endpoints as a function of the parameter t. It is convenient to make this parameter varying in the range of *[0,1]* on the interval between the endpoints so that t equals *0* in P_1 and *1* in P_2. Based on this assumption, you can find the expressions that are true in the endpoints:

$$\begin{pmatrix} x(0) \\ y(0) \end{pmatrix} = P_1 = A0^3 + B0^2 + C0 + D = D$$

Similarly, for the second point the following takes place:

$$\begin{pmatrix} x(1) \\ y(1) \end{pmatrix} = P_2 = A1^3 + B1^2 + C1 + D = A + B + C + D$$

These two equations are not sufficient to resolve for the coefficients $A, B, C,$ and D. You must use the remaining vector controls to infer two additional equations. The vectors V_1, V_2 specify tangents of the curve at P_1 and P_2 respectively. A tangent of the curve in a point can be computed as a derivative in this point, since the derivative is defined to be a ratio of the rate at which the function changes to the rate of the argument change:

$$f'(x) = {df(x)}/{dx}$$

which has a geometric meaning of the tangent in a point (see Figure 6.12).

FIGURE 6.12
Tangent of a curve in a point.

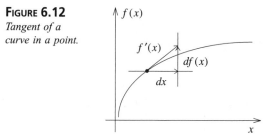

The derivative of a cubic is the following quadric:

$$\begin{pmatrix} x'(t) \\ y'(t) \end{pmatrix} = 3At^2 + 2Bt + c$$

Since the tangents are known at two endpoints, the following two equations can be derived:

$$\begin{pmatrix} x'(0) \\ y'(0) \end{pmatrix} = V_1 = 3A0^2 + 2B0 + C = C$$

$$\begin{pmatrix} x'(1) \\ y'(1) \end{pmatrix} = V_2 = 3A1^2 + 2B1 + C = 3A + 2B + C$$

The four equations that were obtained could be represented in matrix form as follows:

$$\begin{bmatrix} D \\ A+B+C+D \\ C \\ 3A+2B+C \end{bmatrix} = \begin{bmatrix} 0 & 0 & 0 & 1 \\ 1 & 1 & 1 & 1 \\ 0 & 0 & 1 & 0 \\ 3 & 2 & 1 & 0 \end{bmatrix} \begin{bmatrix} A \\ B \\ C \\ D \end{bmatrix} = \begin{bmatrix} P_1 \\ P_2 \\ V_1 \\ V_2 \end{bmatrix}$$

This equation is written in vector form so that D is actually a tuple

$$\begin{bmatrix} D_x \\ D_y \end{bmatrix}$$

and similarly

$$P_1 = \begin{bmatrix} P_{1,x} \\ P_{1,y} \end{bmatrix}$$

This notation is more convenient than two equations (three in 3D), one for each respective projection.

Using Gaussian elimination or any other method for solving systems of linear equation, it is easy to see that:

$$\begin{bmatrix} A \\ B \\ C \\ D \end{bmatrix} = \begin{bmatrix} 2P_1 - 2P_2 + V_1 + V_2 \\ -3P_1 + 3P_2 - 2V_1 - V_2 \\ V_1 \\ P_1 \end{bmatrix} = \begin{bmatrix} 2 & -2 & 1 & 1 \\ -3 & 3 & -2 & -1 \\ 0 & 0 & 1 & 0 \\ 1 & 0 & 0 & 0 \end{bmatrix} \begin{bmatrix} P_1 \\ P_2 \\ V_1 \\ V_2 \end{bmatrix}$$

And, in a somewhat artificial yet convenient matrix notation, the cubic itself can now be rewritten as follows:

$$\begin{pmatrix} x(t) \\ y(t) \end{pmatrix} = At^3 + Bt^2 + Ct + D = \begin{bmatrix} t^3 & t^2 & t & 1 \end{bmatrix} \begin{bmatrix} A \\ B \\ C \\ D \end{bmatrix}$$

If the actual meanings of *A,B,C,* and *D* are inserted into the preceding expression, the following results:

$$\begin{pmatrix} x(t) \\ y(t) \end{pmatrix} = \begin{bmatrix} t^3 & t^2 & t & 1 \end{bmatrix} \begin{bmatrix} 2 & -2 & 1 & 1 \\ -3 & 3 & -2 & -1 \\ 0 & 0 & 1 & 0 \\ 1 & 0 & 0 & 0 \end{bmatrix} \begin{bmatrix} P_1 \\ P_2 \\ V_1 \\ V_2 \end{bmatrix}$$

The four-by-four square matrix is often called a *basis* matrix. In this case it describes the basis of the *Hermite* form. Other forms of cubics have somewhat different basis matrices. The purpose of these matrices is to specify what kinds of controls are used. The vector containing the controls such as P_1, P_2, V_1, V_2 is often referred to as a *geometry vector* or *geometry matrix*, and it specifies the properties for a specific instance of the curve.

In practical applications, it is at times inconvenient to specify tangent vectors directly. In these cases it is often helpful to use an alternative form of cubics where tangents are specified indirectly. One form of cubics that allows you to do that comes from a French mathematician named P. Bézier, who worked in the domain of automotive computer-aided design. This form is given through four control points (see Figure 6.13).

FIGURE 6.13
Control points of a Bézier curve.

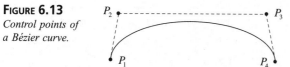

There is a simple relationship between Bézier controls and Hermite controls:

$$P_{1,hermite} = P_{1,bezier}$$
$$P_{2,hermite} = P_{2,bezier}$$
$$V_{1,hermite} = 3(P_{2,bezier} - P_{1,bezier})$$
$$V_{2,hermite} = 3(P_{4,bezier} - P_{3,bezier})$$

This relationship can be expressed in matrix form as:

$$\begin{bmatrix} P_{1,hermite} \\ P_{2,hermite} \\ V_{1,hermite} \\ V_{2,hermite} \end{bmatrix} = \begin{bmatrix} 1 & 0 & 0 & 0 \\ 0 & 0 & 0 & 1 \\ -3 & 3 & 0 & 0 \\ 0 & 0 & -3 & 3 \end{bmatrix} \begin{bmatrix} P_{1,bezier} \\ P_{2,bezier} \\ P_{3,bezier} \\ P_{4,bezier} \end{bmatrix}$$

In order to obtain an expression for the Bézier form, it is easy to substitute the preceding dependency into the computed formula for Hermite forms:

$$\begin{pmatrix} x(t) \\ y(t) \end{pmatrix} = \begin{bmatrix} t^3 & t^2 & t & 1 \end{bmatrix} \begin{bmatrix} 2 & -2 & 1 & 1 \\ -3 & 3 & -2 & -1 \\ 0 & 0 & 1 & 0 \\ 1 & 0 & 0 & 0 \end{bmatrix} \begin{bmatrix} 1 & 0 & 0 & 0 \\ 0 & 0 & 0 & 1 \\ -3 & 3 & 0 & 0 \\ 0 & 0 & -3 & 3 \end{bmatrix} \begin{bmatrix} P_{1,bezier} \\ P_{2,bezier} \\ P_{3,bezier} \\ P_{4,bezier} \end{bmatrix}$$

After multiplying matrices, the sought equation for Bézier forms is obtained:

$$\begin{pmatrix} x(t) \\ y(t) \end{pmatrix} = \begin{bmatrix} t^3 & t^2 & t & 1 \end{bmatrix} \begin{bmatrix} -1 & 3 & -3 & 1 \\ 3 & -6 & 3 & 0 \\ -3 & 3 & 0 & 0 \\ 1 & 0 & 0 & 0 \end{bmatrix} \begin{bmatrix} P_1 \\ P_2 \\ P_3 \\ P_4 \end{bmatrix}$$

Formulas of this type are relatively straightforward to evaluate in the runtime. It is somewhat expensive—after all, there are a number of multiplications to perform. The very first obvious speedup for cubics is, instead of evaluating them as:

$$A \cdot t \cdot t \cdot t + B \cdot t \cdot t + C \cdot t + D$$

to evaluate them as:

$$((At + B)t + C)t + D$$

Taking the common factor outside the brackets cuts the number of multiplications in half in this case. However, even having three multiplications per point is quite expensive. There is a very effective speedup technique developed by de Casteljau that exploits a special property that Bézier curves possess. A Bézier curve can be split into two sub-curves by the process described in Figure 6.14.

FIGURE 6.14

Building a cubic curve by iterative subdivision.

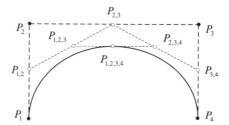

In Figure 6.14, the point $P_{1,2}$ is obtained as the middle of the segment formed by the points P_1 and P_2, and similarly, the point $P_{3,4}$ is the middle of the segment P_3, P_4. The point $P_{1,2,3,4}$ is the middle of the segment $P_{1,2,3}, P_{2,3,4}$. In fact, $P_{1,2,3,4}$ belongs to the original curve separating it into two sub-curves so that the points $P_1, P_{1,2}, P_{1,2,3}, P_{1,2,3,4}$ control the first sub-curve, and the points $P_{1,2,3,4}, P_{2,3,4}, P_{3,4}, P_4$ control the second sub-curve.

As you can see, the subdivision process only involves finding middles of the line segments. For integer coordinates this procedure involves a division by two, which is easily achieved by shift operations with a very small cost compared to arbitrary divisions or multiplications. By applying the subdivision process recursively, you can obtain an arbitrarily large number of points on the curve.

Listing 6.1 illustrates the subdivision strategy.

LISTING 6.1

Finding a Point on a Bézier Curve Using Recursive Subdivision

```
void MI_evaluate_bezier_points(int *b1,int *b2,int *b3, int *b4,
                               int *points,int length
                               )
{
  int b12[T_LNG_VECTOR],b23[T_LNG_VECTOR],b34[T_LNG_VECTOR];
  int b123[T_LNG_VECTOR],b234[T_LNG_VECTOR],*b1234,*last;

  if(length>2)
  {
    b1234=points+(length/2)*3;

    b12[0]=(b1[0]+b2[0])/2; b12[1]=(b1[1]+b2[1])/2; b12[2]=(b1[2]+b2[2])/2;
    b23[0]=(b2[0]+b3[0])/2; b23[1]=(b2[1]+b3[1])/2; b23[2]=(b2[2]+b3[2])/2;
    b34[0]=(b3[0]+b4[0])/2; b34[1]=(b3[1]+b4[1])/2; b34[2]=(b3[2]+b4[2])/2;

    b123[0]=(b12[0]+b23[0])/2;
    b123[1]=(b12[1]+b23[1])/2;
    b123[2]=(b12[2]+b23[2])/2;
    b234[0]=(b23[0]+b34[0])/2;
    b234[1]=(b23[1]+b34[1])/2;
    b234[2]=(b23[2]+b34[2])/2;

    b1234[0]=(b123[0]+b234[0])/2;
    b1234[1]=(b123[1]+b234[1])/2;
    b1234[2]=(b123[2]+b234[2])/2;

    MI_evaluate_bezier_points(b1,b12,b123,b1234,points,length/2+1);
    MI_evaluate_bezier_points(b1234,b234,b34,b4,b1234,length/2+1);
  }
}
```

Points on the curve will be stored in this array.

Currently found point is to be stored here.

Subdividing the sub-curves.

3D Curves and Patches

3D cubic curves are formulated in exactly the same way as plane curves. They only differ in the size of the vectors. Each has three *(x,y,z)* instead of two *(x,y)* components. However, even though the curves are at times important primitives, as far as solid modeling is concerned, surface patches are much more interesting and important. A *bicubic* patch is formulated as a set of cubic curves. There are 16 controls associated with a patch. The patch itself is a cubic curve in every section. The formula for the patch can be represented as:

$$\begin{pmatrix} x(t,s) \\ y(t,s) \\ z(t,s) \end{pmatrix} = \begin{bmatrix} t^3 & t^2 & t & 1 \end{bmatrix} [M][G][M]^T \begin{bmatrix} s^3 \\ s^2 \\ s \\ 1 \end{bmatrix}$$

Note that there are two parameters involved: *s* and *t*, hence the name *bicubic patch* to indicate that it is cubic in two directions. In this formula, *[M]* is a four-by-four form matrix ($[M]^T$ is its transpose where $M[i,j] = M^T[j,i]$), and *[G]* is a four-by-four geometry matrix containing data that represents the controls of the patch. Despite the fact that, like cubic curves, different forms can be given for the patches, for the majority of practical applications the most interesting are Bézier forms. For these, all 16 controls are points. Thus, in the preceding formula, *[M]* will be a Bézier basis matrix and *[G]* will contain 16 points controlling the properties of the patch. Figure 6.15 illustrates a model built from two Bézier patches and Figure 6.16 shows a patch with a wireframe mesh of its control points.

FIGURE 6.15
An object built from two bicubic patches.

Having an analytical expression for the patch allows you to use this primitive in a screen-to-world visualization process. Similar to the cases of other primitives, such as spheres or cylinders, it is possible to simultaneously solve the patch equation with the equation of the cast ray.

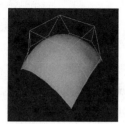

FIGURE 6.16

A bicubic patch and its control mesh.

For the world-to-screen method, it is important to be able to compute coordinates of points belonging to the bicubic patch. This procedure is quite straightforward. The formula suggests the following strategy: For some parameter s, you find points T_1, T_2, T_3, T_4 belonging to the four curves on the patch. Thus, you can find T_1 from $[P_1, P_5, P_9, P_{13}]$, T_2 from $[P_2, P_6, P_{10}, P_{14}]$ and so on. (see Figure 6.17). At that stage the equation becomes:

$$\begin{pmatrix} x(t,s) \\ y(t,s) \\ z(t,s) \end{pmatrix} = \begin{bmatrix} t^3 & t^2 & t & 1 \end{bmatrix} [M] \begin{bmatrix} T_1 \\ T_2 \\ T_3 \\ T_4 \end{bmatrix}$$

This equation means that the points T_1, T_2, T_3, T_4 are in fact the control points for a 3D cubic curve with the parameter t. You can further proceed with evaluating along the parameter t to obtain points on the patch.

By moving along both parameters, it is possible to find an arbitrary big set of points belonging to the bicubic patch (see Figure 6.17).

FIGURE 6.17

Computation of points belonging to the patch.

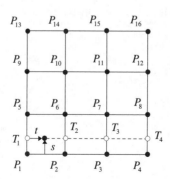

To speed up this process you can, of course, use the subdivision strategy discussed for Bézier curves.

Even though the procedure allows for finding a set of points belonging to the patch, it still doesn't give a lot of hints on how to rasterize bicubics on the screen. Surprisingly enough, rasterization of bicubic patches is most often done by tessellating them into polygons. A discretely spaced grid of points belonging to the patch is computed to build a polygonal mesh. The existing polygonal pipeline is then used to rasterize the mesh.

There appears to be a bit of a contradiction in this strategy. After all, trying to avoid approximating surfaces with polygons is the main motivation for considering bicubic patches in the first place. Unfortunately, you often must use polygonal approximation due to the complexity of rasterizing bicubics directly. Furthermore, the kinds of tools and pipelines available usually dictate polygonal approximation. Most often, there already is a polygonal pipeline in place, in many cases even implemented in hardware.

An alternative solution is to employ forward differences and move across the patch at a small rate, plotting the screen pixels during this process.

Even though you often do end up using polygons for final rendering of bicubics in the world-to-screen viewing process, at least two big advantages of these primitives remain. The bicubics are very convenient in modeling due to their simplicity in manipulation and minimal storage requirement. Moreover, during the visualization process you can perform rotations, scalings, and translations on the control points and turn the patch into the polygonal mesh only for perspective transformation and rasterization.

Let's consider the last statement in more detail. The reason it is possible to do the transformations on the control points is due to the way the cubic curves composing a patch are formulated:

$$
\begin{pmatrix} x(t) \\ y(t) \\ z(t) \end{pmatrix} = \begin{bmatrix} t^3 & t^2 & t & 1 \end{bmatrix} \begin{bmatrix} -1 & 3 & -3 & 1 \\ 3 & -6 & 3 & 0 \\ -3 & 3 & 0 & 0 \\ 1 & 0 & 0 & 0 \end{bmatrix} \begin{bmatrix} P_1 \\ P_2 \\ P_3 \\ P_4 \end{bmatrix}
$$

This expression can be rewritten as

$$\begin{pmatrix} x(t) \\ y(t) \\ z(t) \end{pmatrix} = A_1 P_1 + A_2 P_2 + A_3 P_3 + A_4 P_4$$

where A_1, A_2, A_3, A_4 are some scalar values obtained from multiplying basis and parameter matrices where

$$\begin{bmatrix} A_1 & A_2 & A_3 & A_4 \end{bmatrix} = \begin{bmatrix} t^3 & t^2 & t & 1 \end{bmatrix} \begin{bmatrix} -1 & 3 & -3 & 1 \\ 3 & -6 & 3 & 0 \\ -3 & 3 & 0 & 0 \\ 1 & 0 & 0 & 0 \end{bmatrix}$$

Applying a coordinate transformation represented by a matrix *[T]* to the control points can be represented as

$$\begin{pmatrix} x'(t) \\ y'(t) \\ z'(t) \end{pmatrix} = A_1 P_1[T] + A_2 P_2[T] + A_3 P_3[T] + A_4 P_4[T] =$$

$$= (A_1 P_1 + A_2 P_2 + A_3 P_3 + A_4 P_4)[T]$$

This last expression is equivalent to saying:

> It doesn't matter what is performed: Either applying affine transformation on the controls followed by computing points on the cubic curve, or computing points on the curve followed by applying the transformation to them.

However, this fact is not true for the perspective transformation. The reason is that perspective transformation *(x/z,y/z)* is not linear. This difficulty was the basic motivation for developing rational curves that are presented as a ratio of two polynomials. However, the rational curves and patches are relatively expensive to work with.

With the process in place that allows representing, transforming, and drawing bicubic patches, it becomes important to consider how a model consisting of multiple patches can be built. In the case of polygonal models, neighboring polygons share vertices and edges, thus forming a continuous surface. A similar approach is employed in the case of bicubic patches and cubic curves. Whereas it made little or no sense for polygons, when talking about two connected bicubic patches you can differentiate various kinds of continuity at their joining. *Geometrical continuity* is achieved by two Hermite curves when the directions (but not the magnitudes) of the tangents are the same at the joining. If the magnitudes are the same as well as the directions, it gives a higher order of continuity at the joining. From a purely practical point of view, higher orders of continuity imply smoother transition from one patch to another. Figure 6.18 demonstrates the joining of two curves.

FIGURE 6.18

Joining of two curves.

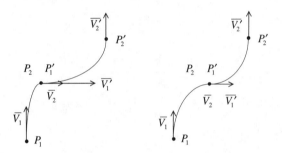

As you can see, achieving proper continuity becomes important when modeling complex smooth surfaces or curves using multiple individual pieces. If the model is to be created interactively, the decision on the kind of joining is often left to the modeler. On the other hand, when trying to create a synthetic model through some sort of sampling process, turning a set of sampled points into a continuous surface might become relatively complex. *Cubic b-splines* may be considered in this or similar situations. Cubic b-splines represent essentially just another form of cubics. However, two neighboring pieces share multiple control points, which provides a high degree of continuity in the modeled curve or patch.

A solid body modeled with bicubic patches may be represented in a data structure similar to that of a multi-polygon model (see Figure 6.19). The only difference is that instead of vertices, several patches may be sharing some common control points.

FIGURE 6.19

A data structure for a model composed of bicubic patches

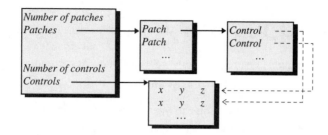

The viewing of this model is also similar to that of the polygonal model. In the case of world-to-screen rendering, you first apply the required geometric transformations to the control points. You further tessellate the patch into the polygons and use the standard polygonal pipeline to draw the object on the screen.

In the case of screen-to-world viewing, it is important to find the intersection of a ray with a bicubic patch. Since there are equations for both, such an intersection (or intersections) can be found by solving both equations simultaneously.

A number of refinements and extensions to these schemes are available. First of all, you can employ some strategy to trivially reject the patch when it is outside the viewing pyramid. There is a property of the Bézier cubic curves and bicubic patches according to which all points of the curve or the patch are within the convex hull of the control points. This property makes the computation of the bounding volume particularly easy. Only control points have to be considered in such a computation.

You can also mix polygons and bicubic patches in the same model. Some of the real-life objects can be partially curved and partially planar, and although bicubic patches can represent planes, they have higher overhead. Alternatively, the construction of the polygonal mesh before the rasterization stage can be done adaptively, depending on the curvature. Little or no subdivision is done if the patch is mostly planar and a lot of subdivision is performed if the patch is highly curved.

Overall, modeling using bicubic patches allows for representing highly sophisticated objects. Although this approach provides some degree of implementational challenge, especially on the level of tools for creation of the models, the rendering process can be done in a very efficient and simple manner.

Landscapes

Many graphics applications require some representation of the outdoor world. For some, such as flight simulators, this is the most important object.

In the simplest imaginable case, you can model the outdoors as an infinite plane populated with different objects that are associated with the outdoors, such as trees or buildings. However, since the landscapes are not planar, for many applications, such as flight simulators, it is important to find a modeling scheme that allows representing ragged terrain. This section overviews several techniques to model landscapes.

When thinking of a landscape, you most often imagine some surface (see Figure 6.20). Previous sections have considered techniques that allowed for modeling complex surfaces using planar patches or patches of simple curved surfaces such as bicubics. Although the general strategy still applies, the landscapes warrant special treatment in this case due to special properties and requirements that exist.

FIGURE 6.20
A landscape.

Most of the techniques to represent landscapes take advantage of several properties. A landscape is assumed to be a non–self-intersecting surface. You can also assume that it can be represented as a function of two variables ($f(u,v)$). This means that there is a single value $f(u,v)$ representing heights associated with every (u,v) pair of coordinates of the landscape's area. This assumption is a relaxation since, for one thing, the earth is round rather than flat.

Moreover, even locally, in an actual landscape, such a fact may not hold true (see Figure 6.21).

FIGURE 6.21
*An actual
landscape may
not be a function.*

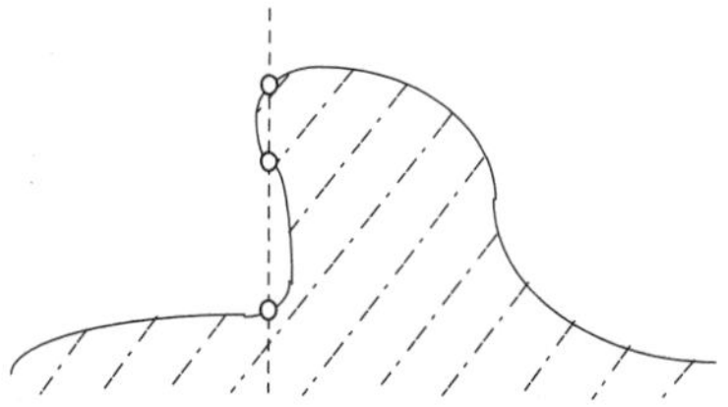

As shown in Figure 6.21, multiple values may be associated with some *(u,v)* pairs in the actual landscape. However, since landscapes are mostly smooth on the larger scale, representing them as functions is an admissible relaxation. Of all the possibilities that arise from this assumption, the one that is exploited most often is to represent a landscape as a table of heights presampled for a grid of *(u,v)* coordinates, often referred to as the *height field*. The sampled points define a polygonal mesh used to approximate the surface. As an alternative to this approach, you can split the *(u,v)* plane into some regular cells and define a curved bicubic patch within each cell. This strategy can even allow for representing surfaces that are not functions as in Figure 6.20. However, additional overhead and complications in, for instance, hidden surface removal, make the latter strategy somewhat less attractive. The reasons for this are examined in Chapter 7.

A number of considerations define which presampling to use. A prime consideration is the ease of storage. A square array is a very convenient data structure to employ in this case. Using it basically implies that you have to do regular sampling and split the surface into square cells. The simplicity of this solution is a definite advantage. A disadvantage is that this method disregards curvature of the approximated surface. When the curvature is low, you may want a larger sampling step, whereas in the localities of high curvature you need smaller steps. Sampling in an adaptive manner allows you to both increase the precision of the representation and to save some storage space (see Figure 6.22).

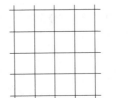
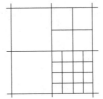

To partly address the problem with regular sampling, a recursive approach where each cell can itself contain an array of sampled points (see Figure 6.22) can be used. When the surface within the cell is mostly flat, it is possible to use a larger sampling step within the cell, whereas when the surface is curved, you use a smaller sampling step. A possible complication with this method may be due to the presence of discontinuities at the joining of some cells. If the sampling steps are different within two neighboring cells, their edges may not fit (see Figure 6.23), tearing the continuity of the surface.

FIGURE 6.23
Discontinuities at the joining of two cells.

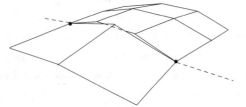

To avoid this complication, you should ensure that only some numbers of subdivisions are allowed, and the points on the boundaries of cells with more subdivisions at least map onto the edges of the neighboring cells.

Since a square array is used to store the sampled points, it is natural to use square or rectangular cells. However, such a cell contains four vertices and four vertices don't necessarily belong to the same plane. Consequently, they may not define a single planar polygon. A common technique to avoid this problem is to split each cell into two triangles. Three vertices that will be present in each of the triangles are guaranteed to be in the same plane (see Figure 6.24).

FIGURE 6.24
Representing cells as two triangles.

The rendering process for these models is similar to the one considered for the general polygonal objects, but with several exceptions. For the regularly sampled representation, *(u,v)* area coordinates are likely to be represented implicitly. Only the height of the point is explicitly stored. However, *(u,v)* coordinates can be easily computed since they are proportional to the indices describing the position in the square array.

The virtual representation of the landscape can model considerable areas of the real world. In the real world you can see only the immediate neighborhood of the current location. Similarly, when viewing an artificial landscape model, you may want to preselect a smaller area from the representation that corresponds to what is considered to be near the observer. Such an approach is extremely beneficial with respect to the efficiency of viewing and can be done independently and prior to clipping, which also may trivially reject some primitives.

Once the preselection is done, the selected polygonal mesh passes the typical stages in the employed viewing process.

Figure 6.25 presents a sketch of a possible data structure. Note that besides storing the height field you may also have to store a square array of structures containing attributes of the cells, such as texture maps or lists of objects, which are placed onto the surface.

FIGURE 6.25
A possible data structure for a landscape.

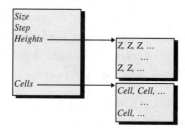

As previously mentioned, the landscapes are very important for such applications as flight simulators. Numerous refinements and speed-ups were developed in that area because a landscape is a fundamental object that must be displayed in that kind of application. One of the techniques used in high-end implementations is to sample the same landscape multiple times with different steps so that, depending on the height of the viewer above the ground, a model of the corresponding scale can be drawn.

Most of the time you use world-to-screen methods to display a landscape. This is at least the case for flight simulators. The representation that was considered suits this viewing process very well. A need for high frame rates among many applications makes using the screen-to-world method much less attractive. However, considering the growth in performance of modern hardware, it is conceivable that ray-casting may become important for applications that portray landscapes at interactive rates, especially those that can afford using specially designed hardware.

Voxel Models

A *voxel* is a *volume element*, similar to a *pixel*, or *pictorial element*. As can be inferred from the name, the purpose of this object is to represent volumetric information. Considering the previously described ways to model solid objects, you can see that all of them are relatively labor-intensive. To create a polygonal or bicubic description of a complex shape takes a lot of man-hours. On the other hand, sampling devices developed to automate creation of synthetic descriptions of real-life objects produce discrete sets of sampled points rather than polygonal, let alone analytical surface information.

In this regard, voxel techniques come as an alternative to more traditional modeling. The idea of this scheme is to represent an object through its spatial occupancy. You can use a 3D matrix, each cell of which models a small, normally cubic volume of space. It can be marked as occupied, in which case the entry in the matrix would be taken up by a value representing some property of that region of space; for instance, a color or density. When the cell is empty, it signals that the corresponding volume in space is not occupied.

This representation is advantageous because it is very simple and it almost directly contains the data that devices such as CATV scanners would be producing. Applications in such fields as medical imaging and remote sensing often resort to using voxel techniques.

There is a big limitation, however. The spatial occupancy matrix representation requires a lot of storage and it is wasteful of storage at times. Consider modeling a room with voxels. All the void space will still have an enormous amount of empty, finely spaced cells allocated for it.

There is an effective alternative to the spatial occupancy matrix. Indeed, there should be a simple way to mark all the void space and allocate storage only for what is really interesting. *Quad* trees and *octal* trees allow for achieving just that. Quad (fanout of four) trees are used in planar applications. The number four relates to the number of children each node that is not a leaf will have. The 3D counterpart of a quad tree is an octal (fanout of eight) tree. The latter has eight children in each node.

Let's consider quad trees first. The strategy to construct a tree of some planar shape can be expressed in several steps.

- You first divide the specified region of space into four equal portions.

- You mark all empty portions in the corresponding leaf nodes with zeros.

- The partitions that are completely occupied are marked with a special designation, for example, with a number, "2."

- You then start the algorithm recursively for all partially occupied portions that are marked with "1" at the current level. To avoid potentially infinite descent through recursive calls, you should stop when the current portion of the space becomes too small (see Figure 6.26).

FIGURE 6.26
Representing spatial occupancy with a quad tree.

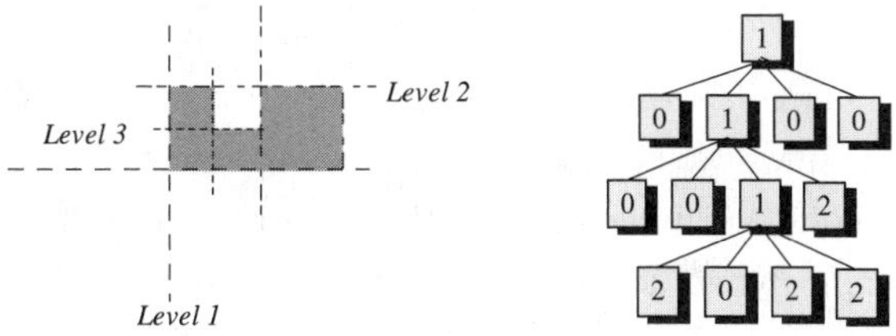

Octal trees use the very same strategy. The only difference is that there are eight cubic partitions to work with at every stage.

Comparing space requirements of spatial occupancy matrices and quad/octal trees, you can see that for sparsely occupied scenes, octal trees offer a considerable saving in storage. However, this saving is achieved by certain complication of the data structure. In this particular case, the rendering process would not suffer in any appreciable way. In fact, quad/octal trees may actually help. Yet, if you want to model a dynamic object—an explosion, for instance—in which certain parts of the model move with respect to other parts, a tree-like structure may become very awkward for that task.

In order to visualize voxel-based objects, it is possible to employ both screen-to-world and world-to-screen viewing processes. In the former case, you often want to find a chain of voxels that are intersected by a given ray. Such a requirement may be present when the voxels are semitransparent and thus many voxels will contribute to the color of a single screen pixel. Considering the fact that each voxel is just a cube, it is not hard to devise a strategy to find the intersections for both occupancy matrix and quad-tree representations.

If you use the world-to-screen visualization strategy, each voxel can be considered as a cube consisting of six faces and, thus, the voxel object can be displayed using a regular polygonal pipeline. This approach requires refinements since the number of faces that you may have to rasterize rapidly becomes too big. Since many voxels that are internal to the model are often completely obscured by the surface voxels, a possible approach is to attempt to locate all the surface voxels and limit rasterization of the model to the surface voxels only. Even when this is done, it is not practical to represent two neighboring voxels as two cubes of six faces, since at least one face will be shared. Moreover, since the voxels are next to one another, this implies that the original object was continuous in that point and so no faces should be appearing in between anyway.

To avoid this problem, it is possible to convert such surface voxels into a nicer polygonal mesh using what's known as the "marching cubes" algorithm, first reported by Lorenson and Cline in the mid-'80s. This algorithm analyzes the neighbors of each voxel and creates a polygon or several polygons to represent a portion of a surface for that locality of space.

Another approach, used in lower-end applications, is to always rasterize a voxel as a rectangular square regardless of the voxel's orientation. This is a relaxation, of course, because a cube doesn't necessarily project into a square. However, assuming that the voxels are usually small and their projections are usually comparable in size to screen pixels, this is a fairly safe approach to pursue. Squares are very cheap to clip against rectangular screen boundaries and then to rasterize into an image bitmap, and thus, due to a simplified primitive you can achieve higher rendering speed for the entire voxelized model.

Summary

Selecting a modeling scheme depends on many factors. Particular goals of an application, expected quality of images, and the rendering method the application is using are some of these criteria.

Wireframe models have a very unrealistic appearance, yet they are convenient for many tasks and could be drawn very efficiently.

Polygonal approximation works very well with rendering algorithms that were considered before (rasterization and texture mapping in particular), but it is neither precise nor convenient in representing curves.

The billboarding technique was used heavily in the times when the polygon budget of applications was very tight.

It is possible to approximate complex surfaces with simple curved patches. This method may also require rendering approximating polygons, but these could be generated dynamically and only very late in the rendering pipeline.

Voxel representation is suitable for models obtained through automated sampling,3 but it has large storage demands. This may also have to be converted into polygons for rendering or drawn in an approximate fashion using tiny rectangles to represent volume elements.

CHAPTER 7

Hidden Surface Removal

All the previous chapters have completely neglected a whole set of problems—notably, those caused by occlusion on the screen of one primitive by another primitive. For instance, when representing a 3D model of an object as a collection of polygonal faces, it is likely that some parts of the polygons are obscured in some projections by other polygons. Only those primitives, or portions of the primitives, that are visible to the viewer at a given view angle must be displayed. For example, in any projection of a cube, you can see at most three faces. You must devise a strategy to determine which of the existing faces can be seen and which are obscured.

When using the screen-to-world viewing method, its very nature assures that the correct portion of any primitive is pictured. In that technique, the visibility is found for every pixel on the screen. The surface that is intersected first by the ray that has originated in the viewer's eye and passed through a given pixel must be visible at that pixel's position. This is because nothing else is in between the eye and the intersected surface. The light reflected from such a surface must have traveled into the eye unimpeded as it would in the real world.

This chapter discusses possible strategies that allow for the elimination of hidden surfaces. Since the most common primitive is a polygon, many of the techniques discussed are applicable to the polygonal models only. Some specialized techniques applicable to polygonal landscapes and voxelized models are considered, as well as a generic algorithm capable of handling any set of primitives.

Although hidden surface elimination is innately achieved in the course of ray-casting, the cost of the computation is quite high. Thus, some of the techniques that are explored in conjunction with the world-to-screen viewing method can also help in ray-casting by reducing the number of primitives so that each ray is checked against a lesser number of surfaces.

Back-Face Culling

The volume of most 3D objects is enclosed by one continuous surface. When viewing such objects, the front side of the enclosing surface can be seen but the back side cannot. A technique called *back-face culling* allows you to eliminate the polygons that compose the back surface of objects from further consideration (see Figure 7.1).

FIGURE 7.1
*Visible and
invisible portions
of the enclosing
surface.*

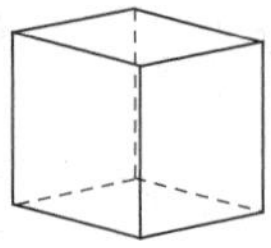

The notion of a convex polygon was already encountered in Chapter 3, "Rasterization." This notion can be extended in the case of a polyhedron, which is a closed surface consisting of interconnected polygons. A polyhedron is convex if the connecting line of any two points within the surface never leaves the boundaries. Concave polyhedrons don't possess this property (see Figure 7.2).

FIGURE 7.2
Convex and concave polyhedrons.

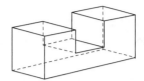

Performing back-face culling on a convex polyhedron also removes all hidden surfaces. Due to the shape of this model, the only polygons that are hidden are the ones that compose the back surface. However, this technique doesn't help eliminate the hidden surfaces of a concave polyhedron because a polygon on the front side of the object may be obscured by another polygon that is also on the front side (see Figure 7.3). Even in this case, the polygons on the back side are definitely invisible and eliminating them does help, if not to solve the problem completely, at least to reduce its complexity.

FIGURE 7.3
Front polygons obscuring one another.

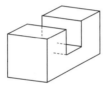

A similar reasoning also applies in the case of the ray-casting algorithm. Although the hidden surfaces are removed automatically due to the nature of that algorithm, back-face culling reduces the scene complexity so that fewer intersection calculations need to be done. This speeds up the viewing process.

You need to devise a technique that will help determine whether a polygon is on the front or the back side of the object's surface. Chapter 5, "Viewing," already discussed normal vectors in the role of describing the polygon's orientation. In this particular case, a polygon is on the back side if its normal is oriented in such a way that it forms an angle greater than 90 degrees with the direction of viewing. The vector and scalar products provide the necessary apparatus for this computation.

First, the normal vector is found using the vector product of some two vectors located in the plane of a given polygon. The two vectors can be computed as the differences of the polygon's vertices. Subsequently, the sign of the scalar product of the direction of viewing and the normal vectors can be calculated to determine whether they form an angle greater than 90 degrees. If that is the case, the polygon in question is culled and discarded from any further consideration in the viewing process.

Determining Back Surface

It should be noted that, by definition, the result of the vector product of two vectors is a vector pointed in such a way that it forms a *right triple* (see Chapter 2, "Geometric Transformations") with the two given vectors. This means that depending on how the vectors in the polygon's plane are chosen, it is possible to obtain a normal pointing in one of two possible directions (see Figure 7.4).

FIGURE 7.4
Order of vertices and the direction of the normal.

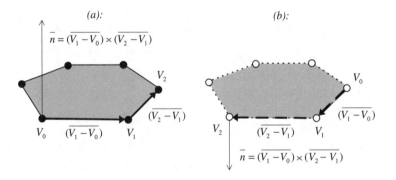

As Figure 7.4 illustrates, if the vectors are built on consecutive vertices V_0, V_1 and V_2, the direction of the normal will depend on the vertices' order. It is convenient to associate the front (that is, outside) surface of the polygon with the counterclockwise order of vertices (see Figure 7.4(a)), which defines the direction of a normal vector. Use of this convention in a consistent manner for all polygons will thus differentiate the outside from the inside of an entire polyhedron.

Depending on the combination of the viewing processes and projection transformations used, back-face culling is applicable in a slightly different manner and may be performed during a particular slot in the rendering pipeline.

The projecting lines of the parallel projection, which correspond to the viewing direction, have the same orientation. Immediately before the projection stage (in the view space) the vector of the viewing direction points along the Z axis and thus can be represented as *(0,0,1)*. This, of course, simplifies the computation of the scalar product that will simply be equal to the z component of the normal vector. Thus, instead of building a complete normal vector in that space, you need only to compute its z coordinate, which is achieved by two multiplications and several subtractions.

The projection lines of the perspective projection intersect in the viewer's eye and have different orientations. You can find the direction of viewing for any point in the world or view space by constructing a vector originating in the viewer's eye and pointing toward that point (see Figure 7.5).

FIGURE 7.5

Finding a back polygon.

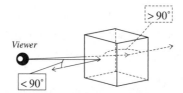

However, in this case, once the model is transformed by the perspective transformation from the view space into the screen space, the direction of viewing becomes constant. This enables you to perform the back-face culling as a simple computation of the coordinate z of the normal vector.

The Place of Back-Face Culling in the Pipeline

Back-face culling can potentially be performed quite early in the pipeline, in the world space or even in the object space. The earlier you discard a back side polygon, the fewer unnecessary operations you have to do. You must also take into account that 3D transformations are performed on the vertices, so performing back-face culling in the object space is advantageous only if you can discard the vertices that don't belong to any of the front side polygons. You can do this by associating a Boolean variable with each vertex and setting it to true every time any polygon containing this vertex is determined to be on the front surface. After examining all polygons, you can discard the vertices for which the true condition was never set. The saving comes from avoiding performing the geometric transformations for the discarded vertices. If you choose not to perform these manipulations, you can do back-face culling in the world space.

Performing back-face culling in the world space allows you to avoid pushing some polygons through an expensive clipping stage. However, the culling itself is just a bit more expensive than when it is performed immediately before the rasterization.

Alternatively, instead of constructing the normal vectors in the runtime, you can precompute such vectors prior to the application's rendering loop and associate one with each polygon. In order to obtain the normals in the world space, you can apply the transformations that were used to transform the vertices into this space. It should be noted that for the purposes of transforming a vector, only the linear parts of the transformation (that is, the rotations and non-uniform scalings) have to be applied. The translations mustn't be applied since conceptually they don't affect the vectors.

Transforming a normal vector from one space into another is somewhat more expensive than just building one using the points in the destination space. However, unit-length normal vectors are also used for the purposes of lighting and, therefore, you can combine computations for both purposes. It is more expensive to build a unit-length normal in some space than to transform one from the space where it is given.

Similar reasoning mostly applies in the case of the screen-to-world viewing process which, as noted, can be modified to avoid seeking an intersection of a ray and a back polygon. Since you don't explicitly transform the coordinates into the view space in this viewing method, it leaves only world and object space for potential culling application.

Back-to-Front Sorting

As seen in the previous section, back-face culling is not sufficient to eliminate hidden surfaces in a polygonal model. In a general case, finding all portions of the polygons that are obscured by any other polygon can be an expensive geometric problem for world-to-screen visualization. It can be solved by performing iterative clipping of every polygon against all other polygons in their screen projections and examining the depth of the resulting pieces. If any piece is farther away in the viewing direction than the clipping polygon, it must be obscured and thus can be discarded. At the end of this process a new set of polygons is obtained, all of which are visible and none of which obscure any other piece.

Without a doubt, this appears to be a fairly expensive solution, which may not be suitable to use. A popular alternative takes advantage of the frame buffer architecture of the graphics hardware. Whenever polygons in the scene may partly obscure one another, you can achieve proper display by just rasterizing the primitives in the back-to-front order. The polygons that are closer to the viewer will be rasterized later, overwriting pieces of any other polygon that was rasterized previously. This is known as a *painter's* method. The specific algorithms in this class differ in their approach to achieving back-to-front order of rasterization, and they range from sorting to space subdivisions.

Note

It must be noted that when rasterizing polygons is too expensive (for instance, when using complex texture mapping and lighting), it may be unwise to rasterize in the back-to-front order. The reason for that is because it is known that many polygons will get overdrawn and a lot of resources will be spent in vain. It is hard to define a cut-off line when the overdraw problem becomes too severe to ignore, yet you must be aware that at times the initial, seemingly inefficient solution may become appropriate to use.

In order to obtain back-to-front ordering, sorting appears to be a logical choice to range polygons depending on their depth along the viewing direction. If you employ the perspective transformation, you cannot apply the sorting in the view space since the viewing directions vary for different polygons. The viewing direction becomes constant just before the rasterization stage and that is where the sorting procedure can be applied.

In order to sort along the viewing direction, you must find a criterion for polygon comparison. The simplest solution is to compare the maximum z coordinates (farthest from the viewer) among all vertices in one polygon against those in the other polygon. Comparing an average z coordinate may be an alternative choice.

Sorting Algorithms

There are many different sorting algorithms. The most straightforward ones have complexity of $O(n^2)$. That means that in order to produce a sorted list, these algorithms employ a number of elementary operations, which is proportionate to n^2—the number of polygons. An example of such a sorting algorithm is a *bubble-sort*. In this algorithm, you compare an object in the list with its successor and if the sorting criterion doesn't hold, you interchange their positions. If you perform the comparisons for every object in the list starting from the first one, a single object must travel to the correct position in the list—not unlike a bubble being pushed up to the surface of the water. It roughly takes *n-1* comparisons to place a single object into a correct location. This translates into complexity proportionate to about n^2 elementary operations to sort the entire list (see Figure 7.6).

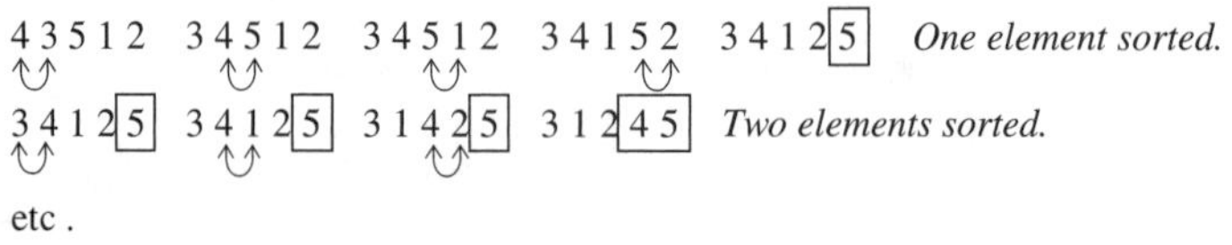

FIGURE 7.6
Bubble-sort.

4 3 5 1 2   3 4 5 1 2   3 4 5 1 2   3 4 1 5 2   3 4 1 2 5   *One element sorted.*

3 4 1 2 5   3 4 1 2 5   3 1 4 2 5   3 1 2 4 5   *Two elements sorted.*

etc .

An algorithm with square complexity is a fairly costly one. In the case of the sorting problem there exists a class of algorithms that improve on the complexity up to $O(n \lg n)$. All algorithms in this class employ a variation of a divide-and-conquer strategy.

For instance, the *quicksort* algorithm separates a list into two sublists. In one sublist all the objects are smaller than a certain preselected pivot value, whereas in the other list all objects are greater than or equal to this value. If you apply quicksort recursively to both sublists, you get a completely sorted original list. This method gives average $O(n \lg n)$ complexity, which is intuitively understandable since the separation of the list into sublists follows a tree-like pattern (see Figure 7.7).

FIGURE 7.7
Quicksort.

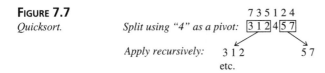

The complexity of $O(n \lg n)$ is a limit to how efficient a sorting algorithm can be. However, one class of sorting algorithms achieves better complexity indications by exploiting the fact that numbers that are sorted, as a rule, come from a limited range. For instance, a representation of an integer number often utilizes only 32 bits of storage, which places limitations on the magnitudes of numbers that can be represented. *Radix sort*, an algorithm from this class, works in essentially linear time ($O(n)$) but it is likely to have bigger space requirements or may use different assumptions on what an elementary operation or unit of storage space is. Thus, it is not always possible to choose this algorithm over some $O(n \lg n)$ algorithms.

Radix sort relies on the fact that you can very easily sort an array of numbers that come from a limited range. For instance, if the only allowable sorting keys are in the range $[0,3]$, you can place objects tagged with such keys in order by the following process. You count total numbers of elements tagged with each key. These numbers define offsets at which elements of each group must be placed in the resulting list. For instance, objects tagged with ones must follow objects tagged with zeros and thus are located in the resulting list at the offset equal to the number of elements tagged with zeros. You pass through the original list again, this time placing objects into the resulting list at the known offsets.

This particular algorithm is known as *counting sort* and it is feasible for sorting keys in a very small range. Radix sort requires a limited, but not necessarily small, range and it works by invoking a process similar to counting sort multiple times, each time sorting along different sets of bits in the search keys (see Figure 7.8).

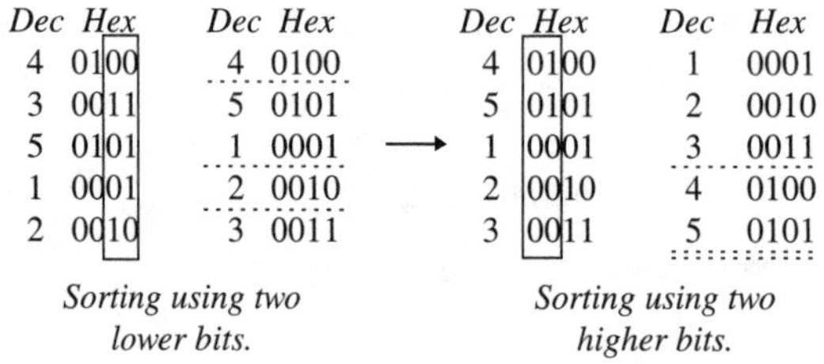

FIGURE 7.8
Radix sort.

Dec	Hex		Dec	Hex		Dec	Hex		Dec	Hex
4	0100		4	0100		4	0100		1	0001
3	0011		5	0101		5	0101		2	0010
5	0101		1	0001	→	1	0001		3	0011
1	0001		2	0010		2	0010		4	0100
2	0010		3	0011		3	0011		5	0101

Sorting using two lower bits.   Sorting using two higher bits.

From the example in Figure 7.8, you can see that this algorithm is essentially $O(n)$; however, it requires multiple passes through the list and thus its effective performance may be worse than that of the quicksort. Generally, quicksort performs better for lists of small or average size. The advantage of radix sort becomes appreciable only in the cases where lists are very long or the range of sorting keys is very narrow.

Any of the preceding algorithms can be applied for the purposes of placing polygons into back-to-front order. However, the performance of the discussed algorithms depends on the level of disorder in the list about to be sorted. Many $O(n^2)$ algorithms work well when the list is almost entirely sorted, requiring in this case only a few operations to finish the work. Straightforward implementation of a quicksort works well on the lists in the state of high disorder, and radix sort is practical only in the cases of very big lists or narrow ranges. In 3D graphics applications, you often want to slowly rotate polygonal objects. In these situations it is often the case that the order of the polygons doesn't change much from frame to frame, and you can achieve good performance with a seemingly inefficient algorithm. On the other hand, if you want to ensure good average performance for any situation, quicksort is often a logical choice.

Comparing Polygons

These sorting algorithms were examined based on the assumption that there is some sorting criterion that allows you to compare two polygons and place them in back-to-front order. Unfortunately, that is not quite the case. The criterion of comparing maximum z coordinates is not always correct (see Figure 7.9).

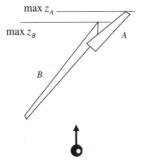

FIGURE 7.9
Failure of maximum z criterion.

In Figure 7.9, the polygon A should be painted first based on maximum z criterion, yet it obscures polygon B, so it should be rasterized later than B and not earlier. A similar situation can be imagined in the case of using average z criterion as well.

In certain situations, you can live with this problem. When it is guaranteed that polygons in the scene will be of roughly the same size, sorting based on maximum or average z is admissible. This happens, for instance, when you tessellate an analytical shape such as a bicubic patch into polygons. When it cannot be guaranteed that the polygons will be roughly the same size, you can attempt to use a more complex sorting criterion. If it is possible to find a point that belongs to the intersection of the screen projections of two polygons, you can further compute the depth at that point for both polygons and compare these using the result as the sorting criterion. In order to locate such a point, however, it may be necessary to resort to finding intersections of every edge in one polygon against every edge in the other polygon, and also checking the situation when screen projection of one polygon is contained in the projection of the other polygon.

Such a strategy may work relatively well when each polygon has a small number of edges. When this is not guaranteed, you may have to make certain relaxations and use a more sophisticated solution. For example, if you assume that the polygons are convex, the approach outlined in the following paragraphs is possible.

First, you need to find the polygons' *common tangent*, the line that connects two polygons and leaves all vertices of both polygons on one side (see Figure 7.10). You then need to further descend the resulting *sail* or *hourglass* polygon to find an intersection, or show that one doesn't exist (see Figure 7.11).

In order to find a common tangent, you can start examining lines that are continued from the edges of the two polygons starting from the vertices having the least *y* coordinates, for instance. Since in a convex polygon, a line continuing an edge leaves all vertices in one of its half-planes, such a line is a tangent. You can examine the relationship of such tangents in both polygons. For example, in the situation shown in Figure 7.10, edge *d* is located in the right half-plane of the line continuing edge *a*. You can take the next pair and conclude that the same situation holds: edge *e* belonging to the second polygon is in the right half-plane of *b*. However, when you take consecutive edges the situation has reversed: edge *c* of the first polygon is now in the right half-plane of *f*, which belongs to the second polygon. Since the tangents have crossed (when turning from direction *b* to direction *c* in one polygon and from direction *e* to direction *f* in the other polygon) the relationship has changed. Hence, there should exist a tangent, common to the two ranges of angles, which leaves vertices in both polygons in its right half-plane. Such a tangent is exactly the line connecting the points *A* and *D* (see Figure 7.10).

FIGURE 7.10

Finding a bridge between two polygons.

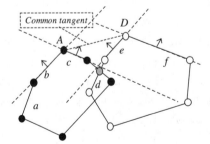

It must be noted that it is possible that the tangents will never cross. If that is the case, the situation is encountered when one polygon is contained inside the other one, and therefore any point of the smaller polygon can be used for depth comparison.

The common tangent serves as a bridge connecting two polygons. It also defines a sail-like shape formed by two crossing convex chains, one from each polygon (see Figure 7.11).

FIGURE 7.11

Finding the intersection point.

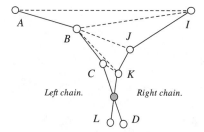

In order to find the intersection of the two chains, you can start iteratively reducing the size of the problem until the crossing is found. Consider the triangles *ABI* and *IJA* from Figure 7.11. Clearly, either one or the other should be an *ear*; that is, a triangle that doesn't contain any other vertex inside. This can be tested by checking if *B* is on the inside or on the outside with respect to *AJ* and, similarly, where *J* is with respect to *IB*. Having determined this way that *ABI* is an ear, you can cut it off and proceed with the sub-problem of the original—a sail with *BI* on its top. Eventually, *CK* becomes the current top of the sail, at which point the test will fail for both *D* being on the inside of *CL* and *L* being on the inside of *DK*. This means that the intersection has been located as the crossing of *CD* and *KL*. The depth of both polygons can be computed at that point, enabling you to figure out which of the polygons is closer to the viewer.

It should be noted that the two polygons may not intersect, in which case there will be an hourglass polygon instead of a sail polygon. It is not difficult to adjust the suggested strategy to tell when this is the case.

An obvious speed-up technique for such methods involves using binding volumes (extends) and avoiding expensive calculations when the relation of the polygons is obvious. If, for example, the minimum *z* of one polygon is farther away than the maximum *z* of another one, you can be sure of the order of polygons (see Figure 7.12).

Figure 7.12
Comparing extends of polygons.

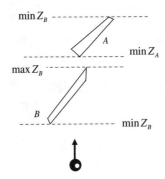

When z extends do overlap, only then do you need to use the expensive comparison.

Well-Founded Order

Besides being computationally expensive, sorting contains internal problems even with the complex way of comparing polygons just described. You can't really find a criterion of polygon comparison that gives a well-founded order. Essentially, an order is *well-founded* if any set of elements contains the least one. This is not the case with polygons. Without well-founded order, the principle of induction that sorting is built upon can't really be applied (see Figure 7.13).

Figure 7.13
An arrangement of polygons that are difficult to compare.

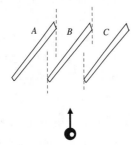

In Figure 7.13, the polygons A, B, and C should be rendered in exactly this order: A then B then C, since B partly obscures A, and C partly obscures B. However, if it will be necessary to compare A and C during the sorting process, it will be difficult to do so. These polygons have absolutely the same maximum and average z coordinates, and their projections on the screen don't intersect. You will be tempted to say that they are "equal" and that it doesn't matter in what order they are rendered. But that's not true—polygon B imposes order on A and C, and so their order does matter. The situation is even worse in a mutual overlap arrangement of polygons (see Figure 7.14). This arrangement illustrates that there might not be the least polygon in a set of polygons.

FIGURE 7.14
Mutual overlap of polygons.

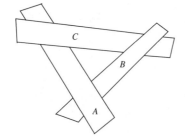

In the example in Figure 7.14, the following relationships take place: $A<C$ and $C<B$ but $B<A$. But this, of course, contradicts what you expect if the order is well-founded. By transitivity, if $A<C$ and $C<B$, it could be concluded that $A<B$, which produces a contradiction with the assertion $B<A$.

As you can see, sorting can't handle some special arrangements of polygons such as the mutual overlap. There are also severe difficulties in the cases of one polygon piercing another one. In the latter case, some polygons must be split before sorting can even be applied. Despite the complications, the sorting approach is still usable, but you should keep the limitations in mind.

Order Lists

As mentioned in the previous section, hidden surface removal for a generic polygonal model can be quite costly. However, in many situations an object that is represented possesses some special properties, which can be exploited to ease hidden surface elimination. For example, in the case of landscapes represented as height-fields, it is easy to obtain the back-to-front ordering of polygons thanks to the regular nature of the representation method, according to which the landscape is divided into a grid of square cells.

Consider a situation where a viewer is located on or above the surface of the virtual landscape within the boundaries of some cell. You can divide the whole landscape into four rectangular sublandscapes, as shown in Figure 7.15.

FIGURE 7.15

Height-field traversal.

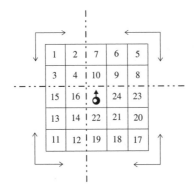

Due to the regularity of the representation, the projections of these four sublandscapes onto the viewer's screen practically do not intersect. The small number of intersections that may appear with perspective transformation can be easily fixed by rendering the sublandscapes in the order of their size, from the smallest to the biggest.

Within each of the partitions, it is easy to obtain the back-to-front order of polygons by just starting from the corner polygon farthest away and proceeding toward the cell occupied by the viewer, column by column or row by row. The polygons composing a cell that is occupied by the viewer must be rasterized in the last turn. For example, the order of cell rasterization for the landscape in Figure 7.15 is as follows:

- 1,2,3,4;

- 5,6,7,8,9,10;

- 11,12,13,14,15,16;

- 17,18,19,20,21,22,23,24,25;

Effectively, this traversal guarantees correct visibility in any projection. However, each cell, as noted in the previous chapter, is likely to be composed of two triangles. The order of their rasterization will be different depending on the angle at which the scene is viewed (see Figure 7.16).

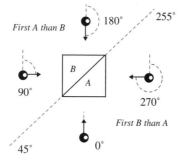

FIGURE 7.16
Order of triangles in a height-field cell.

From Figure 7.16, it is clear that when the view direction is in the range from 45 to 225 degrees, polygon *B* should be rendered after polygon *A*. Otherwise, when the view direction is different, the polygons are rendered in the reversed order: *A* after *B*. At exactly 45 or 225 degrees, the order doesn't matter since projections of the polygons onscreen will not intersect.

Quad Trees and Octal Trees

The very same property of regularity that helped for landscapes also helps to find a back-to-front sequence of voxels stored using an octal tree, or, in this matter, stored using a spatial occupancy matrix. In both cases you can employ a method very similar to what was discussed for height-fields, extended to deal with three dimensions instead of two.

An octal tree is a recursive structure where the same property of regularity is true in each level of subdivision. Thus, the same traversal order can be applied at every level to obtain the back-to-front order of elements for the entire structure.

A quad-tree is a planar counterpart of an octal-tree. Consider, for the sake of simplicity, traversing the quad-tree pictured in Figure 7.17. Depending on the viewing orientation, there are four different traversal orders, each for a particular range of orientations.

FIGURE 7.17
Order of quads in traversing of a quad-tree.

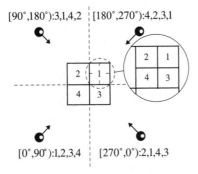

As Figure 7.17 illustrates, to traverse any sub-tree, you use exactly the same order, which in its turn, may cause traversals on even lower levels of subdivision.

The very same strategy is applicable in the case of octal-trees. By extending the preceding method into three dimensions, there will be eight different traversal orders, each applicable in a particular range of the orientation angles.

Portals

Another example of how visibility can be solved in a special situation can be demonstrated in a model describing an indoor scene. Consider a collection of volumes (rooms), connected by portals (doors) (see Figure 7.20). In the simplest example, the rooms are convex polyhedrons, which can be drawn with correct visibility just by applying back-face culling.

Consider the example in Figure 7.18. The goal is to determine what is visible to a viewer located in room *A*. Clearly, if the polygons that compose room *A* will be visible, then all portals leading from room *A* will be visible. To draw screen projections of the portals correctly, parts of the rooms where the portals lead have to be drawn. In order to draw the parts of these visible rooms correctly, the polygons and portals composing them have to be drawn as well.

FIGURE 7.18
Set of indoor volumes.

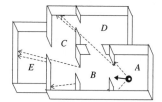

The very language that describes the preceding strategy suggests recursion. Consider the neighborhood of a room where the viewer is located. It is possible to construct a graph where nodes will represent rooms and edges will represent portals (see Figure 7.19).

FIGURE 7.19
A graph of indoor volumes.

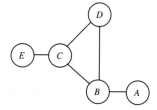

By first drawing the polygons in the room where a portal leads and then drawing all polygons in the current room, the correct visibility is assured. This translates into traversal of the graph where you first recursively apply the traversal to the nodes of the graph (rooms) connected to the current node and then apply the visualization algorithm to the current node itself.

It should be noted that in this algorithm, as in any graph traversal, you should be aware of possible cycling. If the algorithm has been applied to a node, it shouldn't be reapplied to it the second time. For the particular example in Figure 7.19, this will work as follows: start at vertex A, proceed to vertex B, and then go to vertex C, from where you go to vertex D. At that stage you can't go anywhere else since B is already being used. Since there is nowhere to go, the room associated with D is drawn. After that you return back to C, from where you go to E first, draw its polygons, and return back and draw all polygons of room C. At that point, you return to B, draw it, and finally draw room A.

FIGURE 7.20

An interior scene with portals.

Multiple refinements are available in this scheme. Clearly, the graph can be very big, so it may make sense to traverse it with certain maximal depth and just stop when you reach, for instance, three or four rooms deep from the one where the viewer is located. Chances are, the rooms that are deeper than that are not visible anyway.

It is also true that you see all the rooms, other than the one you are currently in, only through the portals. Nothing else outside the projection of a portal onto the screen can possibly be visible. Thus, when drawing rooms that are seen through the doors, you can actually clip their polygons against the screen projection of a portal and considerably alleviate the overdraw problem. However, since the projection of a portal is some arbitrarily shaped polygon, such clipping can be fairly expensive. You can improve the situation by clipping against the binding square—the extends of the portal's screen projection. Although some overdraw will occur, clipping against a rectangle can be done much faster than against an arbitrary polygon. Especially in the case of texture-mapped polygons accompanied by a complex lighting scheme, a considerable saving from such refinement can be expected. It should be noted that if you employ clipping against a portal's boundaries, the room traversal algorithm will have to be changed so that it is possible to draw the same room multiple times when reaching it by way of different portals.

Binary Space Partition Trees

A *Binary Space Partition* tree (BSP) is a data structure to represent a set of polygons. It was first described by Fuch and Kedem in 1980. This data structure helps in many ways. In particular, using this partition scheme allows for obtaining a back-to-front list of polygons in $O(n)$ in the runtime using a precalculated tree. The fundamental idea of this method is based on the fact that any 2D plane divides the 3D space into two half-spaces. All points on one side of this plane define one half-space, and all points on the other side define the other half-space. Furthermore, if you have a plane given in any half-space, it will further induce a division of that half-space into even smaller sub-spaces. You can proceed recursively down smaller and smaller sub-spaces using the list of polygons to perform subdivisions and to construct a binary tree. In this tree, a polygon that induces a division will be stored in the node and all polygons in either of the sub-spaces will be in their proper sub-trees. This rule, of course, applies recursively to every node in the tree.

Consider the set of polygons in Figure 7.21. For simplicity's sake, a planar projection where all polygons map into line segments was chosen. Construct (for example) a BSP tree starting from polygon *B* (see Figure 7.21).

FIGURE 7.21
A binary space partition.

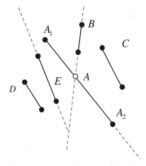

The plane of polygon *B* induces a partition of the space such that the polygons *D* and *E* are in the same half-space and polygon *C* is in the other half-space. From this example, you can also see that polygon *A* crosses the partition plane, and thus can't be unambiguously assigned to either half-space. However, if you split this polygon at its crossing with the partition plane naming the parts as A_1 and A_2, you will be able to place A_1 together with D and E and A_2 together with C. This stage in building a BSP tree is illustrated in Figure 7.22.

FIGURE 7.22
A stage in building a BSP tree.

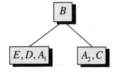

At this point the problem is clearly split into two subproblems. The described algorithms can be reapplied to the lists in the sub-trees. For instance, polygon E can be chosen as a dividing polygon in the left sub-tree and A_2 can be chosen in the right sub-tree. As a result, a tree with the following structure will be built (see Figure 7.23).

FIGURE 7.23
A built BSP tree.

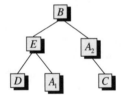

It must be noted that any given BSP tree is not unique. You can find multiple valid binary partitions for the same set of polygons. Depending on the order in which you select the dividing polygons, a different tree will be obtained. For instance, in Figure 7.24, another BSP tree is presented for the same set of polygons.

Although any valid tree suits the algorithm that traverses the tree and obtains the back-to-front order of polygons, some may be more favorable than others due to efficiency considerations. Let's examine the traversal algorithm and then the reasons validating specific tree configurations.

FIGURE 7.24

An alternative construction.

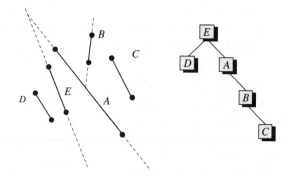

Consider a scene consisting of a small set of polygons with a precomputed BSP tree and a viewer located somewhere in this scene (see Figure 7.25).

FIGURE 7.25

Using a BSP tree to obtain back-to-front order.

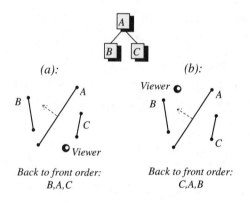

Examine the relationship between the viewer's position and the polygon in the root of the BSP tree. Clearly, the viewer must be located in one of the half-spaces that were formed when the polygon in the root of the tree partitioned the space. It is also true that the polygons that are in the same half-space with the viewer are closer to the viewer than the polygons in the other half-space. Due to this fact, the back-to-front order of polygons is achieved if you first place the polygons from the sub-tree representing the half-space farther away into the resulting list, followed by the root polygon, followed by the polygons of the sub-tree that corresponds to the same half-space where the viewer is currently located. This process is repeated for every sub-tree recursively, most likely with a different relative order of the sub-trees at every level. At the end, this produces the correct back-to-front order of polygons.

A very attractive quality of this algorithm is that it works for any location and orientation of the viewer in the scene. For instance, in Figure 7.25(a) the produced list is different from that in case (b). Both are correct back-to-front orders of polygons in their particular cases. Thus, if a BSP tree is computed for a polygonal model, in the runtime you will only need to invoke an inexpensive tree traversal procedure which, depending on the particular location of the viewer, will produce a correct back-to-front ordering. This will permit you to use the painter's method of hidden surface removal.

In this algorithm, the decision made in every node of the tree depends on the determination of which half-plane the viewer is located in with respect to the node's polygon. You saw such a problem in Chapter 5. It is only necessary to evaluate the plane equation using the coordinates of the viewer as arguments. The positive sign of the result signifies that the viewer is in the half-space pointed to by the plane's normal used to construct the equation. A negative value indicates the other half-space, and the value of zero indicates that the viewer is, in fact, in the plane of the polygon. The latter situation, for the purposes of traversing a BSP tree, means that the projections of the half-spaces on the screen don't intersect and it is possible to choose any order of sub-trees.

Similar computation is also required at the stage where you built a BSP tree. It is necessary to determine in which sub-tree different polygons must be placed. From the implementational point of view, the procedure to precompute a BSP tree can be expressed as follows:

- Of the collection of polygons, one polygon is selected. Its plane equation is computed.

- You check all the vertices of the remaining polygons against said equation. If the results for all vertices are negative, the polygon goes into one sub-tree; if all results are positive, the polygon goes into another sub-tree. If results are positive for some vertices and negative for others, this polygon should be split so that one piece is unambiguously in one sub-space and the second piece is in the other sub-space.

- Once all the polygons are assigned to their proper half-spaces, the tree building algorithm is called recursively for the lists of polygons designated for both sub-trees.

- The algorithm terminates when the current sub-list consists of a single polygon.

The problem of splitting a polygon by an arbitrary plane can be expressed as a clipping problem. It can be solved by an algorithm only slightly different from the one considered in the chapter on clipping. The only significant difference is that during binary search edge clipping, you will use the plane equation of the partitioning polygon to tell the position of the edge's mid-point with respect to the dividing plane. The strategy that was used to combine clipped edges into a clipped polygon remains exactly the same (see Figure 7.26).

FIGURE 7.26

A scene rendered using a BSP tree. Note various polygon splits on the left.

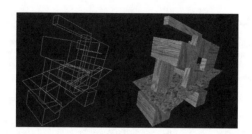

It should be stressed that since construction of a BSP tree is done prior to the application's runtime, either at the application's initialization stage or at the time of creation of the data structures, you need not worry excessively about the efficiency of the algorithm building the tree.

To obtain a back-to-front order of polygons once the tree is created, follow these steps:

- Take a polygon in the root of the tree.

- Compute the plane equation of this polygon.

- Substitute the coordinates of the viewer's current location into this equation and note the sign of the result.

- Finally, recursively apply the same algorithm to the sub-trees in the order dependent on the sign of the noted value.

Recall that the form of the plane equation is $(\overline{X - P}) \cdot \overline{N} = 0$ where P is some point in the plane and $\overline{N}$ is a normal vector to that plane. It is customary to express the same equation in the form of $Ax + By + Cz + D = 0$.

The latter form is obtained by performing the scalar multiplication in the original form so that $A = N_x$, $B = N_y$, $C = N_z$, $D = -(P_x N_x + P_y N_y + P_z N_z)$.

When you traverse the tree in the view space where the viewer is located at the beginning of the coordinates *(0,0,0)*, the result of the formula evaluated for the position of the viewer equals the coefficient D from the plane equation. Thus, BSP tree traversal can be conveniently performed just prior to the perspective transformation stage.

A sketch of possible tree traversal is presented in Listing 7.1.

LISTING 7.1
Traversing a BSP Tree

```
void MI_render_polygons(struct M_polygon_object_order *order,int *verteces)
{
  int plane[4];          Compute equation of the plane of the polygon in the current node.

  if(order!=NULL)                                    /* base case */
  {
    T_plane(verteces+order->m_root->m_verteces[0]*M_LNG_OBJECT_VERTEX,
            verteces+order->m_root->m_verteces[3]*M_LNG_OBJECT_VERTEX,
            verteces+order->m_root->m_verteces[6]*M_LNG_OBJECT_VERTEX,
            plane
           );
    if(plane[3]>0)                          Examining D of the
    {                                       plane equation.
      MI_render_polygons(order->m_negative,verteces);
      M_render_polygon(order->m_root,verteces);
      MI_render_polygons(order->m_positive,verteces);
    }                                       Traverse the sub-trees in
    else                                    different order depending
    {                                       on the sign of D.
      MI_render_polygons(order->m_positive,verteces);
      M_render_polygon(order->m_root,verteces);
      MI_render_polygons(order->m_negative,verteces);
    }
  }
}
```

Now that you know how to create and traverse BSP trees, there are still a few important questions that remain to be answered. At the time of tree construction, you can choose any of the remaining polygons to partition the space. Choosing different polygons causes the construction of a different tree. Thus, it is important to consider whether the choice of a specific polygon can be advantageous for the performance of the algorithm.

Some polygons cause more splits of the remaining polygons (see Figures 7.23 and 7.24). Each polygon has certain overhead associated with pushing it through the pipeline, so the fewer polygons there are, the better. You can use a criterion to select a polygon that causes fewer splits. Of course, if applied locally it may not result in an optimal tree in general, but it appears to help on practice. As an alternative, selection of a random polygon is not sufficiently worse in an average case.

Using a criterion to balance BSP trees so that there is roughly the same number of polygons in sub-trees at every level is not really necessary since it doesn't affect the running time of the traversal. Traversal of the tree always assumes taking each polygon at least once, so balancing doesn't affect the performance—you still have to take each polygon at least once. On the other hand, a balanced tree can be traversed with fewer recursive calls. You can use balancing as a criterion secondary to the condition demanding fewer splits at each stage.

Overall, the biggest advantage to recovering back-to-front order of polygons based on BSP trees is in a fairly low runtime complexity of the algorithm. It must be stressed that this is a general observation for typical scenes. In the worst case of a contrived set of polygons, there may be so many splits that out of original n polygons, n^2 polygons will result. Thus, the performance of the BSP tree is worse than that of an efficient sorting algorithm, which could be as good as $O(n \lg n)$. On average, however, there are not so many splits, and BSP trees behave very efficiently.

This method also resolves the cases of multiple overlap of polygons and piercing of polygons thanks to the proper polygon splitting during the tree creation stage. However, by using a precomputed structure, a certain amount of flexibility is lost. If the arrangement of polygons changes in the runtime, the BSP tree must be altered as well. Cost considerations prevent doing that and, thus, this algorithm is quite unusable for scenes that can be radically changed in the runtime.

It should be noted that the BSP tree is only affected when polygons within the set undergo different transformations. If the same affine transformation is applied to all the polygons in the set, the partition remains valid and the tree is unaffected. Thus, an object that is dynamic in the sense that it moves or changes orientation in the world can still use the same BSP tree. If some parts of the object move with respect to other parts, however, this no longer works.

Beam Trees

Although it is possible to efficiently create the back-to-front order of polygons for use with painter's hidden surface removal by using BSP trees, this has a severe flaw. When you want to draw textured or shaded polygons, overdrawing, which is fundamental for the painter's algorithm, becomes too expensive to ignore. It was noted earlier that a seemingly inefficient solution where every polygon is clipped against all other polygons combined with examining and discarding the obscured pieces may, in fact, be attractive to pursue since it avoids the overdraws. Interestingly enough, BSP trees may help considerably in this latter endeavor as well. A *beam tree* method, which is going to be considered in this respect, may use a BSP tree for both ordering of polygons and tracking which area of the screen has been already drawn to.

The previous section discussed an algorithm that allows using a BSP tree to obtain the back-to-front ordering of polygons. The front-to-back ordering can be obtained in exactly the same way, requiring you only to reverse the order of recursive calls in the BSP tree traversing procedure. Thus, the half-space that is closer to the viewer will be traversed first, followed by the root polygon, and then the half-space farther away to produce the sought front-to-back ordering.

The first polygon in the obtained ordering is the closest to the viewer. Since nothing else can possibly obscure it, this polygon is entirely visible on the screen and thus can be rasterized. All other polygons may be completely or partially obscured by the first one. If you clip the screen projections of the remaining polygons against the boundaries of the first polygon and discard the pieces that are obscured, you have essentially reduced the size of the original problem by one. The new polygon in the beginning of the list is also entirely visible (since it has already been clipped against the original polygon) and the remaining polygons may, again, be partially or completely obscured by the new polygon in the beginning of the ordering.

The need to perform many clippings worsens this approach considerably. To manage the clippings more efficiently, a planar BSP tree can be introduced to track which areas on the screen remain available for drawing. Unlike in the BSP trees considered previously, in this BSP tree the additional leaf nodes will describe the final convex areas formed as a result of the subdivisions and won't have an associated polygon. These areas will be marked as occupied or free. Since functionally the purpose of the 2D screen boundaries clipping is exactly the same—to find a portion of the primitive that can be rasterized—the two processes can be, in fact, unified. Thus, you will start with the BSP tree describing the screen area as free for drawing, and the space outside the screen will be marked as occupied. Figure 7.27 demonstrates the initial BSP tree and the induced partition.

FIGURE 7.27

Beam tree for the empty screen.

Screen partitioning:

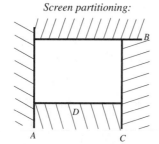

Initial beam tree:

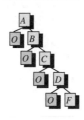

When a polygon must be drawn, it is filtered down the BSP tree. It may get split at some nodes so that the pieces can be unambiguously checked within the proper sub-trees. When a certain piece reaches a leaf of the tree and this leaf is marked as occupied, it is known that this polygonal piece is, in fact, obscured and can be discarded. On the other hand, when a polygon's piece reaches a leaf marked as free, this piece can be rasterized and since the area under that polygon will become occupied after the rasterization, the BSP tree must be updated to reflect that.

Consider the example in Figure 7.28. In that example, a polygon with the edges named *E,G,H* must be rendered. It is first checked against the root of the BSP tree that tracks areas currently available on the screen. The edge *A* that is in the root of the tree splits the given polygon. The smaller piece to the left of *A* should thus be checked against the left sub-tree, and the remaining portion of the polygon should be checked against the right sub-tree. In the former case, the smaller piece reached a leaf node that is occupied and it is thus discarded. In the latter case, the polygon is checked against the edge *B*, and gets split in half with the upper portion getting discarded. The lower portion is checked further, eventually reaching the node describing the screen rectangle (see Figure 7.27, the node marked *F*). At that point you can safely rasterize the remaining piece of the polygon and update the tree using the polygon's edges to induce further partitioning, and mark the polygon's area as occupied and the remaining areas as free. Clearly, when a piece of a polygon has reached a leaf node, this piece is entirely within the region described by the leaf. Hence, any necessary alterations to the tree are local to the sub-tree rooted at the reached leaf (see Figure 7.28).

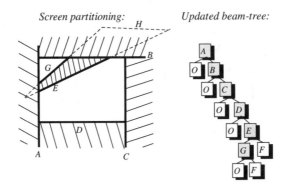

FIGURE 7.28

A beam tree after one polygon has been drawn.

Screen partitioning:

Updated beam-tree:

The BSP tree created in the screen plane tracks the unobscured beams of view, and that's why it is referred to as a *beam tree*. To summarize, in this algorithm you pick polygons from the front-to-back ordering one at a time and filter them down the BSP tree associated with the screen. When a piece or pieces of a polygon get rasterized, the tree is updated, tracking the remaining free space so that each consecutive polygon can be consistently checked. As a result, overdraws are completely avoided at the expense of a still appreciable number of clippings and the implementational complexity of this algorithm.

Another use of BSP trees to help with shadow generation is discussed in the next chapter. Clearly, this partitioning scheme is of great importance when solving multiple problems of computer graphics.

Scan-Line Algorithm

Chapter 6 introduced an alternative representation for a polygonal model where polygons were described in terms of edges rather than in terms of vertices. Such a representation allows you to avoid redundant clipping and is also appropriate for use in the hidden surface removal method that is examined in this section. The idea of *scan-line* hidden surface removal is to shift determination of visibility from the level of polygons to the level of individual pixel lines of the polygons (see Figure 7.29). This algorithm can be thought of as an extension of the generic polygon rasterization that was discussed with respect to concave polygons. As you will see, a lot of ideas in the two algorithms are the same.

FIGURE 7.29
Determining hidden surfaces per scan-line.

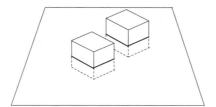

In this method, all polygons in the scene are rasterized simultaneously. The determination of visibility is performed in the plane that is perpendicular to the current scan-line in the screen, where the relationships of the intersected polygons are thus determined. Figure 7.30 demonstrates an example where three polygons are rasterized using this algorithm. As you can see, the information on the order in which polygonal edges are crossed by the scan-line is crucial for this algorithm. Such ordering of edges can be obtained in every scan-line using the same approach as was employed in the algorithm for concave polygon rasterization. Having this ordering, you can determine the visibility in a straightforward manner assuming that the equations of the polygons' planes are available. Examine scan-line number one in Figure 7.30.

FIGURE 7.30
Active edges at different scan-lines.

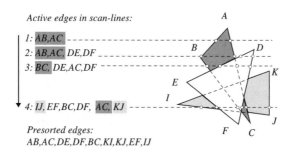

Active edges in scan-lines:

1: *AB,AC*
2: *AB,AC, DE,DF*
3: *BC, DE,AC,DF*

4: *IJ, EF,BC,DF, AC, KJ*

Presorted edges:
AB,AC,DE,DF,BC,KI,KJ,EF,IJ

Scan-line number one in Figure 7.30 only intersects the polygon *ABC,* and thus, you can proceed rasterizing this polygon in between the edges. Scan-line number two intersects two polygons, but the ordering of the intersected edges is such that you finish rasterizing polygon *ABC* before the beginning of polygon *DEF* is encountered. In scan-line number three, this is not the case. You start rasterization of the polygon *ABC* and before it is finished, the edge *DE* belonging to the polygon *DEF* is encountered. At that stage, the visibility must be determined by comparing depths of both polygons in that point.

You can do this by evaluating plane equations for both polygons in that point. In this particular case, polygon *DEF* has lesser depth, and thus its rasterization starts. When you encounter the edge *AC* you can just ignore it since the rasterization of the polygon *DEF* has not been finished yet and the edge *AC* belongs to a polygon that was earlier determined to be further away.

In a sense, each polygon defines a scope in between the endpoints where it is rasterized. If at some point a polygon becomes obscured, you may still have to continue rasterizing it later on. Such a situation is demonstrated in the case of scan-line number four (see Figure 7.30). When you have finished rasterization of the polygon *DEF*, you are still in the scopes of two remaining polygons. Thus, after crossing edge *DF*, you must examine the depth of the polygons *ABC* and *IJK* and, in this case, proceed with rasterization of the polygon *ABC*. When you cross the edge *AC,* you are in the scope of only one polygon that is to be rasterized until it ends.

As you can see, this portion of the algorithm is fairly easy to implement. This algorithm is using the fact that in each scan-line there is edge ordering. As was discussed, such ordering can be obtained by pre-sorting all edges by their minimum vertical coordinate, and in the cases where two edges are found to be equal, using a secondary criterion to compare horizontal coordinates of the endpoints with the maximum vertical coordinate. Having this ordering allows you to update current edges for every scan-line in an incremental manner. Once you find current edges, you must also place them according to the current horizontal coordinates.

It must be stressed that one advantage of this algorithm is in its ability to ignore rasterization of obscured scan-lines. This becomes very important if the polygons in the scene use complex texture mapping or lighting. This algorithm also correctly handles the case of a mutual overlap of polygons, but in unmodified form it can't handle polygon piercing. Using this algorithm also implies making changes to the existing polygonal pipeline since all polygons are rasterized simultaneously, which at times may not be desirable or even possible.

Z-Buffer Algorithm

Most of the methods considered so far have one big limitation: They deal with objects that are modeled as a set of polygons. Sometimes this is not the case. What is being rasterized may be represented in terms of other kinds of primitives. And even with polygonal models, the performance of most hidden surface removal methods degrades disproportionately when the number of polygons is increased.

The algorithm discussed in this section is suitable for any kind of primitive rasterized by any method. It works in essentially linear time; that is, its complexity is proportionate to the number of primitives in the scene.

The idea of the *Z-buffer* algorithm is to even further shift the process of finding what is visible and what is obscured from the level of primitives or scan-lines to the level of individual pixels. In other words, each time you determine that a pixel should be drawn during rasterization of some primitive, you store that pixel's color together with its view space z coordinate (the depth). If at a later time a pixel belonging to another or even the same primitive has to be drawn at the same position, z values will be compared and if the new pixel is actually the one closer to the viewer, it will substitute a previously drawn one. If the new pixel is determined to be farther away, you leave the original pixel in its place. Figure 7.31 shows two primitives being rasterized using the Z-buffer algorithm for hidden surface elimination.

FIGURE 7.31
Rasterization using Z-buffer hidden surface elimination.

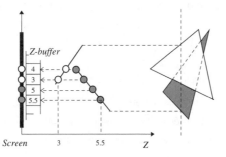

From Figure 7.31 you can see that each screen pixel, besides some unit of storage in the image bitmap, must also have some allocated space to store the current z value. An array of all z values is referred to as *a Z-buffer*, hence the name of the algorithm.

At the beginning of the frame rendering, you must initialize all locations in the Z-buffer with the farthest value of z available at the selected precision. As a result, the first pixel obtained at any location will be necessarily drawn by comparison logic of the algorithm.

Determination of the z coordinate in the case of polygons can be done by linear interpolation. This method was used to interpolate shading intensities in the case of rasterization with interpolative shading and texture coordinates in the case of linear texture mapping. Thus, the z coordinate is kept at each vertex until the rasterization stage, interpolated along edges and then along the scan-lines using values on the edges.

It should be noted that if you employ the perspective projection transformation, the z coordinate in the obtained space doesn't change linearly. It is attractive to use $-C/_z$ instead as the depth measure. This one changes linearly in the screen space.

FIGURE 7.32
The Z-buffer algorithm handling the intersection of objects.

Of the many advantages the Z-buffer algorithm offers, its simplicity is perhaps the greatest one. With the help of this algorithm it is also trivial to solve visibility in cases when some polygons intersect (see Figure 7.32). Because of its simplicity, this algorithm is the one often implemented in hardware. Its generality and essentially linear running time make it extremely attractive for high-end applications. Problems with the Z-buffer algorithm usually arise from the fact that there is a finite and often quite limited number of bits available to represent the z coordinate for each pixel on the screen. At some stage, you may be rounding or truncating the z values, causing artifacts at the pixels where reduction of bits caused wrong determination of visibility. And of course, performance-wise, a certain amount of code has been pushed into the very inner loop of the rasterization. This causes a performance penalty, which makes the algorithm less attractive for applications that operate with moderate numbers of primitives.

It must also be noted that the Z-buffer is an array of considerable size, and although memory limitations become softer and softer with time, for some applications just filling the Z-buffer with the initial value may incur undesirable cost. This algorithm is also vulnerable to the overdrawing problem, since the obscured primitives must be rasterized nonetheless. There are some extensions of this algorithm, however, where lighting and texturing is done as a post-processing step only for those points that survived Z-buffer visibility determination. Those extensions alleviate the overdraw problem but they present certain implementational challenges.

Summary

The problem with hidden surfaces arises in world-to-screen visualization when an image of the virtual world is obtained by projecting primitives from the world onto the screen. Some primitives may obscure other primitives in the screen projection, thus requiring some strategy to eliminate hidden surfaces.

Of the several hidden surface removal strategies you have seen, many are applicable to models represented in terms of polygons only. A popular strategy is to rasterize the polygons in back-to-front order so that the polygons that are closer overdraw previously rasterized polygons that are farther away from the viewer. There are a number of ways to obtain a back-to-front ordering of polygons. The algorithms to do that range from sorting to space subdivision. This strategy, however, wastes resources when rasterization of primitives is expensive because it is necessary to rasterize all, even obscured, polygons. In such situations, it may be advantageous to examine other seemingly inefficient solutions such as iterative clipping of all polygons using a beam tree, which avoids unnecessary rasterization.

The Z-buffer method doesn't impose any criteria on the shape of primitives and it is also the simplest hidden surface removal algorithm. It is, thus, often implemented in hardware. This algorithm also requires performing unnecessary rasterizations. Scan-line hidden surface removal avoids this problem, but it is applicable to polygonal models only. It also demands considerable changes throughout the polygonal pipeline.

Running time of hidden surface removal algorithms is hard to compare since all of them have an elementary step of different complexity. Thus, implementations of algorithms with linear running time may behave worse than implementations of algorithms with more expensive running time. The advantage of the former usually becomes appreciable only when the number of polygons becomes extremely large. The choice of which strategy to use is based on the particular situation and allowable relaxations.

CHAPTER 8

Lighting

The previous chapters have concentrated on the geometric aspects of computer graphics. The modeling, transformation, projection, clipping, rasterization, and hidden surface removal techniques considered permit you to render a contour of the virtual scene on the computer screen. Although object outlines are important for human vision and we can easily recognize objects represented as line drawings, color and the interaction between light and objects give images their visual realism. Modeling color and light is therefore imperative for modern graphics applications.

This chapter discusses how color and light are modeled and handled in computer graphics applications that use the world-to-screen and screen-to-world viewing methods.

Physics of Light and Human Perception

The ultimate destination of the renderings produced with the help of computer graphics is the human eye. Therefore, the way humans see things is of immense importance and must always be taken into account.

What makes humans distinguish red from blue, for instance? And, physically, what is the difference between red and blue? Light is of an electromagnetic nature and is caused by the variation of the parameters of the electromagnetic field over time. These electromagnetic waves are characterized by their frequency (the number of peak intensities of the wave per unit time) or by their length (the distance between two consecutive peaks). Our eyes are sensitive in a relatively small range of wavelengths, from approximately 400 to about 700 nm. Electromagnetic waves that fall into this range are what we call light.

Incoming light is focused by both eyes, which allows for binocular vision. Since each eye receives a slightly different projection of the scene, the human visual cortex can approximate the distance to the object by comparing its two projections (neurons receiving information from both eyes are interlaced in the visual cortex). If the images of an object are roughly at the same place in both projections, the object is farther away. If the images are shifted, the object must be closer. This is very easy to observe by closing each eye in turn and focusing on objects that are close and far away. Binocular vision allows for the exciting possibility of immersive virtual reality 3D graphics, where you make sure that each eye receives its own synthetically rendered image taken from a slightly different angle. When that happens, instead of a flat projection, we are deceived into perceiving the depth of the scene. Of course, graphics applications must rely on special hardware in order to achieve this effect. Such hardware ranges from expensive head-mounted displays, where each eye views its own miniature screen, to inexpensive shutter glasses. The latter obscure their lenses in turns so that each eye receives information in sync with changing images on a computer screen.

The image is projected inside the eye onto the retina and is mostly focused on one small spot. The retina is covered with color receptors. There are two basic types of receptors: *cones* and *rods*. Rods are sensitive to the energy of the light and don't contribute directly to the color perception. Cones, on the other hand, are responsible for color vision. There are three different kinds of cones, each with maximum sensitivity in a different spectral region. The first type is sensitive in the blue part of the spectrum, the second is sensitive in green, and the third is sensitive in red. Receptors most sensitive in the red area do have some sensitivity in neighboring parts of the spectrum, but it diminishes farther away. Blue receptors have less density and thus provide less sensitivity than green or red (see Figure 8.1). This fact has an implication in building color palettes. Fewer bits may be allocated to represent blue than for green or red.

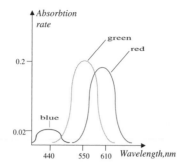

Generally, the combined sum of the three distributions in Figure 8.1 demonstrates human sensitivity to colors of different wavelengths. Our best sensitivity to colors is close to the center of the spectral range.

Monochromatic light can be specified uniquely by wavelength and intensity. However, real visible light is hardly ever monochromatic—it's a pack of waves with different lengths and intensities, so to speak (see Figure 8.2). Real light can be represented by its energy distribution in the visual range. Reddish colors will have peak intensities of their graphs shifted right and peak intensities in bluish colors will be shifted left.

FIGURE 8.2
*An energy
distribution for
some color.*

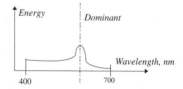

Although necessary from the physical perspective, it is, of course, unreasonable to represent a color as an energy distribution in a computer graphics application. Due to the peculiarities of human vision, it is the dominant wavelength, usually the maximum of the energy distribution with respect to eye sensitivity, that really matters for our perception. And in fact, colors with relatively different energy distributions but with roughly the same dominant wavelengths will be perceived as having the same hue.

Total amount of energy (area under the distribution) relates to perceived *saturation* of the color. The saturation describes the amount of white in a color. For instance, the distribution of ideal white is a straight line across the spectral range without any dominant wavelength, and therefore it has 0% saturation. A 100% saturated color should have only a spike of energy at a certain place and maintain a zero level of energy otherwise. Brightness of color relates to the magnitude of energy, especially that of the dominant portion of the distribution.

On the assumption that representing a color through an energy distribution is both too complex and doesn't take into account the particulars of our vision system, computer graphics opts for different approaches to modeling colors and light/object interactions.

Modeling Colors

Attempts to reproduce colors date back centuries. Color mixing for paintings and color television are perhaps the brightest examples. In all cases, a scheme much simpler than an energy distribution was used, and with quite acceptable results. This section considers several schemes pertinent to computer graphics applications.

Achromatic Light (Black and White)

Total energy of light is very important for human perception. The fact that we can watch black-and-white images and relate them to real life is indirect proof of that. Early television and early computer graphics were black and white. The popularity of this scheme is due, of course, to the simplicity with which a single color can be represented and reproduced. All that is required is one number related to the magnitude of energy of this light. Higher energy translates into brighter color; less energy translates into dimmer color.

When representing lighting effects, such as reflections, it is necessary to have a set of different shades of a color. To achieve that, it is natural to assign a range of indices to different shades, so that increasing the index will correspond to perceiving a proportionately brighter shade.

Generally, such indices are not simply proportional to the energy of light. This dependency is in fact logarithmic. At lower magnitudes of energy, humans need smaller energy increases, and at higher magnitudes bigger energy increases are needed to perceive a proportionally brighter color. This is because our visual system is not very good at detecting gradation in shades at higher levels of energy. Most of the time, this is considered in the characteristics of computer display devices.

Once a system of indices corresponding to varying shades of an achromatic color is set up, it is possible to perform a certain number of operations on lights described in this form. For instance, since the combined effect of two lights must intuitively correspond to the sum of their energies, it can be modeled by summing the indices. Similarly, the indices can be interpolated to find intermediate values between two points with known intensities.

However, it is possible to obtain a greater number than the total number of available shades by adding two indices. Therefore, when there is an upper limit on the number of available shades, a strategy should be devised for how to always produce a valid number as a result of any operation involving colors.

The simplest strategy is to clamp the index at the upper limit so that any color that should be brighter than the maximum is represented by the brightest shade available. Another possible strategy is to attempt to avoid such situations by proportionally scaling all colors so that the biggest obtained color will correspond to the available maximum and the rest will be proportionally smaller.

Although achromatic light is still important for many different technologies, such as producing a hard copy on a printer, modern 3D graphics relies on color as the main tool to achieve visual realism.

Tri-component Color Models

You have already seen that certain properties of light energy distributions are more important for visual perception. Dominant wavelength relates to the perceived hue of the color, and area under the distribution roughly relates to the color's saturation (the amount of white in it). Levels of energy in the dominant portion of the distribution relate to the perceived brightness of the color. These notions are fairly intuitive, and thus one approach to modeling colors is to describe their hue, saturation, and brightness. This is known as the *HSB* system. The space of the color that is possible to describe with HSB can be represented by the cone illustrated in Figure 8.3.

FIGURE 8.3
HSB color space.

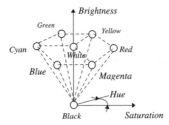

In this system, the hue is measured angularly and the brightness is measured horizontally. Therefore, black is located at the bottom and white is located on the top. The notion of saturation is not well defined for very dim colors, which in the case of the diagram, explains why the range of the saturation increases for brighter colors.

Although this system is intuitively clear and allows specification of colors by human users, it is not very convenient for internal usage in a computer program. For the purposes of a computer program, you are looking for a system that allows for expressing interactions of several light sources; for instance, expressing the combined effect of multiple lights or interpolating between two known colors.

Since the sensitivity of eyes is concentrated around the three spectral ranges (red, green, and blue—often called *prime* or *pure* colors), an individual color can be represented as a weighted sum of its intensities in the respective ranges of these three components. Thus, you can specify a color as

$$\begin{bmatrix} R \\ G \\ B \end{bmatrix}$$

where R, G, and B are intensity levels for red, green, and blue wavelengths, respectively. Representing a color as a triple of values is, of course, a much more workable representation than an energy distribution. Although it is not completely correct, and it doesn't cover the full range of visible colors, its simplicity and additive nature is of great value.

This system is called *additive* because the contributions of pure colors are added together, which produces a combined result.

Because of its additive nature, this system also allows you to express the combined effect of two lights as a vector sum of their respective RGB triples:

$$\begin{bmatrix} R_1 \\ G_1 \\ B_1 \end{bmatrix} + \begin{bmatrix} R_2 \\ G_2 \\ B_2 \end{bmatrix} = \begin{bmatrix} R_1 + R_2 \\ G_1 + G_2 \\ B_1 + B_2 \end{bmatrix}$$

Intuitively, it is possible to consider each color as a point in a three-dimensional space formed by the axes of the pure colors (see Figure 8.4).

FIGURE 8.4
RGB color space.

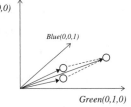

Similar to the situation with shades of achromatic light, there generally is a limited range of intensities that each pure component can assume. Thus, all representable colors can be considered to belong to the insides of a cube (see Figure 8.5).

FIGURE 8.5
Color cube.

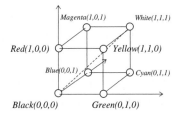

In this cube, shades of gray belong to the diagonal connecting white *(1,1,1)* and black *(0,0,0)*. The space covered by this cube roughly corresponds to the cone of HSB representation. If you look along the diagonal connecting black and white, it becomes apparent that it corresponds to the axis of the cone in Figure 8.3.

Similar to the problem of finite numbers of shades of an achromatic light, in this case it is also impossible to guarantee that by adding the effects of two lights, the result will remain within the boundaries of the cube. A common strategy is to clamp the three components individually when their values overflow the preset limit. An alternative approach is to attempt to avoid an overflow by proportionally scaling all colors. In many cases, however, all possible lights and their interactions are unknown beforehand and thus the first strategy is the one commonly used. In fact, this strategy is so common that special arithmetic instructions are provided in some processors to simplify the task. For instance, MMX extensions in Intel Pentiums have instructions for vector addition and subtraction with saturation. These instructions enable you to evaluate the three components of the color model in parallel. Additionally, the saturation mechanism enables you to limit ranges of numbers. In the course of the instruction execution, if a result is received that exceeds the precision, it is represented as the maximum value that can be stored.

There are many other models that describe colors, such as the YIQ system that is used to describe broadcast TV signals, and CMY, which is often used in hardcopy printer technology. The RGB system, however, is commonly used for the purposes of computer graphics, mainly because it allows you to split most lighting problems into three independent parts, one for each pure color. Because of a system's additive nature, combining the effect of separate solutions for each pure color roughly corresponds to the answer you would expect to see in real life. For instance, this system is fairly well suited for interpolation between two different colors done by combining the effects of interpolating each component individually (unlike an HSB system, which will not always produce an acceptable result in this case). A fourth component, called *alpha*, often extends the RGB system. This component describes transparency properties. The extended RGBA system helps to model complex illumination effects where the light is not only reflected, but also transmitted, by matter.

Chapter 1, "Hardware Interface," explained that the display hardware may support different schemes of representing image bitmaps. In one case, the color of each pixel is represented directly through its RGB value, and in another case the color is specified as a palette index. In the latter method, the palette stores the actual RGB value and is limited in size. In many situations, you may have to convert a bitmap stored in the first representation into the second representation and thus be forced to reduce the number of colors. Since the first representation is almost continuous and the latter one is inherently discrete, this problem is known as *color quantization*.

If you find all unique colors from the original image, there may be more colors than can be stored in a palette. Thus, the number of colors must be reduced in a visually acceptable way. One approach to doing so is to find some set of clusters in the color space so that the colors within the clusters are optimally close to each other, and then substitute a single color for the entire cluster. This problem happens to be quite expensive to solve directly. However, many techniques exist that can efficiently find some approximation and, as a result, a visually acceptable color reduction. One way to do that is with the help of the *median-cut* algorithm, designed by P.S. Heckbert in the early eighties.

The idea of this algorithm, which treats colors as points in 3D, RGB space, is to first find the bounding box around the original set of colors. Then, you can split the problem into two subproblems by cutting the space along the median of the longest side of the bounding box. Figure 8.6 shows the steps in this process, illustrated for simplicity on a planar example that ignores the axis *G*.

FIGURE 8.6
Steps in the color-reduction procedure.

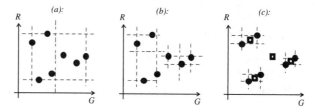

As Figure 8.6(a) illustrates, the space is split along the median of the longest side of the bounding square. You can then proceed recursively, computing the bounding squares for the points in both partitions and performing the splits (see Figure 8.6(b)). In one case the split happens along the *G* axis, and in another case along the *R* axis. You stop the algorithm once the necessary number of clusters is obtained. For instance, if the original set of colors has to be represented in only four palette entries, you stop after two levels of splits and compute the sought colors as the geometric centers or *centroids* (weighted centers) of clusters of points within each partition (see Figure 8.6(c)).

It should be noted that in order to improve the quality of the color reduction, the median-cut algorithm may have to consider the frequency with which the points from the original set appear in the image. This information is used during the computation of the medians and the centroids, so that the median along an axis is computed as the sum of frequencies times the coordinate along that axis divided by the sum of the frequencies. In other words, it is computed as the mean value of coordinates of all points in the cluster. The coordinates of a centroid are computed as medians along the respective axes.

As the following sections demonstrate, to represent illumination effects you need to be able to represent shades of different intensity of the same color. While it is easy to do when the image bitmap stores entire RGB values, it becomes much more complicated in the palette-based representation. In that representation, there is only a limited number of colors available. The colors in the palette can be arranged so that increasing the index corresponds to some brighter color. However, if some of the colors in the palette have completely different hues, it becomes difficult to place them in any order. In such a situation, it may be necessary to logically split the palette into groups of colors within which the increasing index corresponds to a brighter shade.

It must be noted that such groups may still share some colors. For instance, any color under zero illumination is supposed to be black. Since, considering the limitation on the number of colors you have, you can't afford to store the same color multiple times, it may be necessary to resort to using a secondary indexing structure to reflect the sharing. To represent the sharing, it is relatively common to build a two-dimensional array, storing palette indices so that one dimension represents the logical index to a color and the other dimension represents the shade number. Because of the sharing of actual palette colors among some shades of the logical colors, the size of the table may exceed that of the palette.

It should be stressed, however, that increasing the index of the shade roughly corresponds to illumination by a brighter monochrome light. It will require more dimensions in the secondary table if you want to allow light sources of different color. In the constrained palette scheme, such a generalization becomes impractical, however. This is one of the reasons why palette modes are less and less relevant these days.

Modeling Illumination

Previous sections examined the nature of light, its properties, and the approaches to modeling light of different wavelength composition (different colors) for the purposes of computer graphics. However, it is the interaction of light emitted by light sources and the surfaces of objects in the surrounding world that matter for our visual perception of the surrounding environment.

The ultimate goal of 3D graphics is to portray images of virtual worlds as if they were taken from the real world. In this endeavor, particular attention must be paid to modeling light/matter interactions since they are of such great importance for human vision.

There are many different kinds of interactions between light and matter. For instance, matter can *absorb*, *reflect*, or *transmit* light. These effects can be generally explained and modeled based on particle properties of light; that is, by modeling light as a collection of tiny particles. Modeling other effects such as *interference*, *defraction*, or *refraction* requires the aid of the wave theory and are generally more complex. Overall, a sufficiently detailed lighting model that considers multiple effects of light/matter interaction is both complex and expensive to handle in computer programs, especially those that must produce images at interactive rates. Most applications are, therefore, forced into modeling only absolutely crucial interactions, notably reflections. Even this is often approximate and uses a lot of various heuristics to speed up computations. This section considers the components for lighting models that are widely used in computer graphics.

Ambient Illumination

Probably the simplest and oldest illumination model attempted in graphics applications is that of ambient light. In this model, it is assumed that there is no concentrated source of light and that the illumination is equal from any direction, maintaining constant levels throughout the world.

With such illumination, each surface demonstrates its intrinsic reflective capability. The objects that reflect light better appear brighter, and the objects that mostly absorb light appear darker. Obviously, this has to do with what we commonly refer to as the color of a material object. In everyday life, we are used to seeing objects in the fairly uniform white light that is emitted by the sun. What is referred to as the color of a material object is in fact its capability to reflect white light. Generally, reflective capability is described by a coefficient in the range *[0,1]*, with *0* meaning that the object absorbs 100% of the light of a given frequency and *1* meaning that the object is a perfect reflector. Obviously, this coefficient must vary for different wavelengths—most objects absorb in some frequencies and reflect in others. Therefore, the general reflective capability of a material object can be described by a distribution in which the coefficient is given as a function of the wavelength of the incident light. This, of course, is very inconvenient. Furthermore, according to the color models it is possible to represent a color as either a single index (in the case of achromatic light) or a triple (in the case of colored light). In this regard, reflectivity of matter also can be represented either as a single coefficient in the former case, or as a triple of coefficients in the latter case. Generally, this lighting model can be expressed as the following simple equation:

$$I_{reflected} = K_{object} I_{ambient}$$

The intensity value for the reflected light is obtained simply as a product of the intensities of ambient light and the reflection coefficient of a given object. Note that both $I_{reflected}$, $I_{ambient}$ and K_{object} are scalars in the achromatic color model or three-tuples in the case of colored light.

Since the level of ambient light stays constant, you can store $I_{reflected}$ for each surface in the scene, and thus display each object using its own intrinsic color. Of course, such an illumination model doesn't provide even a minimal amount of realism. All that is seen are colored silhouettes of some shapes (see Figure 8.7).

You will have to find a more complex illumination model if you seek realism. However, even with the fairly sophisticated models employed these days, you often have to use an ambient light component to compensate for effects that are not computed, such as multiple reflections of light from matte surfaces, which can be very roughly modeled as ambient light.

FIGURE 8.7
*Ambient
illumination.*

FIGURE 8.7
*Ambient
illumination.*

Diffuse (Lambertian) Reflection

Quite unlike the assumption taken in the case of ambient light (that is, light is considered to be uniform from any direction), in the real world, the light is often emitted by a particular light source. Thus, the light often falls onto some surface from a particular direction. In order to model reflection in this case, you must consider both the location and the type of the light source as well as the properties of the reflecting surfaces. You can differentiate between point light sources, which emit equally well in different directions; spotlights, which have a predominant direction; and directional light sources. The latter occur when a light source is remote from the modeled scene so that the direction of light doesn't change significantly across the scene. Light sources of all types illuminate the material objects present in the virtual world. These objects reflect some of the light falling onto their surface.

The *Lambertian* or *diffuse* model of reflection is based on the assumption that light is reflected equally well in all directions (see Figure 8.8).

FIGURE 8.8
Diffuse reflection.

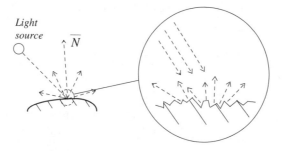

This model generally holds for matte surfaces. The roughness of these surfaces is such that each tiny region consists of a large number of microfaces that are oriented almost randomly in space, and therefore reflect in all possible directions (see Figure 8.8). Hence, the intensity of the light reflected in any direction depends only on how much light falls onto the surface. This, of course, is a function of the surface's orientation with respect to the direction of the light. If the surface is facing the light source—that is, it is perpendicular to the direction of the light—the density of the incident light is the highest. If the surface is directed under some angle smaller than 90 degrees, the density is proportionately smaller. This relationship is demonstrated in Figure 8.9.

FIGURE 8.9
Geometry of diffuse reflection.

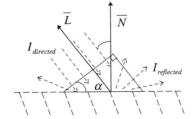

Figure 8.9 illustrates that the same amount of light that passes through one side of a right-angle triangle is reflected from the region of the surface corresponding to the triangle's hypotenuse. Due to the relationships that hold in a right-angle triangle, the length of the hypotenuse is *1/cos(α)* of the length of the considered side. Thus, you can deduce that if the intensity of the incident light is $I_{directed}$, the amount of light reflected from a unit surface is $I_{directed} \cos(\alpha)$. Adjusting this with a coefficient that describes reflection properties of the matter, similar to the approach taken in the case of ambient light, the following equation to describe the diffuse reflection is obtained:

$$I_{reflected} = K_{diffuse} I_{directed} \cos(\alpha)$$

This equation demonstrates that the reflection is at its peak for surfaces that are perpendicular to the direction of light and diminishes for smaller angles. It must be noted that if the angle is more than 180 degrees or less than 0 degrees, this surface is obscured from the given light source and, thus, no light falls on it and no light is reflected from it. However, if you just evaluate the equation in this case, you will obtain a negative intensity of the reflected light, which, to preserve the physical sense, must be set to zero.

From a practical point of view, darkening the surfaces not illuminated directly also presents a problem. In an environment with a single directed light source, all surfaces oriented away from the light will be black. Although such a situation may happen when modeling the emptiness of space, in most practical settings some light will still reach such surfaces by reflecting multiple times off of other surfaces. The diffuse reflection model only takes into account the reflection of the light emitted by a light source and doesn't handle the light reflected by other surfaces. It is practical to adjust the model with the ambient light component that will simulate the multiple reflections as some constant term:

$$I_{reflected} = K_{ambient}I_{ambient} + K_{diffuse}I_{directed}\cos(\alpha)$$

This expression is referred to as the *Bouknight* illumination model, named after its creator. Figure 8.10 demonstrates a sample scene rendered using this model.

FIGURE 8.10
Diffuse or Bouknight illumination.

When this model is implemented, assuming that the properties of surfaces and lights are known, you still must find a way to compute $\cos(\alpha)$, a multiplier that classifies the orientation of the direction of light and the surface. In the previous chapter, the normal vectors were used to describe the orientation of a plane. Suppose that the direction toward the light source is also given as a unit vector named $\overline{L}$. By definition, the scalar product of the two vectors can be expressed as $(\overline{N} \cdot \overline{L}) = \|\overline{N}\|\|\overline{L}\|\cos(\alpha)$ where $\|\overline{N}\|$ and $\|\overline{L}\|$ are the lengths of the vectors. Assuming that both vectors are unit length, you can compute $\cos(\alpha)$ for the purposes of the reflection model as the scalar product of the direction of light and the normal of the surface at the point where you want to find the intensity of the reflected light. Thus, the expression for the Bouknight illumination model can be computed as $I_{reflected} = K_{ambient}I_{ambient} + K_{diffuse}I_{directed}(\overline{N} \cdot \overline{L})$.

In this expression, depending on the particular color scheme used, the terms are either scalars (in the case of achromatic light), or three-tuples (in the case of the RGB color model).

Previous chapters discussed how to find a normal vector. However, until this point, it was never necessary for it to be unit length. Indeed, for such purposes as back-face culling or building a plane equation, a vector of any length, as long as it was pointing in the right direction, was acceptable. Evaluating the light model requires unit length vectors. Clearly, any vector can be scaled to unit length if its present length divides every coordinate:

$$\overline{n} = \frac{1}{\|\overline{N}\|}\overline{N}$$

By definition, the scalar product of a vector multiplied by itself equals the square of its length. Thus, the length can be found by computing the square root of the scalar product of the vector multiplied by itself:

$$(\overline{N} \cdot \overline{N}) = \|\overline{N}\|\|\overline{N}\|\cos(0) = \|\overline{N}\|^2$$

$$\|\overline{N}\| = \sqrt{(\overline{N} \cdot \overline{N})}$$

In the process of computing a unit length vector, the only difficulty may be in finding the square root when computing the length of the vector. This computation can be considered a fairly expensive one. Most of the time, a function to compute the square root is already available in a standard library or even hardware. In some cases, however, it might not be available, which will demand that some algorithm to compute the square root be coded.

A relatively fast way to find the square root is to employ the binary search algorithm. In this method, you make an initial guess of the result and compute its square. If the square is bigger than the argument, the square root is bigger than the guess (at least for the numbers that are bigger than 1). If the square is smaller than the argument, the actual square root is smaller than the guess. By employing the binary search technique, it is easy to proceed in a way that reduces by half the interval on which you search for the square root. When the interval becomes smaller than a certain precision value, you know that an approximation for the result has been found.

Although this method is relatively fast and in most cases requires only a few iterations, it is still necessary to compute the square in every iteration. This implies at least one multiplication per iteration. In many situations, the coordinates of the objects in space are integers, and in computing the lengths of vectors you may be satisfied with an integer number as a result. You can take advantage of this assumption in the following algorithm, which finds the square root by analyzing which of the bits must be set in the result.

In this algorithm, you initially set the highest possible bit in the guess value and compute its square. Since a single set bit represents a value that is a power of two, you can find a square through shifting. If the square is bigger than the argument, this bit cannot be set in the result. If the square is smaller, this bit indeed must be set in the result. You further proceed to set and test the second highest bit. Since the guess value may have several bits set at this stage, you can't compute the square simply by shifting. However, the square of a sum can be computed as follows:

$$(a + b)^2 = a^2 + 2ab + b^2$$

If *a* is the guess value from before the current bit was set and *b* is the current bit, then *(a+b)* is the new guess value with the current bit set. The square of the new guess value can be computed as a sum of three components: The first represents the square computed during the previous iteration and the other two represent the multiplication of values, at least one of which is a power of two. Thus, these components can be computed through shifting. Once the square is computed, you again check whether this bit is present in the result. Proceeding further to the next iteration, the same situation as before reappears.

At the time you exhaust all bits, an integer approximation of the square root will be computed.

An implementation of this algorithm is presented in Listing 8.1.

LISTING 8.1

Computing the Square Root by Iterative Bit Setting

```
unsigned long TI_sqrt(register unsigned long arg)
{
  register int i;
  register unsigned long nprd,msk=0x8000L,val=0,prd=0;

  for(i=15;i>=0;i--)
  {
    nprd=prd+(val<<(i+1))+(msk<<i);    /* iteratively computing the */
    if(nprd<=arg) { val|=msk; prd=nprd; }   /* square */
    msk>>=1;                            /* bit must be in the result */
  }
  return(val);
}
```

Starting from the highest feasible bit.

A bit to test during next iteration.

Note that in the implementation in Listing 8.1, it is expected that integers occupy 32 bits of storage and, thus, the computation starts with the biggest guess value whose square doesn't overflow the available precision.

Specular Reflection

Although the diffuse model can describe reflection from matte objects sufficiently well, many other objects in the world have smooth surfaces that reflect light in a single predominant direction that mirrors the direction of the incident light. This phenomenon is known as *specular* reflection and is exhibited by smooth, shiny, polished surfaces. When the direction of viewing coincides, or nearly coincides, with the direction of specular reflection, a bright highlight is observed. This is the reflection of the light source from the shiny surface (see Figure 8.11).

FIGURE 8.11
Specular reflection.

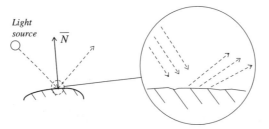

It is clear that a model describing this effect will be dependent on the location of the light source, the location of the viewer, and the orientation of the surface. The highlight at a particular place on the surface is observed when the viewer is located in the direction of the specularly reflected light. If the observer moves, the specular highlight may still be visible as reflected from a different part of the surface. For many materials, the mechanism of the specular reflection is such that the wavelength combination doesn't change much during the reflection. Therefore, the color of the highlight is the same as that of the light source and doesn't generally depend on the color of the reflecting surface.

Generally, a theory describing reflection from shiny surfaces is quite complex. An approximation is commonly used for the purposes of computer graphics. This is called the *Phong* illumination model, named after its creator Phong Bui-Tuong. This model is suited for describing reflection from surfaces that are not perfect reflectors. According to this model, a specular highlight is seen when the viewer is close to the direction of reflection. The intensity of reflected light falls off sharply when the viewer moves away from the direction of the specular reflection (see Figure 8.12).

FIGURE 8.12
Geometry of specular reflection.

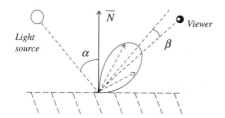

The falloff of the intensity is commonly approximated by $k_{specular} \cos^n(\beta)$, where $k_{specular}$ is a scalar coefficient showing the percentage of the incident light reflected. β describes the angle between the line of reflection of the light source and the viewing direction. Since the color of the reflected light has generally the same wavelength composition as that of the light source, this coefficient is a scalar in any color model. Some implementations neglect this fact and represent it as a tuple anyway. In the expression, the exponent n characterizes the shiny properties of the surface and ranges from one to infinity. The objects that are nearly matte require a small exponent since they produce a large, dim, specular highlight with a gentle falloff. This can be intuitively explained by the fact that such surfaces are not very smooth on a microscopic level and, thus, each tiny region reflects light in a slightly different direction. On the other hand, perfect reflectors have a sharp highlight that is modeled by a very large exponent in the preceding expression, making the intensity falloff very steep.

Objects that are not perfect reflectors also demonstrate a certain amount of diffuse reflection. Thus, the places of the shiny surface where the viewer doesn't observe the highlight show regular diffuse reflection. Considering this observation, the Phong illumination model can be expressed as

$$I_{reflected} = K_{ambient}I_{ambient} + I_{directed}(K_{diffuse}\cos(\alpha) + k_{specular}\cos^n(\beta))$$

Note that the ambient component is also used to compensate for the light that was reflected by other surfaces rather than emitted directly by a light source. Figure 8.13 demonstrates a scene rendered using the Phong illumination model.

FIGURE 8.13
*Phong
illumination.*

From an implementational perspective, you can see that in the expression it is necessary to compute $\cos^n(\beta)$. Similar to the technique used in the previous section, it can be found by using the mechanism of the scalar product of the unit vectors that describe the direction of the specular reflection $\overline{R}$ and the unit vector $\overline{V}$ that describes the direction toward the viewer. Using the scalar products, the equation could be rewritten as

$$I_{reflected} = K_{ambient}I_{ambient} + I_{directed}(K_{diffuse}(\overline{N}\cdot\overline{L}) + k_{specular}(\overline{R}\cdot\overline{V})^n)$$

In this expression it is necessary, however, to use vector $\overline{R}$, which describes the direction of the reflected light. This vector can be found by examining the relationships in the equal triangles that describe the geometry of the specular reflection model (see Figure 8.14).

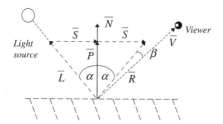

FIGURE 8.14
Geometry of specular reflection.

From Figure 8.14, you can see that vector $\overline{R}$ can be found as a vector sum of vectors $\overline{S}$ and $\overline{P}$. The latter vector is a projection of vector $\overline{L}$ onto the direction of the normal vector. The length of such a projection for a right-angle triangle can be found as $\|L\| \cos(\alpha)$, where $\cos(\alpha)$ can be computed using the definition of the scalar product. Considering the fact that both $\overline{L}$ and $\overline{N}$ are unit length, it is easy to express the length of the vector $\overline{P}$ as $\overline{N} \cdot \overline{L}$. The vector itself can be expressed as $(\overline{N} \cdot \overline{L})\overline{N}$ since it is co-directed with the normal. The vector $\overline{S}$ can be found as a vector difference: $\overline{P} - \overline{L}$. Thus, the unit vector specifying the direction of the specular reflection can be computed as

$$\overline{R} = \overline{S} + \overline{P} = \overline{P} - \overline{L} + \overline{P} = 2\overline{P} - \overline{L} = 2(\overline{N} \cdot \overline{L})\overline{N} - \overline{L}$$

As a result, the expression for the Phong illumination model can be restated as

$$I_{reflected} = K_{ambient} I_{ambient} + I_{directed}(K_{diffuse}(\overline{N} \cdot \overline{L}) + k_{specular}((2(\overline{N} \cdot \overline{L})\overline{N} - \overline{L}) \cdot \overline{V})^n)$$

This formula, of course, is quite computationally intensive, especially considering the fact that it must be evaluated for a very large number of points. In practice, this formulation of the Phong illumination model is often replaced with a slightly relaxed one. Instead of measuring when the direction of view comes close to the direction of reflection, you can alternatively measure when the orientation of the surface becomes such as to produce a highlight for the viewer. This can be achieved by considering an angle between the surface's normal and so called *half-way* vector $\overline{H}$ (see Figure 8.15).

The vector $\overline{H}$ is oriented in such a way that it points halfway between the direction toward the light source and the direction toward the viewer. Thus, when this vector coincides with the normal, the direction of the reflection coincides with the viewing direction and a specular highlight is observed. The Phong illumination model, in this case, can be formulated as

$$I_{reflected} = K_{ambient}I_{ambient} + I_{directed}(K_{diffuse}(\overline{N} \cdot \overline{L}) + k_{specular}(\overline{N} \cdot \overline{H})^n)$$

This approach gives a certain computational advantage, since computing $\overline{H} = (\overline{L} + \overline{V})/2$ is less expensive than computing $\overline{R} = 2(\overline{N} \cdot \overline{L})\overline{N} - \overline{L}$. A further speedup can be achieved if you assume that both the light source and the viewer are located in the infinity, thus making the halfway vector constant along the considered surface. This, however, will have certain undesirable implications for interactive applications because the specular highlight will not move with respect to the viewer's movements as you expect it to.

FIGURE 8.15
Alternative formulation of specular reflection.

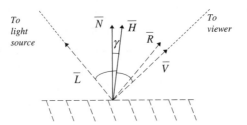

It should be noted, however, that the two formulations of the Phong illumination model are not equivalent and that neither describes the actual physical process of reflection. However, since the goal of computer graphics is to present only a realistic enough portrayal of the virtual scene, you have to employ a computationally feasible technique, which such models provide.

There are many refinements available for this lighting model. Some of the refinements attempt to add considerations for phenomena other than reflections. For instance, you can consider light source and atmospheric attenuation. In the first case, since the light from a point light source propagates equally well in all directions, forming a spherical front, its energy falls off with distance in inverse proportion to the area of the front, which is roughly a square of the distance. Similarly, with atmospheric attenuation, when light is traveling through some uniform media, some of it is getting absorbed. Hence, the intensity also falls off with distance, in this case proportional to the distance traveled. You can also introduce a term into the equation describing the light that is transmitted rather than reflected by the matter. The latter is very important for applications that model transparent or semitransparent objects, such as water or glass. Adding all these effects gives, at times, a considerable improvement to the portrayed scenes. It should be stressed again, however, that the falloff dependencies are often chosen through experimentation and examination of effects produced by different terms rather than through analytical means.

Illumination in Screen-to-World Viewing

So far, only local interactions between light sources and material objects being lit have been considered. However, in real life there often are multiple sources of light and multiple reflecting objects that interact with each other in many ways. Handling lighting for the whole virtual scene is often referred to as a *global* illumination model. Such models are introduced into the framework of the general viewing methods that were considered previously. This section discusses how to add a global illumination model into the screen-to-world, ray-casting process.

When the screen-to-world method is used to compute both the visibility and illumination, the algorithm is often referred to as *ray-tracing* as opposed to *ray-casting*, which is often used in conjunction with visibility determination only.

Local Screen-to-World Illumination

The introduction of the local illumination model into screen-to-world viewing can be done in a very consistent and straightforward manner. Recall that in this viewing method, you cast a ray for each pixel on the screen into the representation of the virtual world. The visibility is solved by examining all intersected surfaces and choosing the one that is closer to the viewer.

In order to add local illumination, it is necessary to locate some attributes of the intersected surface, such as its normal vector and the material properties. These, combined with attributes of a light source (notably position and brightness), allow for applying any of the illumination models thus far considered. Multiple light sources have an additive effect because light energy in a point is a sum of contributions from all sources of light. Figures 8.7, 8.10, and 8.13 were generated using ray-tracing algorithms with ambient, Bouknight, and Phong local illuminations, respectively.

However, these local illumination models only take into account the relationships between light sources and a single object. They don't consider effects that result from the presence of multiple objects. For instance, a light source can be obscured from a given point by another surface and it may not contribute to the local illumination in that point, thus creating a shadow. Similarly, light can be contributed locally not by a light source, but by a reflection of light from some other object. Thus, special techniques have to be used to represent the effects of global illumination.

Global Screen-to-World Illumination

Fortunately, the ray-tracing technique, already in place to resolve visibility, can be extended in order to handle some aspects of global illumination. Of the two effects considered, the first one requires that you check the light source visibility in the point where the lighting model is evaluated. Casting a ray, called a *shadow ray*, from the point toward the light source can do this. If the ray intersects some surface before the light source, this light source is obscured and its contribution is not considered. This process is demonstrated in Figure 8.16.

FIGURE 8.16
Computing shadows.

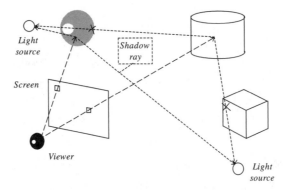

It must be noted that you are looking for the first intersection in between the light source and the point where the light model is evaluated. Therefore, the complexity of casting a shadow ray is somewhat smaller than that of a visibility ray. You stop after locating the first intersection, so you may not have to examine all objects. You must also be careful not to consider the intersections that occur after the light source or before the point.

This can be achieved by constructing a ray with a co-directed vector that is a difference of the light source position and the given view point. With such a ray, intersections before the point will resolve with a negative parameter t and intersections after the light source will resolve with a parameter t larger than one.

Adding considerations for shadows considerably improves the realism of the rendered images. Figure 8.17 demonstrates a scene produced using the ray-tracing algorithm extended to generate shadows.

FIGURE 8.17
Ray-tracing with consideration for shadows.

Figure 8.17 demonstrates that all the shadows are sharp, precisely delimiting illuminated regions from shadowed regions. In many realistic environments, however, the shadows have softer edges, where the illuminated region softly becomes shadowed. This is because real-life light sources are not ideal points but have a certain surface area. To obtain more realistic soft shadows, you must somehow compute not just whether the light source is visible, but also how much of it is visible. Thus, regions just on the edge of the light source visibility will gradually become shadowed as the area of the visible light source diminishes.

As previously noted, illumination in a point can be contributed to by the light that comes not directly from the light source, but rather is reflected into the given point by some other surface. Thus, the illumination model can be generalized in a way to include both the direct contribution of light sources and the contribution of light that is reflected onto the surface by the environment:

$$I_{point} = I_{lightsource} + I_{environment}$$

With the most popular Phong illumination model, and specular reflection in particular, it is easy to find some additional contributions of the environment by the process known as *recursive ray-tracing*. In specular reflection, there is a predominant direction of reflection.

Earlier, this direction was examined to find out whether some light source produced a specular highlight in a point. In this case, you must examine this direction to also find if there is something else in the environment that may create a highlight. Thus, by applying the ray-tracing algorithm recursively, you can cast a *reflection ray* in the direction from which the light should have arrived if it was reflected by objects in the environment, and include the obtained value as a contribution to the local illumination model. Figure 8.18 illustrates a process in which both shadows and environmental reflections are computed.

FIGURE 8.18

Computing shadows and environmental reflections.

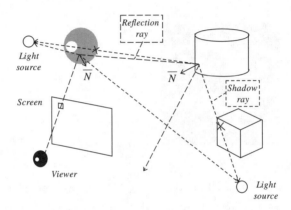

Of course, this process is recursive. In order to compute proper lighting, you may have to spawn yet another reflection ray somewhere along the path. In practice, there is always a limit to the number of times a ray can bounce because, at some point, the possible additional contributions become quite negligible.

The contribution of the environmental reflection must also be weighted by a coefficient that depends on the reflecting capabilities of the surface. Although this coefficient is logically the same for any light—either coming from a light source or coming from some bright object—it is common to separate the two so that you can have a better handle on the production of images. Figure 8.19 demonstrates a rendering computed by recursive ray-tracing.

FIGURE 8.19
Ray-tracing with consideration for shadows and environmental reflections.

The reflections in Figure 8.19 contribute nicely to the realism of the image. It should be noted that such reflections may show parts of the world that are not directly visible to the viewer. It is expensive to model extra objects in the virtual world and to always compute light interactions between objects that are never directly visible. In such situations, you can place the objects that are directly visible inside a cube, the internal polygons of which carry texture maps representing static pictures of the environment that is not directly visible. By doing that, you can avoid extra modeling effort since the pictures may even be taken from the real-life environments. It also shortens the depth of the recursive rays, which speeds up the computation.

Generally, ray-tracing can be coded in a very compact implementation thanks to a uniform framework that is used to solve different tasks, such as visibility, shadows, and different components of the illumination model.

It must be noted that the ray-tracing algorithm can be extended in a number of ways to account for other illumination effects. For instance, the refraction of light through semi-transparent objects can be described. Casting a recursive ray into the proper direction inside the object can help with semi-transparency.

There are also possibilities to account for light attenuation by introducing a function that describes how the intensity of light diminishes depending on the distance traveled.

It is often interesting to attempt to model irregularities of surfaces. You can do this by assigning a texture map to the surface where each cell stores its own diffuse reflection coefficient, rather than having a single coefficient for the whole surface. To model irregularities even further, it is possible to associate *bump-maps* with the surfaces. These describe how the normal vector is perturbed across the surface so that a slightly different direction of reflection, for instance, would be computed in different points.

Combining these and many other possible effects is quite straightforward under the unifying framework of ray-tracing, and you can produce quite impressive images using this technique.

However, there are a number of problems with recursive ray-tracing. Often there are some unnatural visual clues present in ray-traced images. Specular reflection is treated differently depending on the nature of the light. There is an approximating function in the case of light sources that allows for producing extensive highlights. On the other hand, the contribution of the environment is computed by following the reflected ray. If the same strategy is used for light sources as well as environment, all highlights produced by light sources will be one pixel big at most. In other words, an adjustment for surface imperfections is made for light sources but not for environmental reflections. Because of this dual strategy of treating two kinds of light differently, reflections will often look too good, giving the ray-traced images a surreal look.

Another fundamental problem with the modification of the Phong illumination model that allows computing specular reflection of the environment is that it doesn't consider the contribution of light reflected by the environment in a diffuse manner. Any diffuse surface emanates light in all directions. Some of this light must end up in the point where you evaluate the illumination model. The model, however, doesn't consider that, and the only possible modification is not feasible. Since the light reflected somewhere in a diffuse manner can arrive at a given point from potentially any direction, the only solution is to shoot rays into all directions to find the necessary contributions. Considering that this is also a recursive process, the scheme is not computationally feasible. The next section returns to this problem and briefly considers a method that resolves illumination of multiple diffuse surfaces.

Overall, ray-tracing is one of the most important tools of computer graphics. When visual appearance is very important and the task is not interactive, this method is extremely attractive. Its computational demands, however, make it less than admissible for many interactive tasks. It is also possible to resort to ray-tracing for preprocessing some of the illumination effects of an application, such as precomputed shadows, by using world-to-screen viewing.

Radiosity

As noted in the previous section, ray-tracing generally ignores interactions between diffuse surfaces, or to be more precise, it accounts for such interactions complementing illumination with a dubious ambient light component. However, in many practical settings these interactions are predominant. For example, consider purely diffuse surface *B* in Figure 8.20. Surface *B* is directed away from the only light source in the scene. Thus, according to the model of diffuse illumination, it is essentially dim except for ambient light. This, however, is not quite true. This surface is placed next to a diffuse surface *A*, and some light reflected from *A* must illuminate surface *B* (see Figure 8.20).

FIGURE 8.20
Contribution of diffuse reflectors to the illumination.

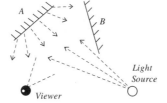

In order to account for such interactions, computer graphics turned to the theory of heat transfer. The idea is that in a closed environment, there is a balance of energy. Assuming that a hypothetical surface is capable of both emitting and reflecting light, the amount of light emanated by a surface patch (referred to as the *radiosity* of the patch) is in balance with the light produced internally plus the reflected light that is contributed by other patches. This can be expressed as follows:

$$B_{patch} = E_{patch} + k_{patch} B_{environment}$$

In this equation, *B* expresses the radiosity of the patch, *E* expresses its emission intensity, and *k* expresses its reflective capability. When the scene is modeled by a set of plane surface patches, assuming that they are small enough so that radiosity across the patch is constant, the equation can be restated in such a way that the radiosity of each patch is described in terms of the radiosities of other patches:

$$B_i = E_i + k_i \sum_{j \neq i} F_{i,j} B_j$$

In this equation, $F_{i,j}$ is a coefficient that describes how much light from patch j reached the currently considered patch i. As you can see, the radiosity approach allows for the uniform treatment of light sources and reflecting surfaces. A patch with a non-zero E is a light source. Coefficients F are referred to as *form factors*, and they essentially describe the geometry of the scene. In order to compute the form factors, you must take into account the orientations of the two patches, their areas, and whether or not the patches are obscured from one another. This may prove to be an expensive geometric problem, but once the form factors are computed, the radiosity of each patch in the scene can be found by solving a system of linear equations. By grouping all unknown radiosities B, the following system of linear equations results:

$$B_i - k_i \sum_{j \neq i} F_{i,j} B_j = E_i$$

This can be restated as the following matrix equation:

$$
\begin{bmatrix}
1 & -k_1 F_{1,2} & \cdots & -k_1 F_{1,n} \\
-k_2 F_{2,1} & 1 & \cdots & -k_2 F_{2,n} \\
\cdots & \cdots & \cdots\cdots & \cdots \\
-k_n F_{n,1} & -k_n F_{n,2} & \cdots & 1
\end{bmatrix}
\begin{bmatrix}
B_1 \\
B_2 \\
\cdot\cdot \\
B_n
\end{bmatrix}
=
\begin{bmatrix}
E_1 \\
E_2 \\
\cdots \\
E_n
\end{bmatrix}
$$

Note that when using the achromatic color model, each element of this equation is a scalar, and for the RGB model, each element is a three-tuple. In the latter case, there are in fact three matrix equations, one for each of the pure wavelengths. By solving the equation, you obtain the radiosity values for every surface patch. The scene can then be rendered by any of the visualization processes that account for found radiosity when drawing each patch.

It must be noted, however, that by assuming that the radiosity is constant across every patch, a relaxation is made. The effects of this relaxation are negligible only when the patches are very small. Thus, every practical scene must be subdivided into a large number of patches, which considerably increases the size of the matrix equation and the time required to solve it. On the positive side, the radiosity considers only diffuse reflections, which are the same in all directions and thus independent from a position of the viewer. Therefore, when the scene has static geometry and lighting, the same radiosity solution can be reused for any location of the camera.

Overall, radiosity is a very powerful technique that allows you to render extremely realistic images. However, by definition this algorithm doesn't consider specular reflections, and it is difficult to introduce them into the radiosity framework. A popular approach is to use radiosity as a preprocessing stage before ray-tracing the scene. Doing it properly is not trivial, however. Some specular effects are caused by diffuse interactions, such as reflection of a diffuse surface against some specular surface, yet specular interactions may give rise to diffuse interactions. Accounting for all possible effects in a two-step process may not be feasible, thus many implementations limit themselves to the most common effects only.

Illumination in World-to-Screen Viewing

Unfortunately, unlike with screen-to-world methods, the introduction of illumination, both local and global, into world-to-screen viewing is much less elegant. Recall that with this method, an image of the virtual world is created by projecting individual primitives onto the screen space and then rasterizing them into the image bitmap. In ray-tracing, the illumination model is applied in every point in the world that is found to be visible on the screen. A similar approach is also possible in world-to-screen viewing. When you rasterize a primitive, you can evaluate the illumination model just before a point is to be placed into the image and thus adjust the pixel's color. There are several problems that are immediately apparent. World-to-screen algorithms in general, and rasterization algorithms in particular, are built for speed and interactive frame rates. These algorithms minimize the processing required to plot a single pixel. By evaluating the illumination model per pixel, the complexity of the very inner loop of visualization is pushed up considerably. Additionally, with the popular back-to-front rasterization strategy to eliminate hidden surfaces, many pixels in the image are overdrawn multiple times, thus throwing out the results of some expensive computations to illuminate pixels which were later overdrawn. In this respect, some approaches to hidden surface removal attempt to minimize on such situations. However, the fundamental problem remains: It is expensive to evaluate the illumination model in each rasterized pixel, let alone to consider global illumination effects.

Local World-to-Screen Illumination

A common strategy to deal with the problem of local illumination is to evaluate components of the model only in specific places on the primitive and to interpolate everywhere else. This is called *shading* the primitive. Gouraud shaded polygons that demonstrate an example of this approach were discussed in Chapter 3, "Rasterization." In its general framework, world-to-screen viewing can't really handle global illumination effects such as shadows and environmental reflections. Thus, these effects are achieved either by using special add-on techniques or they are not implemented at all. As the strength of computers increases, the latter alternative becomes less and less suitable so that dynamic illumination effects take the center stage today in most graphics applications.

This section briefly discusses shading algorithms, and then examines some techniques used to compute global illumination effects. Both types of algorithms (shading and global illumination effects), with few exceptions, are designed for polygonal patches. This is not a very big limitation, because for many other reasons, such as feasibility of fast rasterization or hidden surface removal, this primitive is the preferred one.

Obviously, the type of shading depends on the particular illumination model used and the relaxations that the developers are prepared to make. For instance, if you are prepared to assume that illumination stays constant across any polygon, the illumination model can be evaluated just once for each polygon, and regular rasterization can be done with the obtained color. This process is referred to as *ambient* or *flat* shading (see Figure 8.21).

FIGURE 8.21
Flat shading.

Of the three models considered (ambient, diffuse, and specular), an assumption that illumination is constant across the polygon definitely holds true in the case of ambient illumination. In the case of diffuse reflecting surfaces and the Bouknight illumination model, such an assumption holds true only if the polygon actually models a plane. In other words, it holds true if a polygon doesn't serve as an approximation to some curved surface and if there are only directional lights in the scene (that is, all light sources are infinitely distant). Recall that illumination in this model is computed as:

$$I_{reflected} = K_{ambient}I_{ambient} + K_{diffuse}I_{directed}(\overline{N} \cdot \overline{L})$$

The illumination depends on both the surface normal $\overline{N}$ and the direction toward the light source $\overline{L}$. When you are approximating some curved surface with polygons, the normal vector is not actually constant across the polygon (see Figure 8.23). If there are point light sources, the direction toward them also changes across the polygon. By assuming that illumination is constant, flat shading will produce a wrong result. However, since the goal of computer graphics is often to present recognizable representations of reality, not necessarily an exact copy, you may decide to live with such unrealistic images.

Thus, even in both Bouknight and Phong illumination, you can still decide to use ambient shading. In Phong illumination, if you happen to evaluate the model in the location of specular highlight, the whole polygon will be highlighted, which is quite unpleasant. On the other hand, it is possible to miss some specular highlight altogether, which also is undesirable.

The faceted look of flat-shaded polygonal mesh is also exaggerated due to the peculiarities of the human visual system, particularly the *Mach bands* effect, which is quite noticeable in Figure 8.21. Although each polygon does have constant coloring, it is still possible to see that close to the edge between a pair of polygons, the darker of the two looks even darker, whereas the lighter of the two looks lighter. The receptors in human eyes inhibit the neighboring receptors when brightly lit. Thus, the receptors on the darker side of the edge are inhibited by the neighbors on the lighter side, and thus give a weaker response signal. The receptors on the lighter side aren't inhibited enough because of their proximity to the area of the darker polygon, and thus have a higher response signal. This *latteral inhibition* of eye receptors is quite important for the human visual system. It is the first step for recognizing the contours of objects. For the particular method of flat shading, or even Gouraud shading done without enough shades, it may work to exaggerate a contour where you wouldn't actually want to stress one.

Thus, when the faceted look of ambient shading does become unbearable, a common technique to improve the appearance is to employ *Gouraud* shading. In this method, you evaluate the illumination model in the vertices of the polygons and interpolate the intensity across. Figure 8.22 demonstrates this approach.

FIGURE 8.22
Gouraud shading.

This shading method is generally suitable for the Bouknight illumination model that describes reflection from diffuse surfaces. By smoothing intensity values, this shading technique also conceals the faceted look of the approximation of curved surfaces with polygonal patches.

In order to compute the illumination, you must find the normals in the vertices of the polygons. When you are approximating a smooth surface with planar patches, the normals in the vertices can be obtained by averaging the normals computed for the polygons it belongs to. The normals for polygons can be found by computing vector products (see Figure 8.23).

FIGURE 8.23
Approximating a curved patch with plane polygons.

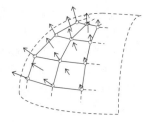

This shading method also allows you to approximate diffuse planes that are unequally illuminated with point light sources. However, it is not particularly suitable for specular surfaces or the Phong illumination model. By definition, interpolative shading allows for only linear change of intensity across the polygon. Intensity response of specular reflection is non-linear:

$$I_{reflected} = K_{ambient}I_{ambient} + I_{directed}(K_{diffuse}(\overline{N} \cdot \overline{L}) + k_{specular}(\overline{R} \cdot \overline{V})^n)$$

Thus, it is possible to completely miss the specular highlight when it happens to be inside the polygon. When the highlight happens to be in the vertex of the polygon, the interpolation still computes a wrong result by proceeding with linear intensity falloff, whereas the Phong illumination model requires a steeper, non-linear one. Similar to the situation with ambient shading, you may choose to live with such problems if the polygons are small enough and quality demands are not high.

When you must portray specular surfaces correctly, it is possible to use the *Phong shading* method (not to be confused with the related, but different, Phong illumination model). With this algorithm, the illumination model is effectively evaluated in every rasterized pixel and only a component of the model is interpolated across the polygon.

Consider the equation of the Phong illumination model presented above. Notably, the normal vector contributes to the computation and, since you often approximate curved surfaces with polygons, it is possible to interpolate the normal across the polygon and use it in the illumination computations at each point (see Figure.8.24(c)).

FIGURE 8.24
Ambient, Gouraud, and Phong shadings.

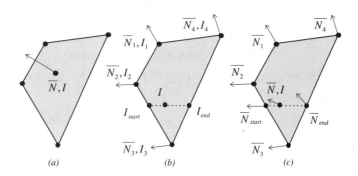

Each component of the normal vector is interpolated separately, thus obtaining an approximate normal direction in each point on the polygon. It must be noted that it is important to have normal vectors of unit length for the computations. This, however, is not preserved during interpolation. Thus, it may be necessary to renormalize the vector at every pixel. The illumination computation to be applied at each pixel using the interpolated normal is still fairly expensive. However, as mentioned earlier, you can speed it up by using the halfway vector alternative formulation and fixing the viewer's position at infinity. You can also attempt to precompute a component of the equation with the exponent $(\overline{R} \cdot \overline{V})^n$ (or $(\overline{N} \cdot \overline{H})^n$ in the alternative formulation) and use table lookups in the runtime.

Some hybrid shading methods also exist that attempt to model specular reflections with a lower cost than that of Phong shading. For instance, Gouraud shading could be extended in such a way that the light intensity of the specular component is computed in every vertex. When rasterization is performed, the diffuse component also computed in every vertex is linearly interpolated, whereas the specular component is interpolated in some non-linear way. The two components are added together to obtain the current pixel color. This method avoids many of the complex calculations of Phong shading, yet it is not without problems. For instance, since the illumination is computed in vertices only, a specular highlight in the middle of the polygon will still be missed.

The considered shading methods allow you to introduce the illumination models in the framework of world-to-screen viewing. However, the presence of multiple objects in the scene may cause other illumination effects, such as shadows or environmental reflections. You have already seen how to resolve mutual illumination by diffuse surfaces. The radiosity algorithm is applicable to world-to-screen visualization as a preprocessing stage. Similar to ray-tracing combined with radiosity, the radiosity solution can be reused in multiple frames, assuming that illumination and scene geometry don't change from frame to frame. It happens, for instance, when you generate a walkthrough or fly-by of the virtual scene. Generally, the demands of interactive visualization are such that other global illumination effects are too expensive to compute in the runtime and they have to be precomputed as well.

The requirements of particular applications have to be analyzed and weighed against the limitation of flexibility that such precomputation unfortunately imposes.

Global World-to-Screen Illumination

There are multiple algorithms that allow you to compute shadows. They can be roughly differentiated into two groups. Algorithms in the first group precompute geometrical information required for the representation of shadows. Other algorithms compute shadows dynamically during the scene rasterization. As just noted, the first class of algorithms can't handle dynamically changing scenes.

There are two approaches to precomputing shadows. A common one is to subdivide the scene in such a way that each primitive is either completely illuminated or completely hidden with respect to every light source. Alternatively, the subdivision can be just fine enough so that all polygons in the screen are very small. With the latter subdivision, an algorithm similar to radiosity will result.

Another approach is to store shadows implicitly in the texture maps associated with the primitives. This approach requires, of course, the presence of a texture map for every primitive. This requires a considerable amount of resources and may not be feasible in some settings. A common solution is to separate a texture map storing basic color from a light map storing illumination intensities. During the texturing process, the colors from both maps are added. This is known as *multi-texturing*. The advantage of this approach is that the light maps can be of significantly lower resolution than texture maps. Textures are often shared by numerous surfaces in the scene, and with this approach it is possible to have a shared texture but separate light maps for different polygons.

To precompute the shadows, you must essentially solve the visibility problem from the point of view of each light source. Fragments of primitives that are visible from the position of the light source are illuminated, whereas everything else must be shadowed. Figure 8.25 demonstrates a *shadow volume* approach.

FIGURE 8.25
A shadow volume.

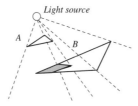

As you can see, illuminated polygons shadow a particular volume of space. This volume can be described as a polyhedron formed from a polygon casting the shadow on its top, and as planes formed by shadows of the polygon's edges. Other polygons can be clipped against this volume, separating into completely shadowed and completely illuminated types. The illuminated polygons must be marked as such for a particular light source so that at the rasterization stage, you know which light sources to use in the illumination of every polygon.

Complexity of this operation is, of course, quite high, but it is possible to exploit some properties of the synthetic scenes to reduce the amount of work. For instance, an individual polygon is most often a part of some polygonal object. Thus, you can compute the shadow volume for a whole object instead of individual polygons. By minimizing the number of shadow volumes, you can reduce the amount of processing and the number of subdivisions quite considerably. It is also important to note that this method is used as a preprocessing step before the runtime. Thus, minimizing the number of subdivisions is more important than performance concerns.

Shadow volumes can be used very effectively with a BSP-tree representation of the world, not unlike the way this partitioning structure was used for the purposes of beam-tree hidden surface removal. With a BSP-tree representation, it is easy to obtain a back-to-front ordering of polygons and it is also easy to obtain a front-to-back ordering. It only requires reversing the order of the recursive calls in the traversing procedure. A front-to-back order obtained with respect to the light source immediately shows which polygons are capable of shadowing other polygons. Obviously, polygons in the front cast shadows onto polygons in the back. Therefore, polygons in the list may shadow their followers but not the other way around. It is possible to use the shadow volume approach and perform the necessary subdivisions while traveling down the list. An important thing to notice is that an effective BSP structure does not change as a result of such subdivisions against the shadow volumes, assuming that you allow multiple polygons in each node of the tree. When you split any polygon into shadowed and illuminated pieces, all these pieces still belong to the same plane and, thus, can be stored in a combined list in the original place in the tree without violating binary partitioning.

Most other algorithms that generate shadows also involve solving visibility from the light source point of view. A *shadow Z-buffer* algorithm is an elegant extension to a popular hidden surface removal strategy, which can be used to solve the light source visibility dynamically. Consider Figure 8.26.

FIGURE 8.26
Shadow Z-buffer.

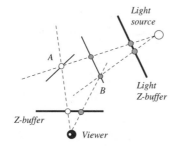

In Figure 8.26 you can see two Z-buffers, one for the image being generated and another one for the light source point of view, referred to as the *light Z-buffer*. If you compute the light Z-buffer before rendering the scene, it is possible to adjust actual Z-buffer–based rasterization to account for shadows. When a pixel has to be drawn onto the screen and into the Z-buffer, you can also find its projection onto the plane in front of the light source and check whether the Z coordinate of this projection is the one actually stored in the light Z-buffer. If that's the case, this point must be visible by the light source and you can illuminate it in the main image. For example, consider point *A* in Figure 8.26. When its visibility is checked in the light Z-buffer, a smaller Z coordinate corresponding to an obscuring point is discovered. Thus, point *A* is shadowed. On the other hand, this is not the case with point *B*, so rasterization of this point has to account for illumination from the light source.

An apparent drawback of this algorithm is in the necessity of keeping a separate light Z-buffer for every light source. Also, by introducing extra processing into the very inner loop of rasterization, the complexity of viewing is increased. What's even worse, due to its nature, the Z-buffer algorithm often overwrites previous values for some pixels. Thus, shadowing and illumination may be computed for points that will not even be present in the resulting image. A possible approach to improve on this situation is to do rasterization of the image first and add shadow computations as a post-processing step.

Thus, you compute the shadowing information for every point that appears in the final image. It must be noted that, in this case, since the illumination model is additive, the same light Z-buffer can be used for all light sources, processing them consecutively and adjusting the image as a result of each computation.

In the section on ray-tracing, environmental specular reflections were solved by using the regular ray-tracing framework. Essentially, the visibility in the direction of specular reflection was computed, thus finding how the environment reflects from a shiny surface. A similar approach, within a different framework, is also possible in the case of world-to-screen viewing. Consider Figure 8.27.

FIGURE 8.27
Computing environmental mapping.

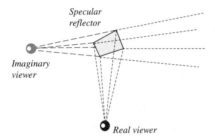

Specular reflector

Imaginary viewer

Real viewer

Figure 8.27 shows a specular reflecting patch viewed by the camera. Obviously, because of its specular capability, this patch will show a reflection of the environment. Since it is known that the reflection direction is mirrored about the normal of the patch, it is possible to compute the reflection as a separate image. You can do this with the help of an auxiliary viewing camera looking in that reflection direction and then applying the image generated for the auxiliary camera as an extra texture map in the original viewing process, perhaps using multi-texturing to augment the actual texture of the polygons.

Multiple invocations of the viewing algorithm are expensive, of course, so it is common to precompute the environmental reflection as texture maps and completely substitute texture mappings for environmental reflections. A popular approach is *cubic mapping*, where a polygon is considered to be inside a cube whose internal surfaces contain pictures of the environment. It is necessary to compute which parts of these internal pictures should be reflected and further use those visible pieces as additional textures.

In some instances, especially in computer games, it may be necessary to have dynamic, geometrically correct reflections. This is done, for example, when modeling mirrors in interior environments. An effect of the mirror can be achieved by proper modeling of the scene (see Figure 8.28).

FIGURE 8.28
Geometrical modeling of a specular reflector.

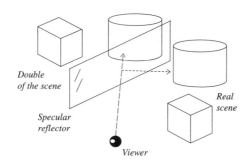

In Figure 8.28, a reflector is modeled by introducing a mirror copy of the scene in the virtual world representation. When this is accompanied by proper color adjustments in the copy that describes the reflection image, a viewer is left with the impression of seeing a reflection of the scene. As with everything else, the decision as to whether to implement such schemes depends on the application's nature and its specific goals.

Summary

Illumination is of tremendous importance in computer graphics. Generally, each color can be represented as an energy distribution in the spectral range. Due to the characteristics of human visual perception, colors can be represented in a simpler manner, such as red, green, and blue triple. Many algorithms that are commonly used to model illumination are of a heuristic nature, such as the Phong illumination model.

When there are multiple objects in the scene, the problem of global illumination arises because the objects reflect light in different ways, contributing to the illumination of other objects. Ray-tracing computes some global illumination effects, such as shadows and specular reflections. The radiosity algorithm resolves all global diffuse interactions so that diffuse colors for all polygons in the scene could be found. Both local and global illuminations are complicated in world-to-screen viewing, mostly because of the performance constraints. Local illumination in the world-to-screen viewing method is approximated by shading algorithms, and the global illumination effects rely on special add-on techniques.

CHAPTER 9

Application Design

The previous chapters examined numerous techniques of 3D computer graphics that allow for modeling and visualization of virtual scenes on a computer screen. All these algorithms must, however, combine together in a structured way inside a real-life computer program. Each level in the rendering pipeline must efficiently communicate with other levels. The rendering pipeline must be built with respect to the data structures representing virtual scenes and the algorithms most suitable for their viewing. The method for removing hidden surfaces must be properly placed in the pipeline. Advantage must be taken of existing hardware resources or common libraries that may take care of parts of the process in an efficient way.

Although writing efficient, readable, and well-organized computer programs can be considered an art rather than a science, this chapter nevertheless attempts to examine some general rules that can aid in this endeavor.

General Approaches to Design

Different applications have different purposes and goals. Depending on the application's value or other external factors, different amounts of resources (including development time) are going to be allocated for the purposes of development. The product itself may be aimed at a particular market and, thus, at a specific hardware platform. Combined with the particulars of the application's domain, these serve as arguments for the decision process producing, as the result, the implementation strategy and the application's design.

Before you consider the design and implementation strategies, it is always helpful to evaluate the application's goals from the point of view of some common criteria. Although the list of criteria is not rigid, some of them are likely to be encountered in most projects. For instance, the desired *quality* of what the application does and its *efficiency* or speed at doing it are two important criteria. *Flexibility*, such as the ability to work with different data formats, is another criterion. Depending on the long-term goals of the project, considerations of *maintainability*, *reusability*, and *portability* may be important as well.

As an example, the performance criterion is likely to be very important for a computer game. Thus, it will be necessary to attempt to stay close to hardware and use all the resources and hardware assistance available. Flexibility may be of lesser importance for a game. Thus, modeling tools and the format in which the data structures are stored on disk may not be a mainstream or a particularly flexible solution. A game is often aimed at a single platform, which allows for using specific, efficient tools and resources available just on that platform. However, for marketing reasons it becomes necessary at times to introduce the same game on different platforms. This undoubtedly affects the design and the decision of which tools and hardware resources can be used.

An application in the field of computer-aided design may not require high frame rates or high efficiency. However, flexibility and portability are likely to be given a high priority.

Photorealism, and hence the quality of the produced images, may be very desirable in the case of an interactive game, yet it is not as important as efficiency and the ability to achieve interactive frame rates. Failure to achieve the former may make the game less attractive, whereas a slow frame rate makes it unusable. On the opposite side of the spectrum, an application generating images for animated sequences to be used in advertising or movies will, most certainly, require the highest possible quality of images with the speed at which they are produced being secondary.

Finally, a flight simulator for the Department of Defense will have a somewhat larger amount of resources allotted for its development compared with, say, a racing game for a Game Boy. Whatever exciting goals may be put forward, at one point or another the goals will have to be matched against available resources.

On the other side of the puzzle are all the different resources that will be available, such as targeted hardware, allocated development time, existing code base, libraries, tools, and so on.

Once you assign the weights to the criteria and figure out what resources are available, it becomes possible to consider the implementation alternatives available for the selected set and attempt to find which strategy provides a match between available resources and foreseen goals.

Before you start to build an appropriate design, it is necessary, of course, to examine all available literature and documented experiences of other developers related to the question. It is surprising how many of the ideas that we believe to be original were actually tried by somebody else before. Knowing what was done before saves a lot of time and minimizes the risk quite substantially.

In reality, it is never possible to satisfy all the criteria that were chosen. Most of them are interdependent and, at times, almost pair-wise exclusive. For instance, quality and speed are often unattainable together. Similarly, portability and efficiency may contradict one another. However, the very purpose of the assigned weight factors is to guide thinking into the most important direction, sacrificing less important factors for the overall project. See Figure 9.1.

FIGURE 9.1
Application design.

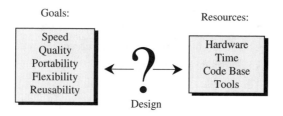

Design

It may require several iterations of going back and forth and adjusting the goals or looking for new resources until a suitable design can be imagined. Even then, there are always unknown variables and some of the solutions or ideas planned for at the design stage may not work as planned once the software development starts.

A common solution is to prototype difficult bits and pieces of the software ahead of actual development so that the risks are minimized.

To satisfy some of the criteria, such as quality and efficiency, you have to choose a suitable algorithmic solution. This has been discussed at length throughout the previous chapters.

Other criteria, such as flexibility, reusability, and portability may depend on the selected algorithm, but also will require special approaches in writing and structuring the code.

For instance, in Chapter 1, "Hardware Interface," you saw a way to provide applications with some portability. It was necessary to separate the application into hardware-dependent and hardware-independent parts and to define the interface between the two. The first part had to be implemented differently depending on the particular hardware so that the remaining hardware-independent part could remain portable.

Producing reusable code and introducing the necessary level of flexibility may also require structuring the application's code in a particular way. In doing so, it often helps to employ specific programming paradigms.

Since the invention of the first computer and its programming mechanism, considerable attention has been paid to paradigms that aid in designing and writing computer programs. First came the abstraction that permits separating the program into independent subroutines or functions, followed by the mechanism to construct derived data types, such as structures and arrays, from basic data types such as integers or characters. The concept of *structured programming*, which appeared a bit later, defined the minimal number of flow control statements (for example, conditional if, while loop, and so on) that should be provided by a programming language. More recently, the paradigm of *object-oriented* programming came about, providing the tools for code sharing and reuse.

Although all the paradigms had a lot of promise in the task of easing programming when they were first introduced, in a sense, those promises were realized only partially. Some of the programs written today are as cryptic and unreadable as those written during the dawn of computers. It is not surprising that the tools and strategies available today don't relieve us from the necessity to analyze and to think. Failure to do that properly, and to only rely on complex tools, can result in incredible debugging problems, loss of performance, and unusable products.

That is not to say that some specific programming paradigms must be ignored completely. Quite the opposite—they should be used but should be employed with care. The following sections look into several such techniques, including object-oriented programming, approaches to scripting, techniques to handle errors, and the idea of state machines.

Object-Oriented Programming

Object-oriented programming is a methodology to shape an application's internal structure. In this methodology, data and code are tied together quite closely, as opposed to the imperative style of programming with separated data structures and procedures/functions. When programming in the object-oriented way, you generally rely on the special features that the languages supporting this paradigm, such as C++ or Objective C, provide. Both of these languages extend the basic C language with additional constructs. Whereas C++ is today's favorite, Objective C was used extensively as a high-level development language for NeXT machines and today it is inherited in the newest version of the Macintosh operating system, MacOS X.

This book is perhaps an inappropriate venue in which to discuss the syntax and other details of these languages. There is an overwhelming amount of literature on that subject. What's interesting, however, are the general ideas of the object- oriented paradigm and how they are pertinent to structuring 3D graphics applications.

In the role of unifying code and data, the important concepts are those of *abstract data types*, *inheritance*, and *polymorphism*.

In languages such as C or Pascal there was a predefined number of data types, such as integers, character, or floats. The derivation rules for new data types were present, but their power was limited. Although it was possible to describe the storage layout of a new data type (such as creating an array of integers or some structure consisting of multiple fields), the new data type was relatively crippled. It was impossible to properly describe the operations that were applicable to the new data type. Therefore, the data types were unequal in their strength: fundamental data types had some inherent operations specifically designed for them. Newly derived data types did not.

The concept of an abstract data type introduced in object-oriented languages improved this situation. In an object-oriented language, you can define both the storage layout for a new data type and the type's particular operations. In this context, types are also referred to as *classes*. Individual instances of the classes are called *objects*, hence *object-oriented programming*. This distinction is the same as between the fundamental data type of integers and a specific integer variable. Particular ways of describing classes in Objective C and C++ are presented in Listing 9.1.

LISTING 9.1

Abstract Data Type Definitions in Objective C and C++.

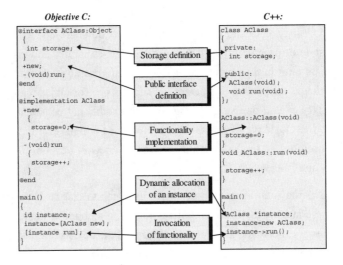

As you can see in Listing 9.1, the two languages, although having different syntax, are relatively similar in the functionality they provide. Perhaps the biggest conceptual difference between the two is that Objective C makes most type-related decisions dynamically in the runtime, whereas C++ performs mostly static typing. Thus, when some ambiguity exists as to which function to call in C++, such problems are resolved during the compile time. In Objective C they are done when the program runs. The former approach often offers an additional level of flexibility although it may incur certain cost, which, in the particular case of Objective C, is quite minimal.

Using the mechanism of abstract data types, you can, for example, describe a data structure for a geometric model. It will be necessary to define the operations that this model can do. Perhaps it can move, display itself, or be illuminated. Further, this data type can be used throughout the application as if it were one of the basic types.

This approach is extremely beneficial for the structure of the programs. The programs are more readable. Furthermore, by providing the valid operations for each data type as its public interface, the parts of the program using this type need not be aware of the type's internal structure. Encapsulated internal structure of the type may even change in the future, but since the use of the type is limited to its public interface, such a change, properly done, doesn't affect the code that employs it. This consideration is very important for the application's maintainability. Well-written types are also good candidates for reuse in future projects.

In 3D graphics applications, a large number of situations exist where the use of abstract data types is clearly beneficial. Besides the models of different geometric entities, this is also the case, for example, with fixed-point numbers and 3D transformations described in the matrix form. All of these have a well-defined set of operations and are natural for implementation as classes.

There are certain dangers that are usually associated with using abstract data types. Although the efficiency of the produced code isn't significantly worse when compiled by most object-oriented languages compared to imperative languages (such as C++ versus straight C), the danger of the efficiency loss comes from the way developers are tempted, sometimes, to write the programs. If you attempt to encapsulate everything and abuse dynamic allocation and destruction of small objects, the cost may become quite significant. For instance, at times it is tempting to encapsulate a 3D vertex as a class. Although this can be valid and helpful in the case of a 3D editor, a rendering pipeline built for efficiency may only suffer from it. The vertices are often manipulated in streams where a different amount of data is associated with a vertex at different stages of the pipeline. There also may not be a significant number of operations pertinent to an isolated vertex in such a pipeline.

Generally, there is little doubt that abstract data types help structure the higher-level modules of applications. Employing it for the lower levels may also be beneficial but should be done with care.

Object-oriented languages also provide other important principles that aid interactions between types. A type can inherit properties of the parent type or even several parent types. This allows different, yet related, modules to share certain functionality and thus, most importantly for development, some source code. For instance, it is possible to organize types describing different 3D models in such a way that a type describing polygonal solid bodies is inherited from a wireframe. Both types rely on the vertex set, and a solid body type can inherit the functionality, enabling you to apply the transformations to this set.

Another important principle is that of polymorphism. It allows you to write generic algorithms that work for objects of different types. The polymorphic types share some functionality interface but may achieve such functionality in different ways. For instance, types implementing different 3D models are polymorphic in the sense that all of them have the ability to render themselves. The rendering may be done differently depending on the type, but the algorithms using this functionality often need not be aware of the details. These algorithms may work with generic models, only asking the models to render themselves when required.

For example, this situation is feasible for landscape visualization for a flight simulator. Such an application is likely to rely on the data structure in which the surface is separated into square cells, each of which may contain some 3D models representing objects located in the described region of the landscape. Naturally, the objects may be of different types, either wireframes representing power line towers, or polygonal models representing buildings, or even sets of points representing lights on runways. The algorithm rendering the landscape must first rasterize the surface polygon and then the objects located on that polygon. If the types representing 3D models are polymorphic with respect to their rendering, the landscape type can be written without regard to the internal structure of the models and rely on their common polymorphic functionality, which enables the models to render themselves. Thus, new models can be easily added or implementation of existing ones can be changed without affecting the landscape class itself.

Summarizing, object-oriented programming is a very important tool to achieve the criterion of code reusability. If used properly, it also helps to create clear and easily understandable code, and at the same time provides an opportunity for code sharing and increased maintainability and reuse of applications.

Error Handling

It is hard to overestimate the importance of good error handling. If testing for critical situations is properly built into the code, the amount of time saved is enormous. Graphics applications are no exception. Perhaps this is even more important for graphics since this kind of application is fairly difficult to debug. Too much data is often flowing between parts of the program (even when drawing simple shapes) and it is not always easy to tell valid data from invalid data. Thus, anything done to catch bugs early on has a potential of saving you many hours, if not days.

Certain mechanisms exist to simplify coding error handling. These range from simple assert macros provided in C to exception handling mechanisms present in C++.

The main difficulty of a straightforward approach to error handling is in the amount of code that must be written. Every function may potentially encounter some critical condition. If the error condition is reported in a function's return value, the calling function must check that value and continue handling the critical situation. This snowballs very fast. Every function must handle its own errors as well as all functions it calls.

The standard library of the C language has two special functions for error handling. These functions help to avoid passing the information about errors that occurred through the chain of function invocations.

This mechanism is quite interesting. The function `setjmp` is used to mark some place in the program as the beginning of the error handler. When invoked, this function returns a value of zero. Further on, some error may occur deep in the chain of function invocations. It is possible to return immediately to the spot marked with `setjmp` by calling the `longjmp` function. When that happens, the execution resumes from the spot where `setjmp` is located as if `setjmp` was just called and now returns a nonzero value (in fact any value specified as a parameter to `setjmp`). See Listing 9.2.

LISTING 9.2

Error Handling in C

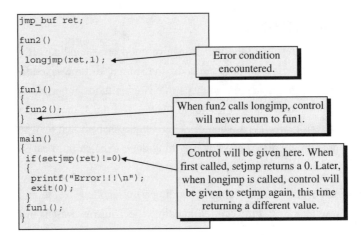

```
jmp_buf ret;

fun2()
{
  longjmp(ret,1);         ◄──── Error condition
}                                encountered.

fun1()
{
  fun2();                 ◄──── When fun2 calls longjmp, control
}                                will never return to fun1.

main()
{
  if(setjmp(ret)!=0)      ◄──── Control will be given here. When
  {                              first called, setjmp returns a 0. Later,
    printf("Error!!!\n");        when longjmp is called, control will
    exit(0);                     be given to setjmp again, this time
  }                              returning a different value.
  fun1();
}
```

C++ has a provision for a similar mechanism. It also allows skipping a chain of invocations to directly reach an error handler. In C++ this is known as the *exception handling* mechanism. There are three special keywords provided: try, catch, and throw. The catch keyword is used to indicate the beginning of the exception handler. The try keyword delimits the statements of the program where exceptions could occur. Every catch block of statements must follow a try block. The throw keyword is used when a critical situation is encountered and control should be given to the error handler (see Listing 9.3).

LISTING 9.3

Error Handling in C++

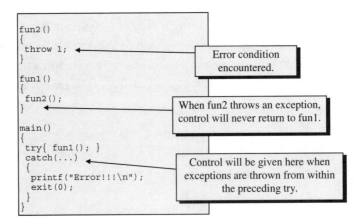

```
fun2()
{
  throw 1;                ◄──── Error condition
}                                encountered.

fun1()
{
  fun2();                 ◄──── When fun2 throws an exception,
}                                control will never return to fun1.

main()
{
  try{ fun1(); }
  catch(...)              ◄──── Control will be given here when
  {                              exceptions are thrown from within
    printf("Error!!!\n");        the preceding try.
    exit(0);
  }
}
```

The main difference between the two mechanisms (`setjmp` and exception handling) is that exception handling permits you to automatically deallocate local objects created on the chain of function invocations, which leads to the place where the exception was thrown. This is not done when `longjmp` is called.

The use of these mechanisms is clearly beneficial. It becomes possible to concentrate error handling in one place and to indicate new critical situations with only minimal effort. Thus, it helps maintainability and reusability of applications.

State Machine

Graphics applications operate with large amounts of data. These data are often passed as parameters to different functions. In many situations, it is possible to minimize the parameter passing and thus potentially increase an application's efficiency. The straightforward technique of *state machines* is discussed in this section.

Consider an example. There are a lot of different parameters specifying how geometric primitives must be drawn. For instance, a polygon can have a base color, a texture map, various parameters describing what shading method should be used, and so on. It also so happens that when multiple polygons are sequentially drawn, many will share the same drawing parameters. For instance, the base color may well be the same for all polygons belonging to a certain object. It is natural to attempt to minimize on parameter passing by exploiting this fact. In a graphics library, some functions could be responsible for setting current drawing attributes and others could be performing the drawing itself. The application that uses the library must first call the functions to specify drawing parameters followed by any number of calls to functions drawing the primitives themselves. The graphics library retains the drawing parameters in its internal storage.

When a primitive is to be drawn, the library uses its current *state*; that is, the current values of its internal variables storing drawing parameters that were previously set (see Figure 9.2). Such a library operates as a *state machine*.

FIGURE 9.2
Graphics library as a state machine.

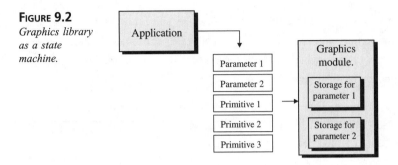

Figure 9.2 illustrates that there is less data passed to a state machine than in the situation when all drawing parameters must be specified for every primitive (referred to as a *stateless machine*), as illustrated in Figure 9.3.

FIGURE 9.3
Graphics library as a stateless machine.

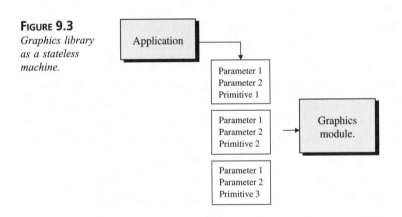

It must be noted, however, that the approach in Figure 9.2 worked only because several primitives shared some parameters. If that was not the case, parameter-setting functions should have been called before every primitive, which would not have produced any savings. Due to a higher number of function calls, the performance may have even deteriorated. Thus, depending on the kind of data expected, it may be perfectly valid not to use the state machine approach.

Another important consideration for the design stage has to do with the media of parameter passing between the application and the graphics library. Many different situations can be imagined. For instance, the application may be linked with the library. If that is the case, both will share common memory and thus a large amount of information can be passed with the help of a single pointer. If a data structure describing a primitive's geometry includes all the drawing parameters (colors, textures, perhaps geometric transformations, and so on.), they all could be passed to the graphics library by just sending one pointer to that structure. If the applications and the library are two different processes (perhaps even running on two different computers), there will be no common memory and minimizing the parameter passing will be a much bigger issue.

Many existing graphics libraries (OpenGL, for instance) partially or entirely work as state machines.

Scripting

The previous sections discussed how to improve code maintainability and reusability by using specific paradigms. Those approaches also helped the criterion of flexibility in the sense that it was easier to adapt an application to changing goals. This section examines a different notion of flexibility. In various contexts, it is necessary to change what an application does in the runtime. For instance, you often want an application to handle different data structures with only minimal effort. It is also necessary, at times, to change some procedural behavior such as motion paths of some objects as displayed by an animation package or a computer game.

> **Note**
>
> For this section, examine the implementation of the data interpreter located in the /3DGPL3/DATA subdirectory on the accompanying CD.
>
> Refer to Appendix A for more instructions about 3Dgpl library.

Naturally, it will be too limiting to have to recompile the program each time such a change needs to be made. An obvious solution is to separate the changing elements from the executable code and store their representations separately on the disk. The data for all volatile components is read by the application in the runtime and is interpreted in a way that is predefined by the application.

The data describing various virtual scenes can be stored in binary form. Such an approach guarantees high efficiency of the reconstruction of this data structure in memory but may limit portability of the data. Information stored in binary form is also less manageable since it is hard to immediately understand its meaning and, thus, it requires a special set of utilities for creation and manipulation. Especially when the volume of information is not very large, it may be preferable to describe such information simply in the textual form. This is not unlike what is done for programming languages. In programming languages such as C or Pascal, you can describe the necessary data structures and functions in some textual form. It is quite common to involve a similar approach and represent changing components of applications with the help of some smaller language. Such languages are often referred to as *scripting languages*. It should be noted that you usually want to address some very specific functionality by employing a script, so it will not be necessary to introduce all the complexity that is hidden behind modern programming languages.

In order to define a language, you must design and properly express its syntax and semantics. *Syntax* describes all valid expressions of the language, and *semantics* describes the meaning and the effect of interpreting the expressions and statements of the language. A *grammar* is a set of formal rules describing the language's syntax. For many practical purposes, it is convenient to represent a language's grammar in *Backus-Naur Form*. This representation describes different elements of the language in terms of other elements or even recursively in terms of the element that is being defined. For instance, in an informal example of a grammar that is presented in Listing 9.4, the element *function* is described as one of the four characters (the vertical line between the characters has the meaning of "or").

LISTING 9.4

A Grammar for a Simple Language

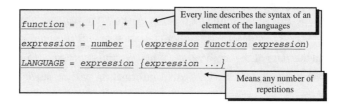

The entire language described in Listing 9.4 is defined by the last line in the listing as any number of elements expression. (In this notation, { E ...} means zero or any number of occurrences of the element E within the curly brackets.) Since the expression is itself an element described with the help of a rule, its grammar is also described by a rule. Thus, an expression is defined as either a number or an application of a binary function to two expressions. This grammar describes (somewhat informally since some components are missing) a sequence of arithmetic expressions such as *(1+1)* or *((1+2)/2)*. You can use the grammar to build a parser that can recognize the validity of strings of symbols written in this language and perform the necessary actions for valid sequences. Each of the rules can be implemented as a separate function capable of interpreting its proper element of the language. Thus, a string of symbols *(1+1)* will be first parsed by rule number three, which will invoke rule number two, which after two recursive calls will find the expression to be valid. This approach is known as *recursive descend*. The interpreting routine may at the same time construct an internal representation expressing the semantics (that is, the meaning) of the interpreted expression. In the preceding example, this may be a *reversed notation* or a *disjoint representation,* which are convenient for evaluation of arithmetic expressions.

Alternatively, instead of coding the parser by hand, you can employ one of the parser generators such as *yacc* (yet another compiler of compilers) or the almost identical *bison*. These produce the C code for a parser when you specify the required grammar in a form similar to that presented in the preceding example. Using such a tool together with a scanner generator such as *lex (flex)*, which produces C code of a scanning routine used to separate the input text stream into lexical units (*tokens*), can considerably reduce the coding effort necessary to build a scripting language. To build a parser in lex it is necessary to describe each token as a regular expression. Regular expressions describe families of strings with the help of wildcards and other special conventions. It is something that is commonly used in the search boxes of many different applications.

For the purposes of 3D graphics applications, you can use scripts to, for instance, represent changing behavior of some animated objects. A script similar to Listing 9.4 may represent arithmetical expressions describing how orientation angles of some entity change depending on the state of the application. Whenever it is necessary to change this behavior, modifying some external files with textual information will be sufficient to achieve the goal.

Many applications employ the technique of scripting. For instance, visualization packages often have their own languages that allow for describing virtual worlds. The same approach is often adopted in computer games, where scripts describe various aspects of the runtime behavior of the characters.

Special Hardware

The ultimate speed-up technique, in the absence of an algorithmic shortcut, is to implement some functionality in hardware. Computer graphics is no exception to this rule and hardware manufacturers attempt to provide some accelerated functionality implemented directly in hardware to speed up these applications. Silicon Graphics, which was founded in 1982 by Jim Clark, still remains at the forefront of these efforts. Although accelerated graphics was originally available only on expensive and exotic hardware, today it is quite common on mass-market platforms (such as PCs). Quite a few different manufacturers, such as 3Dfx, nVIDIA, Matrox, and 3Dlabs, produce fairly cheap graphics accelerators.

Of course, computer graphics has a rich spectrum of different algorithms in its toolkit. Which of these algorithms should be accelerated is an important question. Currently, this is resolved in favor of the functions that are most commonly used and at the same time are simple enough.

Algorithms Implemented in Hardware

Due to these selection criteria (being common and simple), accelerated graphics today encompasses primarily rasterization of primitives and computing geometric transformations. Z-buffer hidden surface removal is also often integrated with the rasterization routines. Indeed, drawing polygons is perhaps the single most important function for the applications that use the world-to-screen viewing method. The geometric transformations are also quite important and an increasing number of manufacturers (including CPU manufacturers themselves) provide some acceleration for these (see Chapter 2, "Geometric Transformations").

However, rasterization of polygons in its general form compounded with shading and texture mapping is not very simple. Since the criterion for the functions implemented in hardware is also their simplicity, some relaxations are often made. Thus, instead of rasterizing a general polygon, acceleration is provided only for triangles and, less commonly, quadrilaterals. These have a fixed number of vertices and triangles and are always convex, which simplifies the task considerably. Chapter 3, "Rasterization," looked at the algorithm for polygon rasterization suitable for implementation in hardware. In that algorithm, polygons were split into parts (triangles and trapezoids) whose base was horizontal. That allowed computing where the pixel lines start and end on-the-fly, without maintaining any data structures. Arbitrary triangles could always be split into two halves so that the bases of the remaining pieces were horizontal (see Figure 9.4).

Figure 9.4
Splitting triangles into two pieces.

Although the fundamental functions for world-to-screen viewing are commonly accelerated, there are practically no graphics accelerators in existence today that help the algorithms of screen-to-world viewing (beyond regular support for geometric transformation, which may be useful). That is because ray-tracing in its general form is already so computationally intensive that even with straightforward acceleration, it may still be unacceptably slow. This may well change in the future. Ray-tracing has a huge amount of parallelism (computation for pixels independent of each other). Thus, when it becomes cheap enough to have one processor associated with every screen pixel, such an ultimate ray-tracing machine could easily eclipse all other solutions and could change the landscape of computer graphics.

Integration of Graphics Hardware

Many different architectures exist for integrating the graphics accelerators. Consider the example in Figure 9.5, which shows a hypothetical architecture containing the CPU and separate accelerators for geometry and rasterization, as well as two kinds of memory.

Figure 9.5

A hypothetical system with hardware acceleration for graphics.

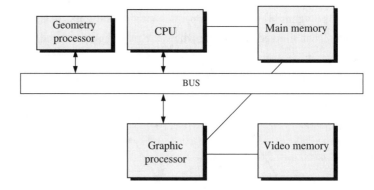

This architecture is not unlike what takes place on the PC platform. Note that Figure 9.5 shows two kinds of memory. The main memory contains the code and the data of the application, whereas the video memory contains data immediately required by the graphics processor. The latter includes the frame buffer itself where the drawing is created. The Z-buffer and textures may also reside in the video memory.

A large architectural question is how to efficiently feed the graphics processor with drawing data so that it is kept busy. The existence of two memories is also something of a problem especially for texture management, which is a large portion of drawing data. Clearly, copying textures from the main memory into the video memory may slow down the process. One solution is to let the graphics processor communicate with the main memory directly. Accelerated Graphics Port (AGP), introduced by Intel, does precisely that. With such an architecture, the textures and perhaps even the Z-buffer could reside in the main memory, which would remove the need for complicated texture management.

Figure 9.5 shows a geometry processor as a separate device. This is often the case on game console platforms, but it may be a part of the graphics processor in accelerators functioning on the PC platform.

To use the graphics processor, the CPU must specify the description of the primitive it wants to draw. Usually, the graphics processor will have a large number of internal registers that are accessible by the CPU. In some of these registers, the graphics processor will expect to see drawing commands. Other registers will store the vertex data. For instance, there could be three groups of registers, one for each vertex of the triangle where the spatial coordinates, colors, and texture coordinates will be expected. This data could be in fixed-point or floating-point form (see Chapter 2) depending on the device. The CPU will set the registers with the appropriate data and issue the drawing command.

The graphics processor will first perform some setup tasks, analyzing the data received and computing values to aid rasterization. At this stage a triangle could be split into smaller triangles whose bases are horizontal. Some sort of clipping may also be done at that point. Each piece will pass through the rasterization circuitry, which will find all pixels that must be changed in the frame buffer to display the primitive. Each pixel will be processed to find its color. This processing depends heavily on the specifics of each accelerator. Figure 9.6 illustrates a hypothetical scenario of the processing during the rasterization.

FIGURE 9.6
Interactions of a graphics processor and video memory.

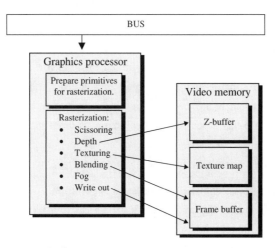

As Figure 9.6 shows, the scissoring test is made. Whether or not the obtained pixel is within the screen boundaries is checked. Most modern accelerators don't perform actual geometric clipping. Geometric clipping is substituted with the scissoring test of all rasterized pixels of the primitive (see Chapter 4, "Clipping"). If, however, true clipping had been done, this stage would have been unnecessary.

Following that, the occlusion check can be made. The depth of the current pixel is thus compared with the corresponding value from the Z-buffer. If the test fails and the current pixel is obscured, processing stops and the next pixel is analyzed. If the test holds, the color of the pixel is determined.

The color of a pixel may consist of many components. The shading value is obtained by interpolating the colors specified in the vertices. The texturing color is obtained with the help of the mapping algorithm and extracted from the texture map (or even several texture maps when *multitexturing* is supported). If the alpha component specifying transparency properties is used, the previous value of this pixel in the frame buffer will also be used. Finally, there could be support for fog implemented and thus the fog color (stored in another internal register of the graphics processor) will be considered as well. All these colors are combined according to certain rules to obtain the final color of the pixel, which is then written back into the frame buffer.

Generally, there are many options to choose from for computing the final color out of the components. Some components could be multiplied together (or *modulated*). For instance, the texture color can be considered a diffuse reflection coefficient and assumed to represent a value from 0 to 1. If that is the case, multiplying it by the shading value (assumed to represent light intensity) has a perfect physical sense as described by the diffuse lighting model. Alternatively, these two simply could be added together, which perhaps has less physical sense but may work well anyway.

The alpha coefficient describing the transparency is commonly used as a blending coefficient. Alpha is added to the color specification as its fourth component (in addition to red, green, and blue prime colors). Alpha could be assumed to be in the range from 0 to 1, where 0 means that the pixel is 100% transparent and 1 means that it is totally opaque. If that is the case, the resulting color can blend together the previous color in the frame buffer with the new color as follows:

$$C_{result} = \alpha C_{current} + (1 - \alpha)C_{previous}$$

The situation is similar in the case of fog. Fogging happens because of atmospheric light attenuation. When light travels through a dense media (fog) some of the light is absorbed and its intensity is thus reduced proportionate to the distance traveled. Thus, the fogging value will depend on the depth of the pixel and the color of the fog. These two are blended and combined with other color components.

Figure 9.6 also illustrates various memory accesses that may occur during pixel processing. Thus, the Z-buffer could be accessed during occlusion testing and the texture map could be accessed to fetch an appropriate texel (or texels). The frame buffer could be accessed twice, once to fetch the previous color to be used in blending computation and the second time to store the result.

In addition to the straightforward functionality outlined here, many graphics accelerators these days provide some advanced features as well. For instance, bilinear mapping and MIP mapping are commonly implemented as well as filtering for the entire image (FSAA) (see Chapter 3). Some modern cards also implement special techniques to improve visual realism. Bump mapping and environmental mapping are implemented in some accelerators (see Chapter 8, "Lighting").

Communicating directly with the graphics accelerator is relatively cumbersome. Normally, there are low-level software libraries that do this task. Thus, a higher-level graphics library or an application often communicate with the hardware through an additional software layer. This layer may provide additional drawing primitives. For instance, it is common to have such primitives as triangle fans and strips at this level (see Chapter 6, "Modeling"). Although the graphics processor may not rasterize such primitives directly, they are nonetheless quite convenient. When drawing a single triangle, the information on all of its three vertices must be placed into special registers of the accelerator. When drawing a fan or a strip, all neighboring triangles share two vertices and that could minimize parameter passing (see Figure 9.7).

FIGURE 9.7
Drawing triangle fans and strips.

(a):

(b):

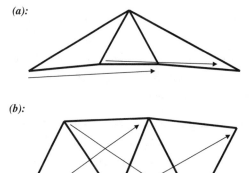

Thus, as Figure 9.7 illustrates, to advance to the next triangle of the fan or strip it is enough to change data related to only one vertex, leaving remaining data in the registers from the previous triangle.

Overall, the accelerators improve considerably as time goes on both in efficiency and the amount of features covered. The unfortunate point is that on the PC platform (the most pervasive at the moment), there is no standard for interfacing with such devices. This creates a fair amount of inconvenience. Fortunately, there are rendering libraries that know how to communicate with different accelerators and provide the applications with a software abstraction layer from the actual hardware. The next section examines some examples of such libraries.

Building Tools

The algorithms discussed in the previous chapters are fundamental for many different 3D applications. Such tasks as 3D transformations and rasterizations must be performed by almost any application using world-to-screen viewing. As common as some algorithms and manipulations are, many have been implemented by various software development kits or libraries. As the previous section showed, some of these functions are even implemented in hardware and, thus, the software libraries provide an interface to these functions as well.

When such hardware or tools are available, this may considerably ease the development tasks.

Since many of the 3D graphics algorithms are relatively straightforward and are in very common use by very different applications, it is attractive to have some basic functionality implemented directly in hardware. Such algorithms as rasterization of flat, shaded, and texture-mapped polygons, and Z buffering along with 3D transformations form such core functionality and are commonly put on accelerator boards. Even some general-purpose processors sometimes provide operations that are especially useful for graphics applications, such as *single instruction-multiple data* vector instructions. These allow performance of the same operation on several arguments at the same time. Using such instructions may allow, for instance, parallel computing of pure components of RGB illumination, thus speeding rendering tasks considerably. *Multimedia Extensions* (MMX) instructions for Intel's Pentium processors implement this approach (see Chapter 2).

As is commonly the case, the amount and kinds of features available in hardware range widely. Fortunately, existing software development kits and libraries can often serve as a common interface to hardware. These libraries may perform software-only rendering on a minimal machine or use hardware assistance when it is available. The following sections discuss the general structure for three such libraries: *OpenGL*, *Direct3D*, and *Glide*. It should be noted that describing these libraries to the degree that allows programming is quite an extensive undertaking, so these sections concentrate mostly on a few basic conceptual issues.

The 3Dgpl graphics library provided with this book is also a tool that helps in building graphics applications. Due to its educational nature, however, there is no support for graphics accelerators. Nevertheless, it should be useful to examine different design choices that were made in it and stages in the viewing process, as well as interfaces between different modules. Refer to Appendix A for more information about that library.

OpenGL

OpenGL is closely based on Silicon Graphics' IRIS GL library. Due to that library's popularity, an industry-wide review board was established to maintain an open, platform-independent standard for a graphics library. As a result, OpenGL is available on a wide range of hardware platforms and operating systems available from such diverse manufacturers as SGI, IBM, Apple, and Microsoft.

OpenGL provides core functionality for 3D transformations, clipping, illumination, and rasterization. This functionality can often be implemented in hardware with OpenGL providing a common interface to different accelerator boards.

OpenGL is designed to function as a state machine. Thus, invocations of many functions set up some parameters that are recalled during subsequent invocations of other functions, such as setting current color or current texture map for the purposes of upcoming primitive rasterization. This is done to enable the OpenGL application to function over the network where a program generates a stream of OpenGL commands on one computer and the interpretation of the commands is done on another computer. Thus, the application program interface of this library is almost entirely procedural and practically doesn't require allocating any data structures.

The approximate logical structure of OpenGL is presented in Figure 9.8.

FIGURE 9.8
Logical structure of OpenGL.

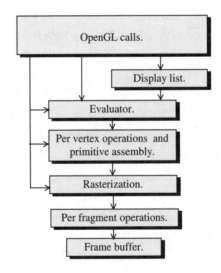

As Figure 9.8 illustrates, the GL commands can be accumulated in a display list for processing at some future time, or sent immediately through the rendering pipeline (perhaps even bypassing some stages). The evaluator stage allows you to approximate curves and surfaces with simpler primitives such as line segments and polygonal patches so that the following stages can operate with simple primitives only. The next stage performs operations on vertices such as 3D transformations and illumination calculations as well as operations on primitives such as clipping. Clipped primitives are passed to the rasterizer, which computes the stream of fragments (pixel addresses accompanied by color, depth, and texturing information), and sends these to the next stage, which is responsible for operations on fragments such as Z buffering, blending, fogging, and changing contents of the frame-buffer.

OpenGL is not tied to any particular architecture or operating system. To allow the applications that access the particular features as well as conform to the necessary standards (such as supported execution flow), additional, auxiliary libraries are commonly provided.

Since OpenGL works as a state machine, geometric information describing a single primitive is passed during invocation of a sequence of OpenGL functions. Such a sequence is started by a call to glBegin, where you specify the type of the primitive you are about to describe. Several types are available, such as GL_POINTS, GL_LINES, GL_TRIANGLES, GL_QUADS, GL_POLYGON and a few others, such as GL_TRIANGLE_STRIP or GL_QUAD_STRIP. The invocation of the glBegin function is followed by the invocations of functions specifying vertex information. Various information can be defined in a single vertex depending on the desired rendering model. The vertex coordinates are specified in a call to glVertex (for convenience, many GL functions have alternative forms that take arguments of different types or arrangements). Current color in a vertex is specified in a call to glColor. It is also possible to specify a normal in a vertex for the purposes of the Phong illumination model with a call to glNormal, and to specify texture coordinates with a call to glTexCoord. The vertex definition is finished by calling glEnd.

The geometric transformations in OpenGL are specified by means of four-by-four matrices. Three different kinds of transformations are involved in the rendering process implemented by OpenGL. These are the transformation from the object space into the view space (called *model-view* transformations), projection transformations, and texture-mapping transformations. The stack of matrices is maintained for each of these (so that it is possible to preserve some matrices for future use) and an application using OpenGL must describe the desired transformation before primitives are passed through the rendering pipeline.

As mentioned before, in addition to the immediate mode where the primitives are passed through the rendering pipeline, it is also possible to enter the OpenGL commands into a display list for combined execution at a later time. It is often the case that creating a display list enables the library to precompute some data, which speeds up the following executions. OpenGL also provides higher-level routines where more complex shapes may be specified for rendering rather than individual primitives. Functions enabling this are provided in the utility library.

Overall, GL implements a wide range of functionality that graphics applications may require. This, combined with ease of use, possible support for hardware assistance, and portability, makes this library a very popular implementation tool.

The overview of OpenGL given in this section is extremely brief. There is a considerable amount of information necessary in order to use the library. There are many books that discuss how OpenGL should be employed and that provide a detailed description of the library (for example, the *OpenGL Super Bible, Second Edition* by Wright and Sweet).

Direct3D

Direct3D is a part of the DirectX software development kit that was first developed by the British company RenderMorphics. That company was subsequently acquired by Microsoft and Direct3D was integrated into the DirectX family. DirectX is available for Microsoft's 32-bit operating systems. This graphics library covers a set of functionality comparable to OpenGL and is also aimed at providing unified access to different accelerator boards.

Direct3D can use hardware acceleration when it is available or perform software-only rendering in its absence. The first is achieved by what's known in DirectX as HAL (Hardware Abstraction Layer) and the second is performed by HEL (Hardware Emulation Layer).

Similar to OpenGL, Direct3D has several layers (on top of HAL and HEL), with the higher *retained mode* layer enabling manipulations with complex geometric objects, whereas the lower *immediate mode* layer represents the actual polygonal rendering pipeline. Figure 9.9 depicts the logical structure of the pipeline as implemented in this library.

FIGURE 9.9
Logical structure of Direct3D.

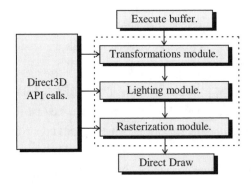

An application using Direct3D must initialize special data structures and set the state of the modules, such as the transformation matrices, light sources, and description of materials. Calling specific functions from Direct3D API takes care of these functions.

There are several ways to draw primitives. The original way is through constructing the execute buffers. These buffers contain geometric information as well as commands that describe transformations and processes that must be performed. The execute buffers are passed through the modules of the pipeline that perform the 3D transformations, lighting, and rasterization, and then invoke functions from another library called *DirectDraw*, which is responsible for frame-buffer access. The modules may perform software-only computations or use hardware assistance if it is present.

Execute buffers are quite cumbersome to work with. Multiple data structures must be allocated, locked, filled up, and so on to construct them.

In the later versions of Direct3D, another method appeared by which an entire primitive could be specified and drawn procedurally (not unlike how it is done in OpenGL).

Direct3D also allows you to use the functionality of the modules for purposes other than rendering. It is possible, for instance, to call the transformation module to transform a set of vertices for some modeling task or for bounding box calculations.

Despite Direct3D's relatively bulky interface and very limited portability of any code that will use it, this library does enable unified access to a wide range of supported graphics hardware, and its retained mode layer is quite convenient for rapid development of a variety of straightforward graphics applications.

An overwhelming number of publications cover the functionality and use of Direct3D. A good introduction aimed at games programmers can be found in *Tricks of the Windows Game Programming Gurus* by André LaMothe.

Glide

The Glide library is a thin interface layer for Voodoo graphics accelerators produced by 3Dfx. It is somewhat more specialized than either OpenGL or Direct3D. For instance, there are no provisions for geometric transformation or higher-level illumination calculations.

Like other graphics libraries, Glide is built as a state machine with various modules having some internal storage where current drawing parameters are specified. These parameters are used when a primitive is passing through the graphics pipeline.

The fundamental drawing primitives in Glide are points, lines, and triangles. Arrays of these primitives are also handled (such as triangle fans and strips).

Hardware rendering of a single pixel is abstracted into three units in Glide: the texture combine unit, the color and alpha combine unit, and the special effects unit.

The texture combine unit performs the texture mapping. Various ways of producing the final color of a pixel are provided in the color and alpha combine unit. The special effects unit performs the depth test and fogging (among other effects).

Although Glide is quite powerful and convenient, it only works for graphics accelerators of a single manufacturer (3Dfx), which is somewhat limiting.

3Dfx provides a detailed outline of the library and multiple code examples illustrating its use.

Design Strategies

There are many factors influencing the design for graphics modules. A particular project may have special requirements. This section considers only a few basic tradeoffs. It also looks at some techniques and approximate solutions that are common.

Viewing Solid Bodies

The ability to view a 3D model of a solid body or a set of solid bodies may be necessary in many different contexts. Computer games, computer aided design, medical imaging, and scientific visualizations are just a few. In these areas it is necessary to visualize 3D models of such diverse objects as animated game characters, parts of a human body, models of cars or aircraft being designed, and so on. As discussed in the first section of the chapter, before any particular strategy can be chosen, it is necessary to first understand the importance of various factors that express the goals of the application you want to implement. The algorithmic solution will then be chosen based on the relative importance of different factors. It is also true that availability of some resources, particularly hardware assistance or some low-level graphics library, may dictate certain design decisions for the rest of the graphics module.

Consider several possible situations that may arise when drawing images of solid bodies. If, for instance, you are interested in generating high-quality images or sequences of images and the performance constraints are relaxed, employing screen-to-world viewing (ray-tracing algorithm) is a possibility. As discussed in Chapter 5, "Viewing," this algorithm has performance constraints, yet it is very natural for the accommodation of various lighting models and global illumination effects such as shadows and environmental reflections. These are extremely important for achieving visual realism.

As for the implementation, an application using ray-tracing can be separated into the major logical modules illustrated in Figure 9.10.

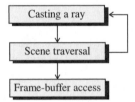

As you saw in Chapter 5, the most basic operation of this method is seeking an intersection of a ray cast from the viewer's eye with some surface of the virtual scene. In order to implement global illumination effects, you may have to cast additional rays from this intersection point by employing the same mechanism as when casting from the eye. This logical structure is represented in Figure 9.10. Of course, this scheme is very much simplified and neglects the internal structure of the modules themselves. For instance, if the scene you are going to visualize is complex and consists of many primitives, you will also have to consider special techniques for space subdivision within the scene traversal module. A more detailed model must take this and other aspects into consideration. However, even this scheme gives a representation of the interdependencies of the modules and an insight into the possible structure of the application. In particular, it is necessary to figure out early on which modules will communicate with one another and define the interfaces for their communication.

The applications that can neglect quality, yet cannot neglect performance, are on the other end of the spectrum. Clearly, the ray-tracing solution becomes less attractive and it is necessary to consider the world-to-screen viewing method instead. You have already seen the necessary stages required in displaying 3D models using this technique. The vertices of the model must pass the coordinate transformation stages. If the perspective projection is involved, volume clipping must be performed prior to that stage. Further, the primitives composing the model are rasterized into the frame buffer. The general outline of the world-to-screen pipeline is presented in Figure 9.11.

FIGURE 9.11
Logical modules of a world-to-screen–based application.

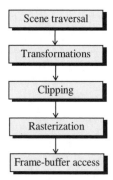

The scheme in Figure 9.11 presents only the basic pipeline. It doesn't show other important aspects of the application that are dependent on additional criteria, notably hidden surface removal and illumination. Clearly, the targeted platform may have hardware acceleration for multiple elements in the pipeline. In particular, geometric transformations and drawing of primitives may already be present. A similar situation occurs if some low-level graphics libraries are available (which may also serve as an interface for special graphics hardware).

Thus, the development tasks can be limited to only some modules, such as hidden surface removal (unless hardware Z-buffer is available), as well as higher-level modeling tasks.

Several hidden surface removal algorithms were discussed in Chapter 7, "Hidden Surface Removal": the painter's method, beam-trees, the scan-line algorithm, and the Z-buffer algorithm. Besides the complexity considerations, some of the algorithms have specific constraints and thus are applicable only in some situations. Moreover, different algorithms also take a different place in the rendering pipeline. The Z-buffer algorithm operates on the image level. The scan-line algorithm is placed at the primitive drawing level. BSP trees operate very early on the pipeline. Some of these algorithms have special constraints. For instance, the BSP tree solution used with the painter's method is feasible only in the case of objects whose shapes are static and are represented as a polygonal mesh. The presence of dynamically changing objects will force you to rebuild the associated BSP trees in the runtime, which is quite expensive and defeats the purpose of the algorithm.

In fact, most hidden surface removal algorithms are applicable to 3D models represented as polygonal meshes. If you possess a technique to rasterize some other kind of primitives directly, for instance a bicubic patch or a sphere, of the algorithms that were discussed in Chapter 7, only the Z-buffer algorithm remains applicable. However, the Z-buffer algorithm, although generic, incurs considerable cost when implemented in software. Thus, in some instances it may be more appropriate to tessellate surfaces into polygonal meshes and avoid using the Z-buffer algorithm, and opt for the painter's method instead.

The presence of complex lighting and texture mappings makes the painter's algorithm less attractive because a lot of expensive work will be lost each time a polygon is drawn over a previously drawn polygon. In this situation, you can employ the scan-line algorithm, the beam-tree algorithm, or a modified Z-buffer algorithm that performs lighting as a post-processing step. The scan-line algorithm can be combined with BSP trees to be used for obtaining front-to-back order of polygons for the calculations that select which polygon is closest on the current span of the scan-line. Similarly, beam-trees may also rely upon the ordering induced by a precomputed BSP tree. However, in both instances considerable modifications of the rendering pipeline must be made. In the former case, all polygons are rasterized simultaneously and may rely on edge-based polygon descriptions. In the latter case, screen boundaries clipping can be easily unified with the beam-tree algorithm, somewhat simplifying the pipeline.

As you can see, model representation and visualization strategy should be considered together. There are many details at work and the creative side of the development process is to apply your knowledge and intuition in the quest for optimal design.

As a result of all such consideration, if the design is still unsatisfactory, you may have to readjust the original set of criteria or look for new resources (although the latter is rarely possible in real life).

Chapter 8 discussed how to introduce lighting and illumination effects into the framework of the world-to-screen viewing method. As you saw, global illumination effects, such as shadows, are quite expensive to compute. In the case of static illumination, the shadows can be precomputed and introduced either into texture maps of the model or as separate, differently illuminated primitives. Handling dynamic lighting in this manner becomes quite expensive.

If you use the Z-buffer algorithm for hidden surface removal, it is possible to augment it to handle light Z-buffers that can compute dynamic shadows.

Viewing Interior Scenes

Viewing interior scenes is often required in such domains as video games and CAD applications for interior design. Of course, any interior scene can be considered a collection of objects. However, interior scenes have some properties of regularity that can be exploited to achieve better performance than in the general case. For instance, you can use the fact that an interior scene is very often a collection of rooms that are convex or nearly convex polyhedrons.

For both visual games and CAD applications, it is very important to generate an interactive walkthrough of the virtual scene. Thus, the efficiency must be very high on your list of priorities.

Although ray-tracing is difficult to use to achieve interactive frame rates in the general case, in many special cases you can exploit some properties of the virtual scenes to achieve suitable performance with ray-tracing. For instance, in many settings the walkthrough doesn't require all six degrees of freedom. After all, many real-life interior scenes are located on a plane such as a floor in a building, and we don't tilt and shake our heads that much while we walk. The polygons representing the scene are likely to be limited in orientation as well. Commonly, there are either vertical polygons representing walls or horizontal polygons representing floors and ceilings. With such assumptions, the ray-tracing can be simplified to a considerable extent. Instead of casting a ray for each pixel in the image bitmap, one ray can be cast for the whole column of pixels, and you can easily find what is intersected at different heights of this column from only a few intersection calculations.

If these relaxations cannot be made, you should consider the world-to-screen method. Although all the considerations related to 3D solid models apply in this case as well, usually the larger number of polygons present in most interior scenes make some hidden surface removal algorithms, such as sorting of polygons, less useful. However, as discussed in Chapter 7, properties of some scenes composed entirely of an interconnected set of convex volumes representing rooms allow for easy computation of back-to-front order of polygons. If the volumes aren't convex, you may associate a BSP tree with each volume, or even build one for the whole scene. The fact that the interior scenes are mostly static makes this solution a very attractive one.

Since it is common to associate texture maps with the polygons picturing interior environments, and rasterization of such polygons is expensive (even when done in hardware), you may have to employ techniques limiting rasterization of hidden polygons, such as the scan-line algorithm. Another technique is to associate with every volume the list of polygons that are visible completely or partially from any point within the volume. Although finding such lists is computationally expensive, it is done as a preprocessing step and the results are stored with the data structure representing the scene. By limiting the number of polygons that can possibly be rasterized in each volume, you can achieve significant performance gains.

Similarly, the lighting can be limited to a particular region so that a light source has no effect outside of the region, or, even better, you can use for this purpose a list of polygons visible from the current volume. However, for proper illumination such global illumination effects as shadows and environmental reflections must be represented. Similar to the situation in the previous section on viewing solids, static lighting and pre-computed shadows can be used as a least expensive alternative. Some dynamic lighting can be added as well. In particular, a light source should be associated with the moving viewer. Since the energy of light dissipates at a rate proportional to the inverse of the square of distance, placing a light source at the position of the viewer is a cheap heuristic method to model that effect.

Some interior scenes require representation for mirrors reflecting the environment. As seen in Chapter 8, one solution is possible through geometric cloning of the scene with respect to the mirror. Rendering the double in a regular way, but with adjusted colors, gives an effect of the environmental reflection.

Viewing Exterior Scenes

Viewing of exterior landscapes is necessary in such applications as flight simulators, video games, geographical information systems (GIS), and so on. Similar to the situation with interior scenes, the special nature of the objects used to model the surface validates some particular approaches to its visualization.

In most cases, you can't reduce the number of degrees of freedom handled in these kinds of applications. After all, handling of all degrees of freedom is essential in flight simulators, for instance. When it can be done (perhaps in a video game), the ray-casting algorithm can be considered. It should also be noted that the ray-casting algorithm is very easy to parallelize. The calculations for casting of rays are computationally independent, and thus, with some special-purpose hardware, this fact can be explored to achieve six degrees of freedom and interactive landscape visualization using the ray-casting algorithm.

Most often, however, world-to-screen visualization is more appropriate. The height-field representation for landscapes was discussed in Chapter 5. With such a representation, the back-to-front order of polygons can be obtained through proper traversal of the model.

Any of the applications mentioned may model landscapes of considerable size. Thus, it is appropriate to render the polygons from the viewer's locality only. It should be mentioned that since the landscapes are fairly smooth, the amount of polygons drawn over previously rasterized polygons is limited, especially assuming the proper use of back-face culling. Thus, you usually don't have to involve the scan-line hidden surface removal or similar techniques to reduce expensive rasterization of polygons that are going to be overdrawn by other polygons.

The illumination and lighting can be largely pre-computed in this kind of application since the landscapes are mostly static. Some local dynamic lighting can be introduced using some subdivision strategy to limit the influence of each light source. In some cases, when modeling surfaces of water in the landscapes, for example, you may want to represent the environmental reflection. This effect can be achieved by cloning the immediate neighborhood of the water surface with respect to the horizon. Rendering the doubles of the polygons presents images of reflections against the surface of the water.

In addition to rendering the polygons representing the surface of the landscape, it is often necessary to display the objects that are located on the surface. Thus, the techniques from the section discussing visualization of 3D solids should be incorporated into the applications dealing with landscapes as well.

Summary

The design stage is very important in the process of building graphics applications. Many techniques, algorithms, and hardware resources are available and it is necessary to understand how these building blocks will fit together.

Many decisions in this process can be made based on the evaluated criteria for the application's goals and the availability of resources. To satisfy speed and image quality criteria, suitable algorithmic solutions should be chosen.

Special programming techniques such as object-oriented programming and scripting should be considered to achieve the application's maintainability and reusability.

Hardware acceleration is perhaps the single most important resource available. Use of hardware accelerations often dictates a particular structure for the remaining parts of the graphics module.

Finally, it is often hard to foresee how proposed designs will work on execution. Prototyping parts that may present problems later on ahead of actual development may potentially save enormous amounts of time.

This book has discussed only the foundation topics of 3D computer graphics. Many other higher-level topics, not covered here, are also important for most applications. Appendix C, "Additional Reading," contains a bibliography of books and articles that discuss many advanced topics in the field of computer graphics.

Appendixes

A

3Dgpl Graphics Library

3Dgpl stands for 3D Graphics Portable Library. The library is written in C, and provides a set of basic tools for 3D graphics applications and demonstrates the techniques that are commonly used. Although it was written with educational goals in mind, and clarity at times took precedence over performance, much of the code can still be used for practical development.

The library is software only, but it is highly portable. Interfaces for MS-Windows and UNIX/X11 are provided with the current versions. Porting to other hardware should be quite easy.

3Dgpl implementation consists of 10 modules that provide functionality for 3D applications at different levels of abstraction, from low level (such as transformation and rasterization) to high level (modeling schemes and hidden surface removal algorithms). With a compact size of well under 10,000 lines of code and a rich number of comments, it should be quite easy to understand the internals of the library and perhaps adapt them for specific use.

Legal

3Dgpl is under the GNU Library General Public License. Please refer to this license (which is included with the library) for the terms and conditions of the library's distribution and use.

Modules

3Dgpl provides tools for both world-to-screen and screen-to-world (ray-tracing) viewing.

Most of the functions and modules described in this appendix are used internally by other modules. Unless it was decided to modify some of the internal functionality, a simple application may be exposed only to the functions from the ENGINE or TRACE modules, aided by a small number of initialization functions from other modules. The source code for each module of the library is placed into a separate subdirectory of the /3DGPL hierarchy. Examine the header files for additional information on the data structures and functions used.

The following sections briefly describe the modules.

HARDWARE Module

The HARDWARE module interfaces resources of a particular operating system or hardware platform. The interface is fairly minimal so porting to other platforms is quite easy. This has been done before, and usually takes a day or less. The rest of the library is mostly hardware independent and should compile and work potentially anywhere. However, 32-bit platforms are strongly recommended.

There are two kinds of functions in this module: The first kind interfaces the display device and the second kind manages the control flow of the applications (see Table A.1).

TABLE A.1 Functions of the HARDWARE Module

Function	What It Does
HW_init_screen	Opens graphical output.
HW_pixel	Packs a pixel from red/green/blue components and stores the result at a specified address.
HW_blit	Moves a frame-buffer into display memory.
HW_close_screen	Closes graphics output.
HW_init_event_loop	Runs rendering loop.
HW_error	Called by other modules when an error occurs.
HW_close_event_loop	Terminates main rendering loop.

Thus, `HW_init_event_loop` must be passed pointers to three functions. Of these three functions, one implements event handling, another implements drawing of a frame, and the third implements processing that needs to be done when there are no events to handle. The function `HW_close_event_loop`, when called from any of the preceding three, causes `HW_init_event_loop` to exit. Hardware and operating system particularities are hidden within these functions and a 3Dgpl application need not to be aware of which operating system it is running under.

GRAPHICS Module

The GRAPHICS module is responsible for rasterization of primitives and, most importantly, it can handle flat, interpolatively shaded, linearly textured, and perspectively textured polygons. At this level, there is also a Z buffer, which can be activated by compiling with the `_Z_BUFFER_` compile-time option defined as opposed to `_PAINTER_`. In the latter case, hidden surface removal will rely upon the painter's approach (see Chapter 7, "Hidden Surface Removal") with various methods placing the polygons into the back-to-front order implemented at the level of the ENGINE module.

Table A.2 details other important functions this module provides.

TABLE A.2 Functions of the GRAPHICS Module

Function	What It Does
G_init_graphics	Allocates the frame buffer and Z buffer.
G_clear	Clears the frame buffer.
G_point	Plots a point.
G_line	Rasterizes a line.
G_flat_polygon	Rasterizes a flat polygon.
G_shaded_polygon	Rasterizes a Gouraud shaded polygon.
G_lin_textured_polygon	Rasterizes a linearly textured polygon.
G_prp_textured_polygon	Rasterizes a perspectively textured polygon.

G_init_graphics allocates the frame buffer and optionally the Z buffer. It is automatically called by HW_init_screen. G_clear is used to clear the buffers prior to the frame drawing. The remaining functions rasterize their respective primitives.

CLIPPER **Module**

The CLIPPER module performs volume clipping, clipping against rectangular screen boundaries, and splitting of a polygon by an arbitrary plane (which is used during the construction of BSP trees, for instance). All of the functions use the binary search technique and are multiplication-free. Table A.3 details the public functions available.

TABLE A.3 Functions of the CLIPPER Module

Function	What It Does
C_init_clipping	Sets 2D clipping boundaries.
C_line_x_clipping	Clips a line against vertical edges.
C_line_y_clipping	Clips a line against horizontal edges.
C_polygon_x_clipping	Clips a polygon against vertical edges.
C_volume_clipping	Approximates bounding box testing.
C_line_z_clipping	Clips a line against the frontal plane.
C_polygon_z_clipping	Clips a polygon against the frontal plane.
C_line_xyz_clipping	Clips a line against an arbitrary plane.
C_polygon_xyz_clipping	Clips a polygon against an arbitrary plane.

The C_init_clipping function is used to specify the clipping boundaries. It is automatically called by HW_init_screen to set the default boundaries. The C_line_x_clipping and C_line_y_clipping functions clip a line against vertical and horizontal boundaries, respectively, and C_polygon_x_clipping clips a polygon to vertical boundaries. The rasterization routines first clip polygons to the vertical boundaries and will perform horizontal clipping per edge, immediately prior to edge scanning, to avoid creating useless horizontal edges in the clipped polygon.

The C_volume_clipping function does approximate accept/reject tests against the viewing pyramid using the bounding box of a primitive. The C_line_z_clipping and C_polygon_z_clipping functions clip respective primitives against the frontal plane, and the remaining two functions, C_line_xyz_clipping and C_polygon_xyz_clipping, clip against arbitrarily oriented planes.

TRANS **Module**

The TRANS module implements the geometric transformations and some linear algebra algorithms, such as Gaussian elimination, which is employed to find the coordinates of vectors used for perspective texture mapping. The module is implemented using both fixed-point (define _FIXED_ at compile time) or floating point (define _FLOAT_ at compile time) precision. Depending on the processor's type, one may be more advantageous to use over the other. Table A.4 details the important public functions this module provides.

TABLE A.4 Functions of the TRANS Module

Function	What It Does
T_init_math	Builds internal tables of trigonometric functions.
T_vector	Constructs a vector from endpoints.
T_norm	Computes the length of a vector.
T_normal_vectors	Computes a normal from two vectors in a plane.
T_normal_plane	Computes a normal from three points in a plane.
T_unit_vector	Changes the length of the vector to one unit.
T_scalar_product	Computes the scalar product.
T_normal_z_negative	Computes only the Z component of the normal.
T_plane	Computes plane equation.
T_vertex_on_plane	Finds position of a point with respect to a plane.
T_translation	Performs the translation transformation.
T_scaling	Performs the scaling transformation.
T_set_self_rotation	Computes matrix for object space rotation.
T_self_rotation	Performs object space rotation.
T_set_world_rotation	Computes matrix for world space rotation.
T_world_rotation	Performs world space rotation.
T_concatenate_self_world	Concatenates object and world rotations.
T_concatenated_rotation	Performs combined rotation.
T_perspective	Performs the perspective transformation.
T_linear_solve	Solves a system of linear equations.

The rotation transformations for object and world rotations use a different order of rotations around individual axes. The matrices describing the two rotations can be concatenated together to obtain a combined transformation from an object directly into the view space.

LIGHT Module

The LIGHT module computes local illumination for world-to-screen applications. The functions listed in Table A.5 are provided.

TABLE A.5 Functions of the LIGHT Module

Function	What It Does
L_init_lights	Sets the list of light sources.
L_init_material	Specifies current material reflection coefficients.
L_light_vertex	Computes local illumination for a point given its position and the surface normal at that point.

The library maintains colors as intensities for pure components of red, green, and blue. Palette-based modes that were alternatively provided in early versions of 3Dgpl are no longer supported.

ENGINE Module

The ENGINE module provides modeling data structures and viewing algorithms for several different objects. There are polygonal objects—a collection of polygons that may be viewed with the help of either Z-buffer hidden surface removal activated in the GRAPHICS module, or BSP tree-based painter's algorithm activated in this module. The former switches on if the _Z_BUFFER_ compile-time option is set. The latter will be activated on defining _PAINTER_.

The objects modeled as collections of bicubic patches are also provided. These are tessellated into polygons just prior to rasterization. Z-buffer or polygonal sorting is used for hidden surface removal.

Another available object represents landscapes that are modeled using a regularly spaced elevation field. Hidden surface removal of the polygons composing the landscape is achieved either through the Z-buffer or through priority list rasterization. The latter (similarly to other objects) is activated on defining _PAINTER_.

There are two functions (detailed in Table A.6) initializing the viewing performed by the module.

TABLE A.6   Initialization Functions of the ENGINE Module

Function	What It Does
M_init_rendering	Specifies the polygon rasterization option used.
M_init_camera	Sets the parameters of the viewing camera.

All of the objects are managed by three similar functions which, in the case of bicubic objects, are detailed in Table A.7.

TABLE A.7   Bicubic Model Management Functions of the ENGINE Module

Function	What It Does
M_init_bicubic_object	Initializes an object.
M_light_bicubic_object	Illuminates an object with the help of the LIGHT module.
M_render_bicubic_object	Renders an object.

Since M_init_... functions compute additional information aiding run-time rendering (normal vectors, for instance), the shape of the models can't change unless M_init_... is called. Initialization of polygonal objects with _PAINTER_ defined causes computation of a BSP tree and thus isn't practical for actual run-time. It should be done prior to launching the main event loop of an application.

Before rendering the objects, the parameters of the camera must be specified in a call to M_init_camera. Coordinates of the camera in the world space, its orientation angles, and the binary logarithm of the perspective focus distance must be passed to this function. Also, since all of the objects supported in the library resort to using the polygonal pipeline at some point, M_init_rendering should be called to select a rendering option of the pipeline. The following options are available: M_POINT, M_WIRE, M_FLAT, M_SHADED, and M_TEXTURED.

SHAPE Module

The SHAPE module helps to automatically build data structures of polygonal models for simple shapes such as spheres and cylinders. The three functions provided are detailed in Table A.8.

TABLE A.8   Functions of the SHAPE Module

Function	What It Does
S_init_shape	Specifies material and texture to use for subsequent model construction.
S_sphere	Builds a sphere.
S_cylinder	Builds a cylinder.

The tessellation ratio could be specified for both spheres and cylinders.

VECTOR Module

The VECTOR module contains a set of basic vector operations to be used by the ray-tracer. The provided functionality is similar to that of the TRANS module, but is tailored for the purposes of ray-tracing. Some of the available public functions are listed in Table A.9.

TABLE A.9   Functions of the VECTOR Module

Function	What It Does
V_zero	Assigns a zero to all coordinates.
V_vector_coordinates	Sets vector coordinates.
V_vector_points	Builds a vector from two points.
V_set	Copies a vector.
V_multiply	Multiplies a vector by a scalar.
V_scalar_product	Computes the scalar (dot) product of vectors.
V_vector_product	Computes the vector (cross) product of vectors.
V_sum	Computes the sum of vectors.
V_difference	Computes the difference of vectors.
V_unit_vector	Finds a unit length vector.
V_plane	Computes plane equation.
V_vertex_on_plane	Finds the position of a point with respect to a plane.

Since speed concerns of the ray-tracing are already poor, only floating point implementation is provided.

TRACE Module

The TRACE module implements a fundamental ray-tracer, which provides the very foundation for this rendering methodology supporting three basic primitives: spheres, cylinders, and polygons.

Only four public functions are provided, as detailed in Table A.10.

TABLE A.10   Functions of the TRACE Module

Function	What It Does
TR_init_rendering	Sets local and global illumination options.
TR_init_camera	Sets the parameters of the viewing camera.
TR_init_world	Computes some auxiliary data aiding the viewing.
TR_trace_world	Traces the scene.

The viewer's camera is specified by the position of the eye, the origin of the viewing plane, and two vectors describing the orientation of the viewing plane.

DATA **Module**

The DATA module interprets script files reconstructing data structures in memory. The syntax of the script is similar to that used for defining static data in C. Listing A.1 describes (somewhat informally) the syntax.

LISTING A.1
Syntax of the Scripting Language

```
type ::= <char> | <short> | <int> | <float> | <ptr> |
         <[>number<]>type | <{>type {type...}<}>
variable ::= name | number | <[>variable {variable...}<]> |
             <{>variable {variable...}<}>
statement ::= <type> name type | <var> type name variable |
              <export> name
language ::= statement {statement...}
```

All data structures used by sample applications (including the textures) are represented in this portable format. The type statement permits description of data structures, the var statement describes the variables (instances of the data structures), and the export statement specifies the pointer that is returned to the calling application.

There are several dangers associated with this module. It is assumed that the data structure described in the application is the same as that in the script file. If not properly maintained, the structures may get desynchronized and crash the application. The efficiency of storing extensive data in the text form (such as textures) is also very low, from both the space and performance viewpoints. However, such script language is quite convenient, especially at the development stage when the data structures may be changing all the time.

Sample Applications

Table A.11 details the 10 sample applications provided in the 3DGPL3/APP subdirectory.

TABLE A.11   Sample Applications

Application	What It Does
window.c	Constructs a window, draws random points.
line.c	Draws random lines.
texture.c	Draws a textured polygon that can be rotated and viewed with different texturing options.
polygon.c	Draws a polygonal model that can be rotated and viewed with different shading/texturing options.
bicubic.c	Draws a bicubic model. The implemented functionality is identical to polygon.c.
surface.c	Draws a landscape. The implemented functionality is similar to polygon.c.
inter.c	Demonstrates BSP tree-based hidden surface removal on an interior scene (compile with _PAINTER_, otherwise the Z buffer algorithm will be used).
group.c	Demonstrates workings of Z-buffer hidden surface removal (compile with _Z_BUFFER_, otherwise the painter's approach will be used).
shade.c	Draws a polygonal model approximating curved objects (spheres and cylinders). Can be viewed with different shading options.
tracer.c	A basic ray-tracer that displays a scene under different local illumination, with or without shadows and environmental reflections.

All sample applications display a string indicating which key presses are handled. Pressing Enter terminates all applications. Many applications handle the arrow keys, which control the orientation of the viewer or the model. For world-to-screen applications, the following keys are responsible for shading/texturing options:

P   Displays key vertices only.

W   Displays model's wireframe.

F   Uses flat shading.

G   Uses Gouraud shading.

T   Uses Gouraud shading and texturing.

Additionally, in `texture.c` it is possible to force the texturing option using the following keys:

L   For linear texture mapping.

P   For perspective texture mapping.

For the ray-tracing sample `tracer.c`, the following keys select local and global illumination options:

A   For ambient local illumination only.

D   For ambient and diffuse illumination.

S   Phong illumination (specular+diffuse+ambient).

H   Phong illumination and shadows.

R   Phong illumination, shadows, and environmental reflections.

The data files for the sample applications are stored in the `3DGPL3/APP/DATA` subdirectory. All data files use the format described in the `DATA` module.

Compiling

Two makefiles are provided:

- `windows.mk`—Configured for MS Visual C++ V4 and above.

- `unix.mk`—Configured for GCC, tested under Linux but should work (perhaps with minor modifications) on other UNIX machines as well.

Note that compile-time options (`_Z_BUFFER_` versus `_PAINTER_` and `_FLOAT_` versus `_FIXED_`) are specified in the beginning of the makefiles.

To compile sample applications under MS-Windows with the help of MS Visual C you will first have to ensure that the command-line tools are properly configured. This includes setting environmental variables indicating where different parts of Visual C are located. Visual C usually has a special batch file `vcvars32.bat` running, which initializes the setting. Once the command-line tools are configured, start a DOS box, go to the `3DGPL3/APP` subdirectory, and issue the following command:

`nmake -f windows.mk *NAME*`

where *NAME* is the name of the sample applications. Alternatively

```
nmake -f windows.mk all
```

compiles all samples.

If you are using UNIX, go to the `3DGPL3/APP` subdirectory and issue the following command:

```
make -f unix.mk NAME
```

or

```
make -f unix.mk all
```

It may be necessary to alter the makefiles to correspond to your particular setup.

APPENDIX B

Common Formulas

Linear Algebra

Scalar (dot) product of two vectors $\overline{A}$ and $\overline{B}$ (see Chapter 5):

$$\overline{A} \cdot \overline{B} = A_x B_x + A_y B_y + A_z B_z$$

Vector (cross) product of two vectors $\overline{A}$ and $\overline{B}$ (see Chapter 5):

$$\overline{A} \times \overline{B} = \overline{i} \det \begin{bmatrix} A_y & A_z \\ B_y & B_z \end{bmatrix} + \overline{j} \det \begin{bmatrix} A_x & A_z \\ B_x & B_z \end{bmatrix} + \overline{k} \det \begin{bmatrix} A_x & A_y \\ B_x & B_y \end{bmatrix} = \det \begin{bmatrix} \overline{i} & \overline{j} & \overline{k} \\ A_x & A_y & A_z \\ B_x & B_y & B_z \end{bmatrix}$$

Geometric Transformations

Translation transformation, where t_x, t_y and t_z describe the translation (see Chapter 2):

$$\begin{bmatrix} x & y & z & 1 \end{bmatrix} \begin{bmatrix} 1 & 0 & 0 & 0 \\ 0 & 1 & 0 & 0 \\ 0 & 0 & 1 & 0 \\ t_x & t_y & t_z & 1 \end{bmatrix} = \begin{bmatrix} x' & y' & z' & 1 \end{bmatrix}$$

Scaling transformation, where s_x, s_y and s_z describe the scaling (see Chapter 2):

$$\begin{bmatrix} x & y & z \end{bmatrix} \begin{bmatrix} s_x & 0 & 0 \\ 0 & s_y & 0 \\ 0 & 0 & s_z \end{bmatrix} = \begin{bmatrix} x' & y' & z' \end{bmatrix}$$

Shearing transformation along the X axis where k describes the shearing (see Chapter 2):

$$\begin{bmatrix} x & y & z \end{bmatrix} \begin{bmatrix} 1 & 0 & 0 \\ k & 1 & 0 \\ 0 & 0 & 1 \end{bmatrix} = \begin{bmatrix} x + ky & y & z \end{bmatrix}$$

3D rotation transformation, where angles α, β, and γ describe the rotation (see Chapter 2):

$$\begin{bmatrix} x & y & z \end{bmatrix} \begin{bmatrix} \cos(\gamma) & 0 & -\sin(\gamma) \\ 0 & 1 & 0 \\ \sin(\gamma) & 0 & \cos(\gamma) \end{bmatrix} \begin{bmatrix} 1 & 0 & 0 \\ 0 & \cos(\beta) & \sin(\beta) \\ 0 & -\sin(\beta) & \cos(\beta) \end{bmatrix} \begin{bmatrix} \cos(\alpha) & -\sin(\alpha) & 0 \\ \sin(\alpha) & \cos(\alpha) & 0 \\ 0 & 0 & 1 \end{bmatrix} =$$

$$\begin{bmatrix} x' & y' & z' \end{bmatrix}$$

Perspective projection, where *focus* specifies the perspective foreshortening (see Chapter 2):

$$\begin{bmatrix} x & y & z & 1 \end{bmatrix} \begin{bmatrix} 1 & 0 & 0 & 0 \\ 0 & 1 & 0 & 0 \\ 0 & 0 & 0 & 1/focus \\ 0 & 0 & -1 & 0 \end{bmatrix} = \begin{bmatrix} x' & y' & z' & 1 \end{bmatrix}$$

Reverse texture mapping equations where $\bar{V}, \bar{U}$ are the mappings of the texture space basis into the view space and O is the mapping of the texture space origin in the view space (see Chapter 3):

$$u = \frac{i(V_z \cdot O_y - V_y \cdot O_z)/focus + j(V_x \cdot O_z - V_z \cdot O_x)/focus + (V_y \cdot O_x - V_x \cdot O_y)}{i(V_y \cdot U_z - V_z \cdot U_y)/focus + j(V_z \cdot U_x - V_x \cdot U_z)/focus + (V_x \cdot U_y - V_y \cdot U_x)}$$

$$v = \frac{i(U_y \cdot O_z - U_z \cdot O_y)/focus + j(U_z \cdot O_x - U_x \cdot O_z)/focus + (U_x \cdot O_y - U_y \cdot O_x)}{i(V_y \cdot U_z - V_z \cdot U_y)/focus + j(V_z \cdot U_x - V_x \cdot U_z)/focus + (V_x \cdot U_y - V_y \cdot U_x)}$$

Analytical Geometry

Line equation where $\overline{C}$ is a co-directed vector and Q a point on the line (see Chapter 5):

$$X = Q + t\overline{C}$$

Plane equation where $\overline{N}$ is a normal vector and P is a point on the plane (see Chapter 5):

$$(\overline{X - P}) \cdot \overline{N} = 0$$

Sphere equation where M is the sphere's center and r is its radius (see Chapter 5):

$$\left\| (\overline{X - M}) \right\| = r$$

Seeking an intersection of a line and a plane (see Chapter 5):

$$\begin{cases} X = Q + t\overline{C} \\ (\overline{X - P}) \cdot \overline{N} = 0 \end{cases} \Rightarrow (Q + t\overline{C} - P) \cdot \overline{N} = 0 \Rightarrow$$

$$t\overline{C} \cdot \overline{N} = (\overline{P - Q}) \cdot \overline{N} \Rightarrow t = \frac{(\overline{P - Q}) \cdot \overline{N}}{\overline{C} \cdot \overline{N}}$$

Seeking an intersection of a line and a sphere (see Chapter 5):

$$\begin{cases} X = Q + t\overline{C} \\ (\overline{X - M}) \cdot (\overline{X - M}) = r^2 \end{cases} \Rightarrow (Q + t\overline{C} - M) \cdot (Q + t\overline{C} - M) = r^2 \Rightarrow$$

$$(\overline{Q - M})(\overline{Q - M}) + 2t\overline{C}(\overline{Q - M}) + t^2\overline{C} \cdot \overline{C} - r^2 = 0$$

Seeking an intersection of a line and a cylinder (see Chapter 5):

$$\begin{cases} X = Q + t\overline{C} \\ (X - M - k\bar{N})(X - M - k\bar{N}) = r^2 \\ (X - M - k\bar{N})\overline{N} = 0 \end{cases}$$

Equation for a Hermite plane curve where P_1, P_2 are the endpoints and V_1, V_2 the tangents of the curve in the endpoints (see Chapter 6):

$$\begin{pmatrix} x(t) \\ y(t) \end{pmatrix} = \begin{bmatrix} t^3 & t^2 & t & 1 \end{bmatrix} \begin{bmatrix} 2 & -2 & 1 & 1 \\ -3 & 3 & -2 & -1 \\ 0 & 0 & 1 & 0 \\ 1 & 0 & 0 & 0 \end{bmatrix} \begin{bmatrix} P_1 \\ P_2 \\ V_1 \\ V_2 \end{bmatrix}$$

Equation for a Bézier plane curve where P_1, P_2, P_3, P_4 are its control points (see Chapter 6):

$$\begin{pmatrix} x(t) \\ y(t) \end{pmatrix} = \begin{bmatrix} t^3 & t^2 & t & 1 \end{bmatrix} \begin{bmatrix} -1 & 3 & -3 & 1 \\ 3 & -6 & 3 & 0 \\ -3 & 3 & 0 & 0 \\ 1 & 0 & 0 & 0 \end{bmatrix} \begin{bmatrix} P_1 \\ P_2 \\ P_3 \\ P_4 \end{bmatrix}$$

General form for a 3D bicubic patch where *[G]* contains the control points (see Chapter 6):

$$\begin{pmatrix} x(t,s) \\ y(t,s) \\ z(t,s) \end{pmatrix} = \begin{bmatrix} t^3 & t^2 & t & 1 \end{bmatrix} [M][G][M]^T \begin{bmatrix} s^3 \\ s^2 \\ s \\ 1 \end{bmatrix}$$

Illumination

Ambient lighting model (see Chapter 8):

$$I_{reflected} = K_{object} I_{ambient}$$

Diffuse (Bouknight) lighting model (see Chapter 8):

$$I_{reflected} = K_{ambient} I_{ambient} + \sum_i K_{diffuse} I_{i,directed} \cos(\alpha)$$

Phong lighting model (see Chapter 8):

$$I_{reflected} = K_{ambient} I_{ambient} + \sum_i I_{i,directed} (K_{diffuse} \cos(\alpha) + k_{specular} \cos^n(\beta))$$

Radiosity equation where $F_{i,j}$ are formed factors, B_i are radiosities, and E_i are emissions (see Chapter 8):

$$\begin{bmatrix} 1 & -k_1 F_{1,2} & \dots & -k_1 F_{1,n} \\ -k_2 F_{2,1} & 1 & \dots & -k_2 F_{2,n} \\ \dots & \dots & \dots \dots & \dots \\ -k_n F_{n,1} & -k_n F_{n,2} & \dots & 1 \end{bmatrix} \begin{bmatrix} B_1 \\ B_2 \\ .. \\ B_n \end{bmatrix} = \begin{bmatrix} E_1 \\ E_2 \\ \dots \\ E_n \end{bmatrix}$$

APPENDIX C

Additional Reading

Abrash, M., "Inside Quake: Visible-Surface Determination," *Dr. Dobbs Sourcebook*, July 1996.

Atherton, P., K. Weiler, and D. Greenberg, "Polygon Shadow Generation," *ACM Computer Graphics (SIGGRAPH)*, 1978 vol. 12, no. 3, pp. 275-281.

Bartels, R., J. Beatty, and B. Barsky, *An Introduction to Splines for use in Computer Graphics and Geometric Modelling,* Morgan-Kaufmann, 1987.

Beatty, J.C., and K.S. Booth, *Tutorial: Computer Graphics,* IEEE Computer Society Press, 1982.

Bézier, P., *Numerical Control: Mathematics and Applications,* Wiley, 1972.

Billmeyer, F., and M. Saltzman, *Principles of Color Technology,* Wiley, 1981.

Blinn, J.F., "Models of Light Reflection for Computer Synthesized Pictures," *ACM Computer Graphics (SIGGRAPH)*, 1977 vol. 11, no. 2, pp. 192-198.

Bouknight, W.J., "A Procedure for Generation of Three-dimensional Half-toned Computer Graphics Presentations," *Communications of the ACM*, 1970, vol. 13, no. 9, pp. 527-536.

Bresenham, J.E., "Algorithm for Computer Control of a Digital Plotter," *IBM Systems Journal*, 1965, vol 4, no 1, pp 25-30.

Cohen, M.F., "A Radiosity Method for the Realistic Image Synthesis of Complex Diffuse Environments," *ACM Computer Graphics (SIGGRAPH)*, 1985, vol. 19, no. 3, pp. 31-40.

de Berg, M., M. van Krevland, M. Overmars, and O. Schwarzkopf, *Computational Geometry,* Springer-Verlag, 1997.

Farin, G., *Curves and Surfaces for Computer Aided Design,* Academic Press, 1990

Foley, J.D., A. Van Dam, S.K. Feiner, and J.F. Hughes, *Computer Graphics: Principles and Practice,* Addison-Wesley, 1990.

Fuchs, H., G.D. Abram, and E.D. Grant, "Near Real-Time Shaded Display of Rigid Objects," *ACM Computer Graphics (SIGGRAPH)*, 1983, vol. 17, no. 3, pp. 65-72.

Fuchs, H., Z. Kedem, and B. Naylor, "On Visible Surface Generation by a Priori Tree Structure," *ACM Computer Graphics (SIGGRAPH)*, 1980, vol. 14, no. 3, pp. 124-133.

Glaeser, G., *Fast algorithms for 3D Graphics*, Springer-Verlag, 1994.

Glidden, R., *Graphics Programming with Direct3D*, Adison-Wesley, 1997.

Gouraud, H., "Continuous Shading of Curved Surfaces," *IEEE Transactions on Computers*, June 1971, pp. 623-629.

Greene, N., "Environmental Mapping and Other Applications of World Projections," *IEEE Computer Graphics and Applications*, 1986, vol. 6, no. 11, pp. 21-29.

Gregory, R.L., *The Intelligent Eye,* McGraw-Hill, 1970.

Hall, R., *Illumination and Color in Computer Generated Imagery,* Springer-Verlag, 1989.

Heckbert, P.S., "Color Image Quantization for Frame Buffer Display." *ACM Computer Graphics (SIGGRAPH)*, July 1982, vol. 16, no. 3, pp. 297-307.

Heckbert, P.S., "Survey of Texture Mapping," *IEEE Computer Graphics and Applications*, 1986, vol. 6, no. 11, pp. 56-67.

LaMothe, A., *Tricks of the Windows Game Programming Gurus*, Sams, 1999.

Levoy, M., "Display of Surfaces from Volume Data," *IEEE Computer Graphics and Applications*, 1988, vol. 8, no. 3, pp. 29-37.

Miller, G., "The Definition and Rendering of Terrain Maps," *ACM Computer Graphics (SIGGRAPH)*, 1986, vol. 20, no. 4, pp. 39-49.

Newman, W., and R. Sproull, *Principles of Interactive Computer Graphics,* McGraw-Hill, 1973.

Phong, Bui Toung, "Illumination for Computer Generated Pictures," *Communications of the ACM,* 1975, vol. 18, no. 8, pp. 311-317.

Sedgewick, R., *Algorithms in C,* Addison-Wesley, 1984.

Sutherland, I.E., and G.W. Hodgman, "Reentrant polygon clipping," *Communications of the ACM,* 1974, vol. 17, no. 1, pp. 32-42.

Sutherland, I.E., R.F. Sproull, and R.A. Schumacker, "A Characterization of Ten Hidden Surface Algorithms," *ACM Computing Surveys*, 1974, vol. 6, no. 1, pp. 1-55.

Toussaint, G.T., "A Simple Linear Algorithm for Intersecting Convex Polygons," *The Visual Computer*, 1985, no. 1, pp 118-123.

Vince, J., *3-D Computer Animation,* Addison-Wesley, 1992.

Watt, A., and M. Watt, *Advanced Animation and Rendering Techniques,* Addison-Wesley, 1992.

Watt, A., *3D Computer Graphics, Third Edition*, Addison-Wesley, 2000.

Wirth, N., *Algorithms and Data Structures,* Prentice-Hall, 1986.

Wolberg, G., *Digital Image Warping,* IEEE Computer Society Press, 1990.

Wright, R. and M. Sweet, *OpenGL Super Bible, Second Edition*, Waite Group, 2000.

Index

C

Windows 95/98/NT/2000 Installation Instructions

1. Insert the CD-ROM disc into your CD-ROM drive.

2. From the Windows desktop, double-click on the My Computer icon.

3. Double-click on the icon representing your CD-ROM drive.

4. Double-click on the file `start.htm` to find out what's on the CD-ROM.

Linux and Unix Installation Instructions

These installation instructions assume that you have a passing familiarity with UNIX commands and the basic setup of your machine. As UNIX has many flavors, only generic commands are used. If you have any problems with the commands, please consult the appropriate man page or your system administrator.

1. Insert the CD-ROM in CD drive.

2. If you have a volume manager, mounting of the CD-ROM will be automatic. If you don't have a volume manager, you can mount the CD-ROM by typing

   `mount  -tiso9660  /dev/cdrom  /mnt/cdrom`

   NOTE: `/mnt/cdrom` is just a mount point, but it must exist when you issue the mount command. You may also use any empty directory for a mount point if you don't want to use `/mnt/cdrom`.

3. Navigate to the root directory of your CD-ROM. If your mount point matches the example listed above, type

   `cd /mnt/cdrom`

4. Open the file `start.htm` with your favorite text editor to find out what's on the CD-ROM.